BEYOND PIETY AND POLITICS

MIDDLE EAST STUDIES

Mark Tessler, *editor*

BEYOND PIETY AND POLITICS

Religion, Social Relations, and Public Preferences in the Middle East and North Africa

by Sabri Ciftci, F. Michael Wuthrich, Ammar Shamaileh

INDIANA UNIVERSITY PRESS

This book is a publication of

Indiana University Press
Office of Scholarly Publishing
Herman B Wells Library 350
1320 East 10th Street
Bloomington, Indiana 47405 USA

iupress.org

© 2022 by Indiana University Press

All rights reserved

No part of this book may be reproduced or utilized in any form or by any means, electronic or mechanical, including photocopying and recording, or by any information storage and retrieval system, without permission in writing from the publisher. The paper used in this publication meets the minimum requirements of the American National Standard for Information Sciences—Permanence of Paper for Printed Library Materials, ANSI Z39.48-1992.

Manufactured in the United States of America

First printing 2022

Cataloging information is available from the Library of Congress.
ISBN 978-0-253-06052-5 (hardcover)
ISBN 978-0-253-06053-2 (paperback)
ISBN 978-0-253-06054-9 (e-book)

Art for the book cover was produced by Hala Aljaafari.

To our families and their wonderful existence . . .

CONTENTS

List of Figures ix

Acknowledgments xi

Note on Transliteration xv

Introduction 1

1 Religious Communities, the State, and Religious Outlooks 10

2 Attitudes of the Devout: The Nature of the Substance or the Nurture of Relationship? 30

3 Empirical Foundations of Religious Outlooks 61

4 The Individual and Contextual Determinants of Muslim Religious Outlooks in MENA 92

5 Islam and Support for Democracy 119

6 Temporal Change in Religious Outlooks and Political Preferences 148

7 Islam and Distributive Preferences 175

Conclusion 196

Appendix A 207

Appendix B 229

Bibliography 233

Index 245

FIGURES

Figure 1.1	Religious Goods and Social Favorability	19
Figure 1.2	State Regulation, Religious Communities, and Religious Outlooks	26
Figure 2.1	Relative Levels of Tension with Society among Various Naqshbandi Communities	40
Figure 2.2	Naqshbandi Communities Relative to Inward-Outward Focus	43
Figure 2.3	Patterns of Political Involvement	51
Figure 3.1	Dimensions and Categories of Religious Outlooks	68
Figure 3.2	Distribution of Responses for Self-Reported Religious Behavior	73
Figure 3.3	Class Shares of Religious Outlooks	78
Figure 3.4	Distribution of the Four Religious Outlooks along Religiosity Index	83
Figure 3.5	Religious Behavior and Religious Outlooks	85
Figure 3.6	Distribution of the Four Religious Outlooks along Religiosity Index	89
Figure 4.1	Multinomial Latent Class Regression (Individual and Contextual Determinants of Religious Outlooks)	97
Figure 4.2	Cross-National Variation in Religious Outlooks	104
Figure 4.3	State-Religion Relations and Religious Outlooks	111
Figure 4.4	Education and Religious Outlooks	113
Figure 4.5	Feeling of Safety and Religious Outlooks	114

Figures

Figure 4.6	Trust and Religious Outlooks	115
Figure 5.1	Religious Expression and the Cost of Repression	126
Figure 5.2	Pairwise Marginal Effect and Predicted Probability Comparisons for Religious Outlooks	141
Figure 5.3	Predictions and Predicted Probabilities for Religiosity	142
Figure 6.1	Change in Class Shares over Time	161
Figure 6.2	Temporal Change in Religiosity and Class Probabilities in Egypt	164
Figure 6.3	Temporal Change in Religiosity and Class Probabilities in Tunisia	166
Figure 7.1	Kernel Density Function for Preferences for Redistribution	179
Figure 7.2	Restrictions on Civil Society and Post-Islamist Attitudes toward State-Led Redistribution	190
Figure A5.1	Religious Outlooks and Mean Overt Support for Democracy by Country	213

ACKNOWLEDGMENTS

THE AUTHORS OF THIS BOOK COME FROM DIFFERENT walks of life. While we share a passion for the study of religion and politics, all three of us have come to this from different backgrounds and outlooks. This book is informed by our different outlooks and the contexts that have shaped them, as well as each author's unique take on the study of religion and politics. The volume is also enriched by the diverse methods in which the authors are trained. It is, thus, appropriate that our gathering of perspectives would lead to this volume, which focuses on the diversity of religious outlooks in the Middle East and North Africa.

The idea for this book came amid a casual conversation during a coffee break at a conference where the authors exchanged thoughts about the lack of depth in the dominant approach to studies in the field of comparative politics on the influence of religion on the attitudes of Muslims. The stimulating conversation that ensued continued through email exchanges and video meetings. We took pleasure in each other's company and learned a great deal about our own challenges, scholarly ambitions, and academic development. This collaboration helped us grow intellectually as it took on a life of its own and transitioned from a journal article to a book project. From beginning to end, this project has been special for the three of us, not only for focusing on a timely topic that has the potential to contribute to the study of Islam and politics but as a project that invites methodological diversity. We learned a lot in researching and writing it and certainly hope it will be of interest to a broad audience by shifting the debate about the social origins and consequences of religion's relational influence on political and social attitudes.

In the process of this book's development, we have become indebted to many individuals. We would like to first recognize Mark Tessler, the Middle East Studies series editor of Indiana University Press, who has been both an inspiration to us and a strong advocate for this project. Amaney Jamal and Michael Robbins invited us to present earlier versions of this project at the special conference Social Justice in the Arab World since 2010: Changing Conditions, Mobilizations, and Policies, at the American University in Beirut. The panel participants and audience at this event were most helpful in their comments. We would also like to thank the Arab Center for Research and Policy Studies in Washington, DC, and especially Tamara Kharroub for inviting us to join a panel at the annual meeting of the Middle East Studies Association in 2017. The panel participants provided great comments about our paper.

The main argument of this book and some empirical observations were presented in front of an intellectual, activist youth group at Istanbul House of Thought (İDE, İstanbul Düşünce Evi). While receiving our book very positively, this group also challenged us to improve our argument and think carefully about the empirical evidence. We thank the İDE members for inviting us and the lecture participants for their valuable insights.

We would like to extend our special thanks to others at Indiana University Press for their support along the path of publishing this book. Jennika Baines, the acquiring editor, remained committed to this project and guided us throughout the process and accommodated our needs. Sophia Hebert, assistant acquisitions editor, helped at various stages. We cannot thank them enough for their encouragement and support. The press staff also deserves special thanks for their help in the editing and production stages. We should also mention the two anonymous reviewers, who provided very thoughtful and detailed comments on the manuscript. Their challenging reviews strengthened our manuscript considerably in its methodological and theoretical vigor, and we are grateful for their assistance in developing this work. In addition to the press's staff, we are deeply indebted to Hala Aljaafari, the artist whose beautiful oil painting was used as the image for our book cover.

We would also like to thank to our institutions and colleagues. Sabri Ciftci thanks Kansas State University (KSU) and his colleagues in the Political Science Department. One could not work in a more positive and supportive environment. Ciftci appreciates all the accommodation provided by KSU throughout his career. John and Karen Hofmeister supported parts of this research through a large endowment for the study of the Middle East at KSU by establishing the Michael W. Suleiman Chair in Arab and Arab-American Studies. Michael Wuthrich is grateful to his colleagues in the Political Science Department at the University of Kansas and the Center for Global and International Studies. Their support in his career development and mentoring have been critical to this and his other research endeavors. Ammar Shamaileh is thankful for the guidance and support of his current and former colleagues and mentors at the Doha Institute for Graduate

Studies, Franklin and Marshall College, the University of Louisville, and Florida State University.

Our families deserve the most significant recognition. Sabri Ciftci would like to bestow special thanks on his wife, Semra, and his four children—Bahadır, Yusuf, İbrahim, and Yiğithan. They have been a great source of inspiration every day. Their questions about the book and their wonderful existence have been great motivations. Michael Wuthrich is extremely grateful to his wife, Aimee, and daughters, Maya and Zoe, for providing rich and meaningful respites from work and research. Their love, patience, and support provide balance and fuel for a healthy research and work program. Ammar Shamaileh is indebted to his family for the seemingly endless reservoir of comfort and kindness they have afforded him. In particular, he is thankful for the unwavering patience and support of his wife, Hala; his mother, Mayada; his father, Atef; and his siblings, Amro and Lelas.

This book would not have been possible without the warmth and support of our families.

NOTE ON TRANSLITERATION

All Arabic and Turkish words are transliterated according to the *International Journal of Middle East Studies* transliteration guide. More information can be found at https://www.cambridge.org/core/journals/international-journal-of-middle-east-studies/information/author-resources/ijmes-translation-and-transliteration-guide.

BEYOND PIETY AND POLITICS

INTRODUCTION

On July 11, 2018, Adnan Oktar, a controversial Turkish preacher and TV personality, was arrested on charges of fraud. Oktar is particularly well-known for two things: he is a fierce critic of the theory of evolution, publishing works on the topic under the pseudonym Harun Yahya, and he does his televangelist preaching alongside his so-called kittens, scantily clad young women who appear on his show with heavy makeup and nightclub attire. For many pious people in Turkey (and likely elsewhere), belly dancing and sexually provocative images—the usual scene on Oktar's TV show—would be considered anything but Islamic.

Oktar's example stands in sharp contrast to that of another religious TV personality, Cübbeli Ahmet Hoca, otherwise known as Ahmet Mahmut Ünlü, one of the top figures of the Naqshbandi order associated with the İsmailağa Mosque community in Istanbul. This community, a powerful Sufi brotherhood, is best known for its conservative religious practices and outlook, which set it apart dramatically from other religious communities in its urban environment. They consider themselves strict adherents to Islamic law, including rigid prescriptions for proper attire for men and women, and they engage in social activism and outreach. In his TV appearances, Cübbeli Ahmet appears with his long beard and religious robe (*cübbe*), giving the impression of a *hoca*, a religious scholar of the traditional mold.

In a country long ruled by strong secularist policies, including the repression of religious attire at various times, Cübbeli Ahmet's appearance stands in sharp contrast to that of Adnan Oktar and his group. However, despite the significant differences in the style of their televangelist preaching and their outlook, each clearly claims allegiance to the same Hanafi school of Sunni Islamic jurisprudence and frequently uses the same Islamic terminology, such as *alhamdullillah* (praise to God) and *mashallah* (God willed it). Moreover, the followers of both figures would describe themselves without hesitation as highly religious.

We can add a third figure to this picture, İhsan Eliaçık, yet another unique religious personality, who has come to be known as a leftist Islamist.

With his relaxed appearance—baggy trousers and plastic slippers—and unorthodox ideas, after 2010, he became the de facto leader of a community of young people calling themselves members of an anticapitalist Muslim movement. While Cübbeli Ahmet has supported the ruling Justice and Development Party (AKP), Eliaçık has been a fierce opponent of the government and openly participated in the Gezi Park protests. He promotes social justice and has invited his followers to resist the tyranny and repression of a state ruled by a religious conservative party. Much like Cübbeli Ahmet and Oktar, he defines himself as a pious Muslim, and if we were to ask his followers about their devotion, it is likely that their responses would not be much different from the members of the other communities.

In a similar fashion, the preaching of Amr Khaled, an Egyptian televangelist of global fame, has been quite distinct from his Salafi counterparts, such as Abu Ishaq Alheweny or Mohamed Hassan. Khaled preached for tolerance and dialogue with the West even after the controversial Danish cartoons denigrating Mohammed, whereas most Salafi televangelists were very conservative in orientation and clearly demonized these cartoons. Following the ouster of President Morsi in 2013, several radical groups emerged in Egypt. Among them was Al-Mourabitoun, formed as a militant group in 2015 by a former military officer, Hisham Ashmawi, who was also affiliated with Al Qaeda. Ashmawi and Al-Mourabitoun operatives have carried out a number of attacks, some of which have targeted civilians, in Egypt and Libya. In his pictures, he always poses with military gear to support his image of a jihadi in the field, and he very quickly rose through the ranks of Islamist militants. He has vigorously called on religious scholars to encourage Muslim youths to join the fight against foreign invaders and domestic tyrants. Like Khaled and Alheweny, Ashmawi is attached to an Islamic social identity and has received traditional religious education. All three men and presumably their followers would define themselves as pious regardless of their distinct social, economic, and political preferences.

These examples from Turkey and Egypt give rise to an important question: If all the religious figures mentioned above and their followers would view themselves as equally devoted to their faith, how can we capture the nuances among these individuals in their religious identity, especially since we often try to do this through large public opinion surveys? If a researcher were able to conduct interviews with members of these various religious communities and ask them how they would define themselves and their general religious practices using a standard survey, their responses would be quite similar: they would all fall on the religious end of a continuum measuring devotion or piety. What distinguishes the religious devotion of these individuals who seem equally religious to an external observer evaluating survey responses? If we were able to differentiate these individuals in their piety, what significance would this have for understanding their attitudes and behavior? This book begins to answer these and similar questions by delving into the many different layers and nuances of piety. It does this by studying the single most important variable in the study of Islam and politics: religion. This volume also examines the ways religion influences individual attitudes toward the broader issues of politics, society, and the economy. Our argument moves beyond linear conceptualizations of the influence of religious devotion that categorize individuals along a continuum of less to more religious based solely on self-assessments and such standard practices as attending services, praying, and reading or reciting holy texts. A linear conceptualization of the influence of religiosity on attitudes masks the rich variation in religious outlooks at each level of individual piety. Is it possible to understand and measure the influence of religion in ways that account for divergent perspectives among practicing Muslims regardless of their reported level of religiosity? More importantly, can we explain political and economic preferences more accurately if we are able to differentiate among these diverse religious perspectives?

Religion plays an important role in shaping political preferences across the Muslim world. A growing body of analytical social science research has examined the interplay between religion and political attitudes, mainly focusing on the empirical association between Islam and democracy but also on attitudes toward Islamic governance models, extremism, and international actors.[1] While quantitative studies of Muslim political attitudes abound, scholars have remained ambivalent about the utility of the "religiosity" variable commonly used in empirical models. This book introduces a novel and multidimensional conceptualization of intrareligious views and investigates this conceptualization empirically. The proposed conceptualization foresees pluralistic religious outlooks stemming from social preferences, contextual differences, and variations among intrafaith communities within a given society. It is our contention that conceptualizing Muslim religiosity in light of these distinct outlooks will help us move the study of Islam and politics forward and avoid the drawbacks of essentializing the impact of Islam on social and political attitudes. This approach is likely to help avoid the limitations of "conceptual stretching" (Sartori 1970), which loads too much on a single concept of religiosity in explaining social and political attitudes. Our analysis introduces various manifestations of religiosity represented in distinct religious outlooks—meaning, cognitive frameworks for understanding the role of religion in relation to social and political orders and norms—to gain leverage in the study of Muslim political attitudes that are usually explained by catch-all measures of piety.

Earlier prominent scholarship on the role of religion and politics in the region clearly established an essentialist position regarding the influence of religion in Muslim-majority societies (Gellner 1983; Kedourie 1994; Lewis 2010). As a corrective to this, the recently burgeoning quantitative studies on the topic have generally used linear measures of religiosity to discredit this reductionist view, but the analysis has yet to move very far beyond addressing basic assumptions regarding how critical aspects of religion other than religiosity might affect social and political attitudes. Despite their methodological limitations, these previous examinations of the relationship between religiosity and political preferences have done much to dispel the notion that Islamic piety exerts a consistently negative influence on political modernization (Ciftci 2010; Robbins 2015; Spierings 2014; Tessler 2002; Tessler, Jamal, and Robbins 2012).

Returning to the examples of Oktar, Cübbeli Ahmet, and Eliaçık, all are clearly religious individuals, but there is a world of difference in their preferences and the preferences of members of their respective religious communities regarding social and political issues. For example, Eliaçık is an individualist with liberal political values and prodistributive economic preferences, whereas Cübbeli Ahmet is a communitarian with strong conservative tendencies.[2] Oktar could be considered a communitarian with liberal views and quite unorthodox behavior. These individuals have different preferences regarding broader social and political issues, such as democracy, women's rights, and economic distribution. It is imperative to account for these differences rather than masking the rich nuances differentiating the attitudes and behaviors of religious individuals with distinct outlooks.

This volume begins to unpack these rich nuances in religious outlooks and in the linkages between these outlooks and social and political preferences. Linear or binary assumptions regarding the influence of religiosity on political outlooks are insufficient to allow us to take the next steps in advancing our understanding of Islam and politics. In contrast, this book's novel conceptualization of distinct religious outlooks, stemming from the dynamics of communal association preferences and state-religious community relations, is better positioned to explain the differences in religiously inspired political attitudes and behavior.

Furthermore, this new framework not only highlights the consequences of religious association and attitudes in the Middle East and North Africa (MENA); it also helps explain several areas of inquiry related to the democracy gap (the lack of democracy observed in the region), radicalization, distributive preferences, nationalism, authoritarianism, and the appeal of Islamism in these societies. For example, rather than operating from an analysis that prioritizes a uniform measurement of religiosity, by employing models of religious outlooks within societies and across cases, we can better understand the factors involved in influencing the distributions of these outlooks and the synergies between religion and nationalism or nation-state formation (Akturk 2015; Grzymala-Busse 2015). This study has the potential to add to the nuanced studies of national identity and state formation in the Middle East by recognizing the context-bound and relational nature of the plurality of religious outlooks as factors that interact with national and ethnic identities, state legitimacy, and nation-state building. In doing so, our approach could also help us better understanding the contingent dynamics and consequences to attitudes toward various political and social issues that predominate among sectarian, ethnic, and national identities in different contexts (Belge and Karakoc 2015; Hinnebusch 2001, 2015, 2020) or the role of economic factors in the formation and survival of states (Cleveland and Bunton 2009).

To tackle these nuances, our analysis uses a mixed-methods design—including qualitative and quantitative case comparison, formal modeling for theory development, and rigorous quantitative analysis of survey data. The emerging data from the Arab Barometer surveys provide the best available measures to evaluate individuals' views about social preferences, state-religion relations, religious devotion, and various political attitudes in a dozen countries in MENA.[3] The work presented here also puts the findings of the analyses into comparative perspective with analyses conducted by others on non-Muslim-majority societies where religion and politics have noticeable synergies. As such, it makes an important contribution to understanding how ordinary men and women in the Middle East construct their religiously informed views about various political issues and contributes to our understanding of the relationship between religion and politics more broadly.

The volume proceeds as follows: Chapter 1 argues that religion influences individual preferences not just substantively—through doctrinal tenets—but also relationally, as a result of the dynamics between one's religious community and the broader society. Most other studies have explicitly or implicitly prioritized *substantive* influences of religion and, thus, measure influence primarily through strength of belief or basic religious practices. We assert, however, that many opinions and behaviors of general interest are likely directed by *relational* (social) influences, stemming from the choices and consequences of associating with a particular community of believers and this community's relative position of tension with the state and broader society. Utilizing recent research in the subfield of the sociology of religion and the literature on religious markets, this study builds a theoretical base for the study of diverse religious communities and discusses the implications of this theory for state policies and religious regulation.

Chapter 2 presents a qualitative case exploration of these theoretical dynamics through examples from Naqshbandi communities in Turkey. Enumerating the rich variation among religious communities within the powerful and widespread Naqshbandi Sufi order, the chapter illustrates how distinct outlooks and orientations to politics have emerged even within a single religious grouping in a religious market and over time. The detailed study of five major Naqshbandi groups and their members' general attitudes toward politics in Turkey illustrates how both the differing levels of tension between religious communities and society and the general state dispositions toward these groups over time lead to patterned approaches to political involvement. This chapter also emphasizes the notion that religion not only relationally influences a community member's approach to politics but that it also does so *contingently*. Therefore, surveys that highlight patterns between outlooks and political attitudes must be understood both contextually and temporally, based on the opportunities and constraints faced by religious communities and their members.

Building on the theoretical framework and observations of the previous chapters, chapter 3 presents a brief background to demonstrate more specific ways that religious outlooks might be theoretically distributed and then enumerates a path that scholars could take to empirically measure these religious outlooks through public opinion surveys using latent class analysis and factor analysis. Using the Arab Barometer surveys, the chapter draws from existing social theory to empirically corroborate the religious outlook categories proposed by our theoretical and conceptual approach. To do this, we use survey questions regarding religious pluralism versus conformity and whether religion should be more or less present in the public sphere. This analysis points to four categories of outlooks that are labeled *religious individualist*, *social communitarian*, *religious communitarian*, and *post-Islamist*. The analysis reveals strong empirical support for our conceptual model proposing a two-dimensional, fourfold classification of religious individuals according to their social preferences.

Chapter 4 presents an empirical investigation of the individual and contextual determinants of religious outlooks in MENA. It reports the results of latent class regression (LCR) models to predict the distribution of religious outlook classes as a function of income, education, life satisfaction, and such contextual factors as democratization, state-religion relations, and economic development. In addition to Arab Barometer surveys, the analyses also utilize the Religion and State Dataset (RAS), Varieties of Democracy data (V-Dem), and Organisation for Economic Co-operation and Development (OECD) data. This chapter confirms that contextual factors have a significant influence on religious outlooks, particularly the state–religious communities relations in a given country. State regulation of religion and government favoritism for certain religious groups significantly shape religious preferences and preferences for various outlooks. Individual factors, including education and perceptions of security or trust, also have sway on these outlooks. The analysis in this chapter shows that shades of religious views do not emerge in a vacuum but have their roots in individual and contextual factors.

Chapter 5 builds on the existing literature and our conceptual model of religious outlooks to develop and test a novel model explaining support for democracy in MENA. The chapter develops a formal model of religious outlooks and democratic orientations, generating several testable hypotheses. The results of these tests highlight the nuanced relationship the religious outlooks share with preferences for democracy. Most notably, the findings of this chapter indicate that religious outlooks play a role in shaping both the *who* and the *why* behind support for democracy. In addition, an increase in Islamic piety appears to increase support for democracy at low and medium levels of religiosity but decrease support for democracy at higher levels of religiosity. This chapter also discusses new insights and contributions of our model to the study of Islam and democracy.

Chapter 6 examines the temporal variation in the predictions emanating from the theoretical model. We focus on Egypt and Tunisia to trace the robustness and case-specific distribution of religious outlook categories between these two cases over time. Empirically, the analysis relies on Waves II and III of the Arab Barometer, and we run a series of measurement models and multivariate regression estimations. This chapter aims to explore the temporal dynamics related to the formation of religious outlooks and shifting patterns of attitudes about economic and political preferences. A detailed account of the evolution of outlooks and attitudes during and in the aftermath of the Arab uprisings of the early 2010s is provided to explain these extraordinary protests and their outcomes from a new perspective. The statistical analysis reveals that, in addition to individual-level and spatial variation, there are also significant temporal changes in religious outlooks, and these changes in turn have implications for political outlooks and attitudes. The temporal changes in religious outlooks of individuals create interesting synergies with organizational strategies. From the Muslim Brothers to Ennahda and various groups of Salafis, the Islamist actors of the Arab uprisings represent the dynamic shifts in communal outlooks that presumably result from the alignment and realignment of various outlooks between and within these organizations. It is not always possible to map changes in individual outlooks onto organizational shifts in ideology and strategy, but the analysis in chapter 6 highlights the various synergies that may occur at both levels. This insight is in line with the differences in outlooks we observe among Naqshbandi communities in Turkey, and it can be applied to distinct religious groups in other Muslim-majority societies as well as the inner structures of violent extremist groups.

Chapter 7 turns to the relationship between religious outlooks and support for state-led economic redistribution. The chapter sets forth an empirical examination of the role religious outlooks play in shaping distributive preferences and preferences for change in the distributive practices of the state. While religious outlooks characterized by communitarian impulses appear to be more homogenous, more likely to support the status quo, and less critical of the regime's policy preferences regarding the redistribution of resources, the relationship between such religious outlooks and preferences for increases or decreases in state-led redistribution are less consistent. The results of this analysis highlight the nuanced relationship that religious outlooks share with support for state-led redistribution and the need for a theoretical and empirical examination that accounts for contextual factors. Subsequently, in this chapter, our attention turns to how a more robust presence of Islamic organizations in associational life may affect support for redistribution among those who possess a religious outlook oriented toward both pluralism and a religious presence in the public domain. In this analysis, a theory is developed that is rooted in the historical development of "moderate" Islamic organizations in Egypt and Tunisia, and the core implication of this theory is subsequently tested on Arab Barometer data. The results of the theoretical and empirical analysis indicate that post-Islamists are more supportive of state-led redistribution relative to members of other outlooks where associational life is limited and less supportive of state-led redistribution where associational life is not. As such, this chapter builds on the notion that these religious outlooks share nuanced relationships with political, economic, and social preferences discussed throughout the book.

The book concludes with a summary assessment of the analyses employed and discusses the applicability of the theoretical and conceptual framework to the broader Muslim world and non-Muslim-majority countries. In addition, it sets forth the implications of our analyses regarding religious outlooks to other issue areas beyond Islam, democracy, and religiously inspired distributive preferences. Finally, the book ends with policy recommendations and a road map for future studies on religion and politics.

Notes

1. Among many studies on Muslim political attitudes, we can cite Ciftci (2010), Ciftci, Wuthrich, and Shamaileh (2019), Driessen (2018), Fish (2011), Hofmann (2004), Isani (2018), Jamal (2006), Rizzo, Abdel-Latef and Meyer (2007), Spiering (2014), Tessler (2002, 2015), and Tessler and Robbins (2007).

2. Here we are using the terminology of "individualist" and "communitarian" consistent with the conceptualization by Davis and Robinson (1996, 2006) in their discussion of moral cosmologies.

3. Other existing data sources did not allow for the adequate construction of religious outlooks to allow empirical testing. For example, World Values Surveys do not include many questions that tap individual opinion about state-religion relations. When such questions are present in surveys, they are not consistently asked across a large sample of Muslim-majority countries.

1

RELIGIOUS COMMUNITIES, THE STATE, AND RELIGIOUS OUTLOOKS

WHAT DO WE MEAN WHEN WE DISCUSS THE influence of religion on social and political attitudes? How does it influence them, and does it always influence attitudes in the same way? For example, is the result equally as predictable when devout Muslims are asked about their attitudes regarding democracy and democratization as when they are asked about dietary prescriptions or conducting loans with interest? We might anticipate that a pious Muslim's attitude toward halal diets or interest in loans would not change much depending on whether they live in Saudi Arabia, the United States, or China. In these cases, we would assume that whatever variance exists is related to level of devotion and, among the devout, doctrinal interpretations of well-known texts. That is, we would expect that people's attitudes and preferences toward these practices would come from the cognitive realm of explicit beliefs, values, the received wisdom from their school of jurisprudence, and interpretations of doctrine. Nonetheless, we might imagine that among the less devout, there might be more freedom and variation in beliefs among Muslims in China or the United States than one would anticipate from the less pious in Saudi Arabia or Jordan.

Now, what if we consider how strictly practicing Muslims in Saudi Arabia feel about the prospect of a policy of state-sanctioned freedom for open proselytization of all religious beliefs in their country in comparison to similarly observant Muslims in China and the United States? Most likely, we would expect devout Muslims in China and the United States to support any political policy that supported religious freedom and protections for religious minorities, and we might also assume that such attitudes would be less prevalent among the devout in Saudi Arabia, Jordan, or Iran. If we flip the script with geographic contexts and insert devout Christians, Hindus, and so on, we would likely predict a similar trend. Why?

Religious doctrine rarely provides an indisputable guide, immune to interpretation and debate, for important social and political questions. This observation might lead us to question the influence of religion on one's broader political attitudes, and in fact many of the empirical studies of the impact of religion on Muslims' attitudes toward democracy and regime type have shown that the relationship is insignificant, weak, or variable from case to case (Ciftci 2010; Jamal 2006; Jamal and Tessler 2008; Tessler 2002, 2015). This finding does not square well, however, with the common perception that religion has a significant influence on individuals' political attitudes. Many have anecdotally observed a consensus of similar political opinions among devout members of a particular faith community. Is there any way to reconcile this "perception on the ground" with empirical data that suggest otherwise?

We believe this disjuncture stems from the fact that religion's influence on people's attitudes can stem from different modes of influence. As has been widely observed, religion potentially informs individual attitudes derived from *substantive*, or doctrinal, guidance. Religious texts often have specific prescriptions or proscriptions regarding certain behaviors—do not eat pork, do not commit adultery, do not charge interest, do not gamble, and so on. When individuals consider specific issues closely related to a particular doctrine of their faith, the response is usually predictable based on the individual's religiosity, religious knowledge, or investment in those beliefs. For the devoutly religious, it might be difficult to follow substantive faith-based rules in a country of a different dominant faith, but these followers are generally still inclined to adhere to the behaviors of their faith. Even in a foreign land, they find like-minded communities and people who help them continue along the right path.

However, beyond the substantive influence of religion and no matter where we live, our religious practice (or lack thereof) necessarily has social—that is, *relational*—implications (Djupe and Gilbert 2008). Most religions strongly enjoin communal association. Every religious community—and by this, we mean a *locally bounded* group of individuals who regularly assemble and engage in religious practices with one another—operates in some sort of dynamic relationship with the broader society, if not also the state. This social reality creates a relational influence that guides individuals' attitudes toward broader political and socioeconomic questions in direct and indirect ways (Djupe and Gilbert 2008; McClendon and Riedl

2019). Religious traditions do have scriptural tenets that touch on political affairs; however, these tend to provide enough wiggle room for contextual realities that even devout "letter of the law" believers are able to interpret politically relevant guidance in religious texts differently. Thus, this salient influence of religion operates not according to textual decree but as a logical consequence of the social context and relational dynamic between an individual's community and his or her place in society. To the extent that the state is involved in regulating religious practices in society, this is also a key component of the dynamic.

In short, attitudes such as ambivalence toward or support for democratization or liberalization, for example, can be derived from the status of a member's religious community within society and whether or not further democratization or liberalization would enhance or impede his or her survival and ability to thrive and grow in that society.[1] Religious communities (i.e., local congregations) of the same dominant religion in a particular society would likely have different political preferences based on their status, or they might support democratization for different reasons. Members of religious communities whose individuals behave and act according to the dominant social norms might prefer the majoritarian elements of democracy—that is, that the government is elected with a mandate from the political majority. Others who find themselves in communities with practices that differentiate them from the broader society might find the liberal and pluralistic provisions that provide foundational protections for minorities to be the desirable components of democracy.

We argue that broader political and socioeconomic questions are not substantively influenced by religion but are influenced relationally and rationally by participation in the social context in which religion is practiced (Campbell 2013). The rest of this chapter is devoted to unpacking these dynamics. We discuss the phenomenon of religious outlooks, which could be understood as religious perspectives toward others primarily derived from religion's relational, rather than substantive, influence on attitudes. To this end, we begin by clarifying the case for existing pluralism among practicing Muslims and providing a theoretical framework for understanding the dynamics that generate nonstatic but patterned distributions of religious communities and religious outlooks within a society. The link between an individual's broader political preferences, his or her religious outlooks, and local religious communities are discussed in the context of the state's role in this relationship.

The Case for Religious Pluralism in Muslim-Majority Societies

It might seem that the case for intrafaith pluralism would be a foregone conclusion. However, this assumption has not always been the working framework in studies of political opinion and religious attitudes, especially in Muslim-majority societies. Studies conducted in the US, for example, began to move away from the simplistic usage of religiosity as a meaningful variable separate from congregational affiliation several decades ago (Gilbert 1993; Jelen 1993; Leege and Welch 1989). In the United States, this happened as a response to observations in the 1980s and 1990s that Christian traditions (such as mainline Protestant, Evangelical, Catholic, Black Protestant) and denominations were increasingly showing distinct political trends that required measures other than generalizable Christian practices to account for meaningful trends in political attitudes.[2] In surveys of Muslim-majority countries, however, the movement away from such simple measures to a nuanced treatment has occurred far more slowly. The religious practice and belief questions of large cross-national and national surveys tend to ask generic questions regarding prayer, Koran reading, and attendance that aggregate rather than distinguish adherents to the majority faith (or even multiple faiths).

Clearly, the reliance on such questions to generate an index of religiosity fails to consider the impact that social interactions or relational influences within distinct religious communities might have on an individual's religious outlook (Gilbert 1993). As Djupe and Gilbert (2008) have shown, however, the local congregation is far more influential than the overall denomination on the political views of its congregants, although congregations vary significantly in their ability to influence their members' political views. Furthermore, they found that the strength of attitudinal affinity between individuals and their religious community is not their religiosity according to the traditional measures (praying, weekly attendance, reading sacred scriptures) but their level of social activity within their community. All of this adds up to an important challenge to the assumption that using measures based on religious practices in surveys will tease out linear attitudinal trends from nonreligious to religious.

To illustrate the challenges of using such general measures in the US context, it would be easy to imagine that a Catholic, an Episcopalian, a Baptist, a member of a Black congregation, and a Latter Day Saint would all report that they are Christian and express a similar level of religious practice—church attendance, regular prayer, and so on. Yet it is fairly easy to recognize that these groups might differ not only in doctrinal beliefs but in political opinions and preferences (Campbell 2004; Jelen 1993) and that this variation could even be found at the intracongregational level (Djupe and Gilbert 2008; McClendon and Riedl 2019).

If we are looking for parallels in Muslim-majority societies, even though Islam does not have the extensive denominational diversification that exists within Christianity, its decentralization of religious authority into very broad schools of jurisprudence or *madhāhib*—that is, among Sunnis, Ḥanafī, Shāfiʿī, Ḥanbalī, and Mālikī—leaves a great deal of latitude to local congregations and their leadership. This should serve to heighten, not reduce, diversity in practices, beliefs, and attitudes across local communities, which is at least part of the reason that the governments in Muslim-majority societies in the Middle East and North Africa (MENA) have made attempts to oversee religious activity through state-run or state-supported organizations (Fox 2008). Although, as we will discuss below, the supply-side of a regulated religious society does have implications on the proportion and distribution of types of religious communities, undeniable diversity exists at the congregational level (Putnam and Campbell 2010), even in highly regulated Muslim-majority countries (Ayoob 2009; Stark and Finke 2000).

There are several reasons why the study of religion and attitudes in Muslim-majority countries has not advanced at the pace of such public opinion studies in the United States, in particular, but also Western Europe. First, it is important to acknowledge that there has historically been an influential trend in the literature on the Middle East region that reflects what Edward Said referred to as an Orientalist tradition in Western scholarship. The scholarship in this tradition has tended to essentialize the Other and especially Islam as it pertains to the life of Muslims in the East (Said 1978). This type of scholarship, which prioritized interpretations of Muslim societies through their ancient sacred texts, created a set of assumptions about Islamic culture and Muslims which still dominates scholarship on the region, if only in the efforts of various scholars to challenge some of the commonly held claims from this tradition, whose literature still casts a long shadow. Studies in this line of research have continued to make the same assumptions about Islam, measuring religion's influence through binary categories of religious versus nonreligious and equating Islam with sharia law. Such reductionist approaches have naturally neglected the pluralistic and dynamic nature of Islam (Ahmed 2015; Ayoob 2009). Thus it was a critical advance when Tessler (2002) and others sought to measure the religious-nonreligious binary and demonstrate its lack of significance and inability to explain attitudes toward political considerations such as support for democracy.

Beyond the impact of these older paradigms in the study of Muslim-majority countries, studies of religion in the MENA region have also lagged behind those in the US and Europe because of inadequate funding: countries such as the United States actively fund research into US politics and society through nuanced public opinion surveys and experiments that are simply not a financial priority for most Muslim-majority countries.[3] Even when funding is available and large national and cross-national surveys investigate opinions in these countries, the nature of many of these political regimes and their frequent desire to censor questions of political delicacy—including questions about the participants' involvement with specific religious communities or orders—prevents the kind of experimental designs and analysis that have been particularly illuminating in the US and elsewhere.

Although these constraints on the study of religion and attitudes in most Muslim-majority societies may seem to have brought us to an impasse, we believe there is still a way forward, even considering the current limitations of public opinion surveys in MENA. If there is, as we assume, religious variation at the communal level—regardless of whether we can currently measure this via surveys—an implication of this would be a dynamic connection between these communities and the existence of a variety of religious outlooks. By *religious outlook*, we mean an individual's broader cognitive framework for understanding the role of religion regarding social order and interactional norms. Why would there be a connection between various religious communities and religious outlooks? As Kellstedt and his colleagues (1996, 175) write, "The principal mechanisms for the worldly realization of religious beliefs are religious communities." How communities interact and understand themselves necessarily has social consequences that transcend the boundaries of the congregation itself, and this broader dynamic establishes how the congregation and its individual members place themselves within the society. To link this all together, it will be helpful to draw from the literature on religious markets (Stark and Finke 2000) to understand how various communities are distributed throughout society. We can then establish the connection between state regulation of religion and posture toward these religious communities and likely patterns of religious outlooks and political attitudes among members of these groups.

Religious Markets and Variation among Religious Communities

It may not be readily apparent why an individual's association with a religious community and its position in society and in relation to the state (rather than received doctrine) will strongly shape his or her religious outlook. In this regard, Stark and Finke's (2000) theory of religious markets offers a simple but useful analogy for generalizable assumptions of religious pluralism within a faith community—such as among Muslims in a Muslim-majority society—and we will use this theory as a basis to explain how diversity among communities could be logically distributed within a bounded society.

Stark and Finke (2000) propose that religious communities within a society are distributed according to the logic of supply and demand within a particular religious economy or market—that is, the broader politically and socially bounded community of faith. Absent heavy state intervention in the "supply" of options for religious participation, individuals select and prioritize different levels of religious practice and activity, spanning options from low intensity and lower costs to high intensity and higher cost. Locally bounded religious communities fit into these larger preference categories, which Stark and Finke (2000) refer to as "religious niches." These niches indicate the major categories of variation in the pattern of provision of services and experiences (i.e., benefits) offered by religious organizations within a religious economy along a scale determined by the increasing levels of costs but also religious "goods" accrued to the individual through participation.

In an unregulated market, it is assumed that the distribution of communities across the scale of niches will resemble something like a normal curve. On the far-left side of the scale, the "liberal" niche includes communities that require minimal cost but provide minimal rewards; in other words, their members are unencumbered by high demands and expectations, but such congregations also provide few benefits to these individuals and encourage high levels of free riding—that is, attempting to partake in common goods without sharing in the costs involved to produce them—reducing the overall corporate benefits that are seen as coming from participating together in spiritual activities or experiences.[4] At the other end of the niche scale are "strict" communities, which offer maximum costs and maximum rewards. These come from the tendency of communities in this niche to have high levels of exclusivity accompanied by similarly high levels of imposed costs that reduce free riding and bring valuable "club goods"—such as euphoria from intense group participation in spiritual activities, higher expectations of reciprocity, support and sacrifice from others, and deeper bonds of relationships—to its members (Iannaccone 1992). To the extent that the full array of options is open to the social market, the vast majority of individuals will nonetheless cluster in religious communities that fit the niches in the middle—the "moderate" and "conservative" niches. Communities in these niche options offer a religious experience that most evenly balances the costs and rewards within the particular social context, with conservative options leaning more toward strict and moderate leaning more toward liberal options.

Membership in a local religious community, whether a church, mosque, or other religious communal organization, involves cost-benefit trade-offs that ultimately establish the overall distribution of congregants. Where an individual's choice is free and unregulated, religious market theory anticipates that few would bother with liberal religious communities offering great freedom but little spiritual benefit and would instead replace such communal affiliations with secular alternatives if this is an available option. In other words, they would opt out of the "faith market" completely, leaving only a small proportion of the faith adherents in the liberal niche. Similarly, relatively few would be predicted to select the strictest options that have a higher religious club goods payoff because they come at the expense of other social goods, which are often lost to the individual due to the level of tension with society that such membership brings. According to Stark and Finke (2000), the vast majority of people within a religious market will select a trade-off toward the middle, which balances social goods, networks, and norms with religious goods, thus locating most individuals in moderate and conservative niche communities (in Stark and Finke's categorization).[5]

This trade-off between social and religious goods and the distribution of these trade-off decisions can be understood most simply within the framework of the conceptual scale put forward in Benton Johnson's (1963, 543) distinction between church and sect. He writes, "The distinction between church and sect involves a single variable the values of which range along a continuum from complete acceptance to complete rejection of the environment." In other words, "churches" in Johnson's definition are communities that are fairly comfortably integrated into the particular society. "Sects" are those communities that exist in much higher tension with the society around them. Stark and Finke (2000) similarly understand their religious niches as representing scaled categories of tension between religious communities and society. Most individuals will choose communities that allow them to maintain and integrate into social networks outside of the community yet provide them a certain measure of religious club goods at a reasonable personal cost or investment; hence, the authors envision an unregulated market with a distribution of individuals across the niches that approximates a normal curve (Stark and Finke 2000, 196).

Even in highly regulated religious markets within a dominant faith community (see Driessen 2014)—such as Sunni Islam in Turkey, Shia Islam in Iran, and many other countries in the MENA—evidence of a distribution across religious niches can be observed. In many places in the region, state regulations act to constrain practices and surveil communities that operate in the strictest niches. Simultaneously, state regulation or significant social censure also create tension for individuals and communities positioned within the liberal niches. Nonetheless, although the state may work to limit the supply of the niches on the extreme edges, as Stark and Finke (2000) propose, the natural demand for such a variety of options still leads to diversity in communal practices and, at times, even produces hidden communities. Introvigne (2006), in his discussion of religious markets in Turkey, delineates well-known religious communities in Turkey in distinct niches. Turkey, since its founding, has subsidized and attempted to regulate the public sphere to promote a particular strand of Sunni Islam compatible with a secular state through the Ministry of Religious Affairs (Diyanet İşleri Bakanlığı) (Lord 2018; Ozgur 2012). Beyond the fact that this state institution appoints imams and provides their weekly sermon materials, it has also regularly operated in such a way as to try to normalize expressions of Sunni Islam and ignore or obstruct Alevi Muslims[6] (Lord 2017). Yet the diversity of religious communities observed by Introvigne persists.

Why would such a distribution be inevitable among adherents to a particular faith, especially when that faith is the dominant belief system of that polity? This is where the discussion of a preferred equilibrium of goods comes into play (fig. 1.1). According to this model, individuals in a society can choose from three different types of social currencies related to the broader faith community in society: autonomy, social favorability, and religious club goods. Of these three, the currency relating to social favorability is the most transferable concerning one's larger community context. By operating squarely within the empowered norms of society, this social favorability gives an individual "capital" that can be applied in social, economic,

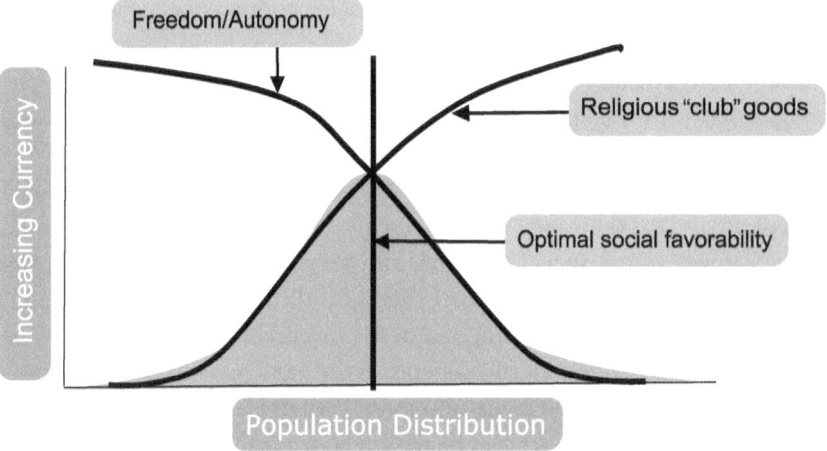

Figure 1.1. Religious Goods and Social Favorability

religious, and political domains. For this reason, a larger portion of society will choose a level of religious association and practice that allows them to maximize the benefits of social favorability. The more a religious community's behavior matches social norms, including a socially normative range of religious participation, the more they benefit from social favorability.

There are some, however, who personally prefer the narrower religious club goods currency. To the extent that social favorability allows currency exchange across a wide number of domains, religious club goods are a currency with a poor exchange across domains but with immense value for those investing in the singular religious community. As an individual increases in the pursuit of religious benefits and participation beyond the social norm, he or she increasingly loses broader social favorability as a consequence of practicing nonnormative and exclusive behavior. Iannaccone (1992) explains why religious communities would increase costs (often the loss of social favorability) and encourage communal exclusivity (in short, to counteract free riding), but the consequence is that religious identities associated with exclusive participation will constitute a smaller proportion of the total number of adherents to the broader faith community. As the line moves right from the median point (i.e., maximal social favor) in figure 1.1, one could imagine also that the trade-off between social favorability and religious club goods roughly begins to mirror an economic trade-off between club goods and material wealth. In other words, as one's tension with society increases through greater religious participation and investments, the potential social favorability cost this brings can also be economically costly.

Similarly, to the extent that individuals prefer self-determination and autonomy in their actions and behaviors, they will trade some social favorability for the ability to live their lives the way they want, make their own decisions, and set their own moral priorities. Here, too, there are potential consequences across social, political, and religious domains for investing in this particular currency, whether that is by affiliating with communities in the liberal niche or by opting out of the dominant faith altogether. The nature of the consequences will depend on the particular society's or state's posture toward those who favor autonomy. Nonetheless, it is an investment that some will always prefer and be willing to trade for (see fig. 1.1).

Religious Communities, the State, and Religious Outlooks—a Dynamic Model

Stark and Finke's (2000) propositions provide a model that helps us understand generally why religious communities within a society vary in their practices and levels of tension with society around them. This model helps us understand the fluidity and diversity of religious participation preferences within a religious economy. While it acknowledges that regulation plays an important role in determining the possible distributions of individuals across religious niches, it does not address how these distributions of religious communities and their respective levels of tension affect political attitudes. Nor does it effectively address all the implications of state regulation on these communities (Driessen 2014).

To better grasp the intersection of public opinion and religion in these countries, it is necessary to examine the link between communities, religious regulation, and individual attitudes. Considering the observed diversity of attitudes toward religiosity and democracy across countries (Ciftci 2010; Collins and Owen 2012; Driessen 2018; Fish 2002; Jamal 2006; Speirings 2014; Tessler 2002), what features of the national context can be considered to help us predict how attitudes toward democracy or regime types might be distributed within a country and cross-nationally? Can we find a basis for the proposition that the attitude of a member of a religious community toward politics and the state is based not primarily on doctrinal beliefs, per se, but on where that individual's religious community is positioned relative to society and the state and the resulting rational outlook based on that existing social dynamic?

Other studies have given us some clues in this regard. State structures and practices do make a difference. For example, regarding state-society interactions, Belge and Karakoç (2014) provide a clue to how communities' relations with the state translate into different attitudes. In their surveys involving four national contexts, Christian religious minorities showed significant and positive support for autocracy in their communities (Egypt and Jordan) while ethnic minorities (Amazighs in Morocco and Kurds in Turkey) showed significant and negative support for autocracy. As the authors point out, the critical factor distinguishing support among these religious and linguistic minorities is most likely not the ideological difference between religious and ethnic groups but the minority groups' relational status to the existing regime. In other words, the long-standing protection of the rights of Christian minorities by autocratic regimes in Egypt and Jordan explains their support for autocracy; this was not a consequence of their doctrinal principles. Similarly, it is likely that the relatively poor social and political standing of the linguistic minorities within autocratic or illiberal regimes engendered greater antagonism toward their autocratic states and a search for alternatives. Thus, Belge and Karakoç (2014) highlight the potential salience of the sociopolitical standing of one's socioreligious community and congregation on that person's attitudes toward the state and regime type.

Regarding the implications of other patterns of state-society dynamics, Buckley (2016) has shown how national social contexts translate into preferences regarding religious elites' involvement in politics. Using survey data and a qualitative case study, he provides what some would consider a counterintuitive portrait, showing that in countries where religious participation is lower, support for religious elites' involvement in politics is higher. Here he sees that individuals who support clerical involvement in politics do so largely out of desperation. If there are ways for religious elites to influence state-society-religion dynamics, devout adherents will not prefer to have their religious community's identity sullied by "dirty politics" or cause division in the ranks of the pious due to partisan alignment (Grzymala-Busse 2015). Thus, the stronger the religious community's position, the less likely that its devout members will want their elites to be involved in politics. They already have what they want. Buckley's study highlights that the relational dynamic—between religious communities on one side and the state and society on the other—affects political preferences independent from substantive doctrines. The logic determining the attitudinal preferences is not religious beliefs but relational realities.

While Buckley analyzes the individual's outlook regarding politics and the state, Anna Grzymala-Busse (2015), in *Nations under God*, looks at these same dynamics at the level of the state. Her purpose is to highlight various ways in which the state has or has not incorporated the political preferences of the religious elites within the dominant national faith. She accounts for a number of factors, such as the role that religious elites played during nation building, whether the dominant faith has a social monopoly, and the manner in which the religious elites attempt to influence the state—through church-state arrangements or partisan alignment. Grzymala-Busse places much of the focus of her work on the politics of religious denominations at the elite level, corresponding to a heavier emphasis on predominantly Catholic countries where such top-down views of the church in a society are more appropriate. Elite politics, of course, is not the primary focus of this study; nonetheless, her work very nicely demonstrates that the way in which the state and society perceive the religious establishment at a macro faith-community level has a huge impact on whether religious views are incorporated into the political structure and policy.[7]

Although Grzymala-Busse's analysis is at the level of entire faith communities, the principal dynamic is transferable to the study of smaller subsets within the larger faith community—for example, religious niches, denominations, and locally bounded religious communities. Some local religious communities and denominations operate within religious niches that find more approval or acceptability from the state and society at large. Others, of course, receive less approval. We would expect to find differentiation in the extent to which these communities find themselves within the political mainstream, and these dynamics would subsequently affect communities' and their members' attitudes toward the state and preferences regarding politics and policy between religion and state. Hence, these elements can help us explain what Buckley observed in his study.

Michael Dreissen (2014) brings together the literature concerning the political economy of religion and the issue of religious regulation in many Muslim-majority societies. While adhering to the logic of religious markets in general, Dreissen tackles the question of why levels of religiosity are so high in many of the highly regulated Muslim-majority societies. Stark and Finke (2000) argue that state regulation of religion may drive down the rates of practice and belief, and such observed patterns are consistent in Western

Europe and elsewhere. Although there is evidence of depressed levels of mosque attendance in Iran and Saudi Arabia (Moaddel 2010; Tezcür and Azadarmaki 2008), which would fit Stark and Finke's general proposition, this is not generally the case for Muslim-majority countries. Dreissen (2014) argues that the critical divergence is that the consequences of regulation in authoritarian countries are different than in democracies and that the type of regulation the state engages in makes a difference. In countries where the state provides incentives and support for the dominant faith, such encouragement leads to higher levels of participation compared to states that primarily use coercive and restrictive means to regulate religious practice.

This distinction could also help explain why certain individuals would inherently avoid religious attendance in Iran (Kazemipur and Rezaei 2003; Tezcür and Azadarmaki 2008) and Saudi Arabia (Moaddel 2010). In both cases, the intertwining of religious institutions with the state creates an environment geared largely toward regulating religious behavior in public rather than incentivizing it. Adhering to religious norms is an expected behavior, not something that should be rewarded. In these regimes, the rewards to religiosity go to a select few. Especially in Iran, where the mosque has become an explicit mouthpiece for the regime, the regular population of the mosque often comprises those who have been individually incentivized to be present—that is, pensioners, members of the state bureaucracy, and the Basij corps. The complex marriage of state and religion in Saudi Arabia has also relegated religious behavior to an expectation; the state's investments in self-legitimizing incentives operate from the state to the citizen directly through the distribution of rents. In other words, one can generally see an element of co-optation in most states' incentives and favoritism toward religious communities, whose favor toward the state can serve to provide legitimation. The balance and need for incentivizing religion primarily occur in states where religious authorities are highly respected but are, nonetheless, differentiated from the state proper, such as in Egypt, Jordan, and Morocco. In Iran and Saudi Arabia, the marriage has been consummated; gestures toward desirable religious elites to garner state support from their communities are unnecessary. Instead, the state-entangled religious elites primarily work to pressure the state to ensure that public behavior is regulated to reflect the preferred religious norms.

In general, though, unlike in democracies, in authoritarian contexts where religion is highly regulated, even if reduced options do not fit an individual's religious niche preference, such individuals have a much harder time opting out of communal religious participation entirely. Stark and Finke (2000) also argue, as Driessen (2014) notes, that while strong incentives and coercion operate to direct people toward Islam, there is relatively open diversity among individual communities. As we have discussed above, the nonhierarchical nature of Sunni Islam allows for a level of flexibility at the community/mosque level that is hard to regulate, although many regimes have tried. Where more diversity is allowed at the level of the mosque, perhaps this increased variety addresses the demand for various niches, which also increases participation in ways predicted by unregulated markets. Thus, participation in Muslim-majority states that are both authoritarian and favorable in their promotion of certain faith communities (those that exemplify what state elites consider the ideal norms of participation) could be said to have push and pull factors driving individuals toward religious communities that more or less meet their niche demands.

If we combine the consideration of various religious niches that operate in varying degrees of tension with society and the state, we can begin to anticipate probable patterns in attitudes from members in these different religious communities. Scholars have noted that the level of distinction between the members of the religious community and the broader society has sway over the extent to which individuals' outlooks are affected by their religious association (Djupe and Gilbert 2008; McClendon and Reidl 2019). Thus, the more the religious community resembles the broader society (low tension, high social favorability), the less likely that religious association will have a strong, unique influence on their political attitudes. The broader network of social interaction for individuals in these low-tension religious communities will cause the social influence of their religious association to be more diffuse because it has more competitors for influence in the society at large (McClendon and Riedl 2019, 8).

For individuals in religious communities whose tension with society is higher, the influence of their religious association on their political attitudes and outlooks will be relatively higher and more consistent across individual members (Djupe and Gilbert 2008, 14; Gilbert 1993). Groups, either in the liberal or strict niches, who experience tension with both society and the state will generally have either political attitudes that favor pluralism and liberalization or, less frequently, antisystem radical attitudes. To the extent that they seek system-based solutions, groups that realize that they are in a socially marginal position will most likely see pluralism (i.e., "live and let live") as their path to social survival within their country's political system. This is because they often realize that their marginal position concerning the state and society will not engender popular support for their religious preferences; in fact, pressure for the political implementation of their points of view would likely encounter a costly repressive response. Outside of violent and revolutionary appropriation of the apparatuses of the state, the rational course of action for such groups would be political quietism or support of policy that provides acceptance of religious pluralism in beliefs and practices. Tilly's (2005) discussion of Waldensians in Europe in his introduction to *Trust and Rule* points out very nicely these dynamics in the historical context of a community in a high degree of tension with society.

On the other hand, state regulation or changes in state positions toward religious communities with nonnormative practices could lead to other predictable patterns. Pious communities and their members, whose religious practices and investments put them on the margins of social norms and who experience far more tension with society than they do with the state, will tend to take political attitudes that support the political status quo (Belge and Karakoç 2015). In these contexts, such religious communities see the current political order as a protector that allows their community to survive despite social disfavor. This understanding will strongly mitigate their likelihood to hold preferences for major changes in political institutions or regime type that would upset the status quo. However, contexts in which the tension between the state and the religious community is much higher than the tension between the group and society—in other words, in situation in which members of these groups see society as generally having a posture of support for their religious community vis-à-vis an oppositional state—will likely encourage political preferences that would challenge the status quo. Thus, where a group believes that they have social support that exceeds their existing favor with the state, they have good reason to push for political activism where such opportunities are available. Social support can be used for leverage to push for political change in the existing system, which—depending on the system—could encourage democratic or nondemocratic impulses. Many of the traditional Islamist organizations and parties that operate within their national context could be seen as fitting within this category, where members of these religious communities perceive that they have garnered a measure of support in society in the face of a seemingly religiously oppressive state.

Figure 1.2 provides an overall illustration of this dynamic between religious communities, state regulation, and religious outlooks, by which we mean

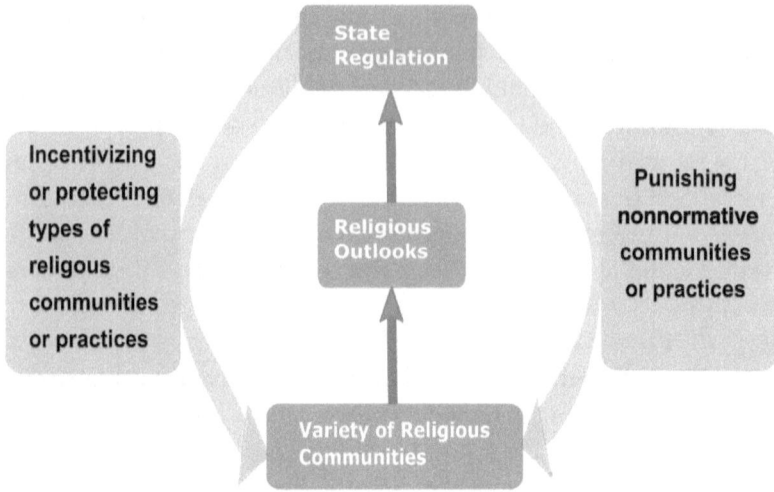

Figure 1.2. State Regulation, Religious Communities, and Religious Outlooks

cognitive frameworks for understanding the role of religion in relation to social and political orders and norms. The state interacts with religious communities through their practices of incentivizing or punishing religious behavior. Religious outlooks should not be seen as static, and they generally form as a logical outgrowth of the state-society relational dynamic with one's religious community. Unlike a preference for level of religious practice, which strongly guides one's choice of religious community, because outlooks are most often (though not always) cultivated through the community-society-state interaction, the arrow is more likely outgoing from community to outlook. Religious outlooks need a context regarding how their community would best fit within the broader social domain. Thus, it is more likely that people's outlooks develop from the context of the community that they have chosen rather than their outlook determining their community preference, although the opposite is also possible. The relatively weaker arrow from religious outlooks to state regulation represents the fact that these attitudes toward state-society and religious preferences have a variable impact—and likely a weak one—on state policy and practices regarding religion.

While all of this would lead us to assume that the individual country-level context is important for understanding how a variety of religious outlooks might be distributed in a country, the discussion of these dynamics among religious communities, the state, and society also highlights the path toward understanding and anticipating patterns across countries. Outlooks are primarily an individual's rational preference framework regarding religion-society relations, stemming from that person's understanding of the state-society relational dynamic with his or her religious community. As a result, one can anticipate that patterns of punishing or supportive regulations by a state would lead to different patterns of distributional proportions for various religious outlooks across countries and across faith traditions. In short, we propose that a probabilistic logic operates between states and religious communities that could help explain the variation in the distribution of religious outlooks among individuals within a country. Attitudes toward religious pluralism and religion in the public sphere are strongly influenced by (1) where one's religious community is located within the religious market and (2) how regimes behave toward these communities situated in varying degrees from the normative center. Thus, we anticipate that political outlooks formed by members of different religious communities would shift in generally predictable ways across the distribution curve of the broader faith community (or religious market) in the country and in relation to the tension dynamic—that is, the interactive levels of tension between the individual's religious community and society and between that community and the state.

Conclusion

This chapter has highlighted many of the dynamics that this book will examine and further articulate in the subsequent chapters. The premise of this work is that attitudes and outlooks among the devout are diverse, a fact that has often been missed in the linear assumptions behind empirical measures of religiosity in survey data based on understandably general indicators. We argue that the diversity of political opinions and preferences among the devout should not be seen as random but rather as based on a number of shaping factors. Although many would assume that such diversity comes from substantive differences in formal doctrine, this chapter builds a theoretical argument that for the broader preferences and outlooks regarding politics and society, the relational influence of religion and religious association might be even more important.

Individuals choose to associate with religious communities that offer differing levels of participation and goods, which also come with differing levels of cost to the individual for their participation and inclusion in the community. Within the broader society, these communities exist in varying degrees of tension with society and in relation to the state. We believe that this dynamic has a major influence on individuals' attitudes toward politics, political orientations, and society. It is not only doctrine but more significantly how the community chooses to live and act relative to the normative practices of the broader society that profoundly influences how they filter political and social preferences and positions. The positions that religious communities occupy relative to other religious communities and the social status quo in a country should generally inform political attitudes and regime preferences, as well as preferences for general economic policy. We believe attitudes regarding these elements could be influenced by religion, but this influence is filtered through a social context for religious practice that must be taken into account. For attitudes on these larger political and economic preferences, it is not substantive religious doctrine that is likely the determining factor but that individual's religious community's relative position and interaction with society.

This would lead us to a number of conclusions regarding the dynamic between religion, individuals, and their political attitudes and orientations. First, this dynamic leads individuals from different religious communities in society to form different—and sometimes completely contradictory—political attitudes and orientations. This is because the context of their religious community association and that community's interaction with society and the state. The implications of these dynamics lead to different filters through which an individual's political attitudes and orientations are formed. For those in communities who are highly socially normative and whose members receive a high degree of social favorability, the religious filter is likely less influential and competes with many other potential associations.

Second, it must be reiterated that this relationship is dynamic and not static. While an individual's preferences for religious practice and participation may be generally static, to the extent that their social or political context changes, we would also expect some movement in their political attitudes and preferences over time unrelated to their doctrinal beliefs or religious community affiliation. From time to time, significant social and political events may play a catalyzing role in creating this shifting of outlooks. In the context of MENA, these have included constitutional revolutions, such mass uprisings as the Arab Spring, social revolutions, and civil war (as in Algeria). These events are likely to alter the relational dynamics to bring about new calculations that significantly inform religious outlooks.

Before we tease out the evidence for the patterns and implications of these diverse religious outlooks in existing survey data, it would be helpful to look more closely at the pattern of political behavior of members in particular religious communities over time. A closer view of the dynamics in specific communities (where we have greater descriptive depth and can control for competing variables, such as different state contexts and doctrinal difference) will assist us in understanding how these dynamics might operate in specific environments. It is to this task that we now turn.

Notes

1. This idea is similar to An-Naim's (2008) theory proposing that democracy would be an acceptable form of government for Muslims to the extent that they could be part of civic debate and have a chance to influence policy according to their religious beliefs.

2. Putnam and Campbell (2010) have observed the increasing salience of religiosity as a variable to measure political attitudes, but even here, they see a major role for religious communities.

3. Recently, there has been a surge of studies using survey experiments and large-scale public opinion surveys in the Arab Middle East. See Bush and Jamal 2015; Corstange 2014; Grewal et al. 2019; Masoud, Jamal, and Nugent 2016; and Tessler, Jamal, and Robbins 2012.

4. This could be seen as comparing the experience difference between attending the game of a sports team with a raucous, highly participatory crowd and viewing the same game quietly and passively in a largely empty stadium. The outcome of the game might be similar, but the opportunity for engaged participation in the event qualitatively enhances the experience for the individual participating.

5. From this discussion, it should be evident that this model does not cover overall distribution of groups in a society, as those who would be classified as nonreligious will leave the religious market. Therefore, the discussion is limited to those who choose, even nominally, to remain in this market.

6. Alevis are diverse heterodox communities in Turkey that share some of their broad religious tenets (such as the belief in the Twelfth Imam and veneration of 'Ali) with Shia Muslims.

7. For a study of the dynamics of the state regulation of religion in the Tunisian and Moroccan case, see Feuer 2018.

2

ATTITUDES OF THE DEVOUT

The Nature of the Substance or the Nurture of Relationship?

The previous chapter emphasized the relational influence religion can have in filtering individual attitudes toward politics and society. We propose that this influence can also be dynamic: individual attitudes and orientations shift as social and political contexts change. By positing the importance of religion's relational influence on the broader issues of politics and society, we understand this influence to be shaped by both social identity dynamics and conformity to the shared opinions of one's ingroup. This implies, of course, that the weaker these religious associational ties are, the more likely it is that other associational ties will influence individuals' views. This can occur when individuals place a higher value on these other ties or to the extent that opinions are diluted through associations with groups with competing viewpoints (McClendon and Riedl 2019). The relational influence of religion appears to be heightened where the level of distinction between a particular religious community and their broader social context is high. In other words, we would anticipate that the filtering influence of religious communities on political attitudes would be stronger for individuals who associate and participate with religious communities that are in higher levels of tension with their social environment.

In this chapter, we explore these questions through a case comparison of a set of religious communities in Turkey from the Naqshbandi orders. A close study of different communities of Naqshbandis is beneficial as it allows us to examine our theoretical propositions while controlling for a number of contextual variables and being able to draw from accessible information about these groups over time. Naqshbandis combine Sunni Islam with Sufi practices, and their spiritual tree spans from Central Asia to India over the course of many centuries. The Khalidi-Naqshbandi variant that is predominant in Turkey emphasizes religious orthodoxy, the importance of sharia, and the sunna of the Prophet Muhammad and has come to represent the dominant expression of greater religious devotion in Turkey (Yavuz 2003). But a particular advantage of examining this group is that—outside of its shared ideological framework and highly participatory, close-knit communities—the Naqshbandis in Turkey show a great deal of subcommunal diversity. Famously situated under the umbrella of the Naqshbandi order are very distinct and identifiable groups, such as the Süleymancı, Menzilci, İskenderpaşa, İsmailağa, and Erenköy communities (*cemaat*). The Sufi tendency to place a high degree of obligation on members toward the community also allows us to classify a large proportion of the members of these well-known variations of the Naqshbandi order in Turkey as devout. If we apply the classification of Stark and Finke (2000) regarding religious niches to the Turkish religious economy, all these groups would be classified as falling within the niche categories of conservative (more generally) or strict (in the case of the İsmailağa community).

Our focus on the single case of Turkey and subcommunal variation among Naqshbandis also comes with methodological advantages. As Gerring (2006, 1) succinctly says, "Sometimes, in-depth knowledge of an individual example is more helpful than fleeting knowledge about a larger number of examples. We gain better understanding of the whole by focusing on a key part." A single case can also help obtain high levels of construct validity (George and Bennet 2005). To the extent that our analysis proposes a dynamic interaction between religious communities, the state and society, and the religious outlooks of individuals, the in-depth study of the Naqshbandis will be useful for teasing out these dynamics in a way that cross-sectional survey data cannot do. This approach will unfold nuances about the contextual determinants of religious outlooks. A final methodological advantage of studying the subcommunal variation within the Naqshbandi order in Turkey relates to the possibility of neatly describing the explanatory mechanisms underlying the complex web of synergies between state-religion relations, communities, and religious outlooks.

Studying Naqshbandi communities offers ideal opportunities to explore the issues we advance in subsequent chapters. First, the Naqshbandis in Turkey provide multiple observations within a single case. By looking at the approaches to politics by distinct Naqshbandi communities tied together by the same ideological order, we have a natural control for the possibility that different attitudes toward politics by these communities could be caused by important differences in the essential doctrines of these groups. Within the Naqshbandis, it is not primarily ideology but communal and individual practice that distinguishes the groups. Though it is impossible to say that any two communities have the same doctrinal understandings, the unity across these Naqshbandi groups is far greater than the differences in beliefs. In fact, in a study of theological differences between two of the most distinct communities—İskenderpaşa and İsmailağa—the most profound takeaway from the study was their surprising similarity in religious perspectives on fairly minute questions (Hülür 1999). Thus, to the extent that we find distinct or varying political approaches in the two communities, we can more effectively rule out important doctrinal—that is, substantive—differences as the cause.

Many people familiar with Turkish society are also aware of a similar large community stemming from the Kadiri order of brotherhoods that are primarily represented in Turkey by the subbranches broadly under the textual authority of the *Risale-i Nur* (*Epistles of Light*), written by Bediüzzaman Said Nursi. The largest and most controversial branch in this tree is the community that closely follows the spiritual guidance of Fethullah Gülen. Although there are many similarities between the membership and broader spirituality of the Naqshbandi and Kadiri/Nurcu groups, we believe that the benefit of focusing on one major Sufi order is preferable. Adding communities from different orders or doctrinal ideologies, however slight, would open the possibility that different attitudes among sublevel communities were due to doctrine, given the possible weight of this variable as an explanatory factor. Nonetheless, had we chosen to explore the communities branching from Said Nursi, our knowledge of those groups suggests that the observations of attitude patterns among individuals in their communities would be similar.

The Naqshbandis also offer an ideal study population because an examination of communal approaches to politics benefits from the Turkish context. The Turkish state and the nature of state-society-religion relations in the country have fluctuated significantly across its short history. Within the last one hundred years, the state's approaches to religion and society have changed markedly at least a half-dozen times and have ranged widely, from animosity to ambivalence to favor. This allows us to observe whether the political approaches of religious communities change when political stances on religion change. Because these fluctuations happened over such a short period, observed changes in political attitudes are less likely to be attributable to generational or slow-moving doctrinal or ideological changes and more likely to be a result of variables relevant to the present study.

Thus, one country and one large religious order within that single country provide us with numerous observations to discuss while simultaneously controlling for critical alternative explanatory variables such as doctrinal difference or gradual doctrinal change. We believe that it is likely that such dynamics could be observed in other countries in the region or other Muslim-majority societies, but the Naqshbandis also provide us with the additional benefit of extensive existing research on multiple prominent communities that is available for us to draw from. The number of scholars and the level of scholarship on religion in society in Turkey allow for a richer exploration of these groups over time than is easily available to us in communities in other countries. Furthermore, the general availability of information about these communities in Turkey also provides accountability for our analysis and any interpretations we might make. The sublevel groups discussed in this chapter are widely recognized as the most well-known Naqshbandi communities. The widespread familiarity with and knowledge of the various communal orders among the Naqshbandis in Turkey discussed in this chapter also helps to allay concerns that we have only chosen for study particular subsets of the Naqshbandi orders because they were likely to confirm a theoretical or ideological agenda. Hence, we discuss *all* the large communal manifestations of Naqshbandi orders in Turkey of which there is broader knowledge.

The following section briefly provides the national and political context in which Naqshbandi communities in Turkey are operating. We then introduce the relatively well-known communal orders, their social and religious practices, and their characteristic approaches to politics in the country. We follow this with a discussion of how these groups might have changed their political practices and attitudes over time in the face of important changes in the behavior of the state toward religion. As will be seen below, the various Naqshbandi groups demonstrate a variety of distinct behaviors toward politics that tend to correspond to the level of tension or exclusivity those communities prefer in relation to the broader society surrounding them.

Religious Communities in the Turkish Republic

Since the founding of the republic in 1923, the Turkish state has not been entirely consistent in its approach to religion in the public sphere. At numerous points, the policy and attitude of the state were even self-contradictory, relying on religious identity while simultaneously discouraging practice (Çağaptay 2002; Kaplan 2006). One could imagine that such shifts in policies might have shaped how devout individuals oriented themselves toward politics and affected their preferences for political and institutional alternatives in governance.

As many scholars now attest, the institutional modernization, centralization, and secularization of the Ottoman regime had begun long before the Turkish Republic emerged from the empire's ashes following World War I (Berkes 1964; Zürcher 2004). However, the institutional steps taken by Ataturk to secularize society through increased differentiation between the sacred and profane through regulation of Islam in the public sphere brought the issue of state-religious society relations to the forefront for a great number of individuals living in the country. In 1924, laws were passed to abolish the caliphate, nationalize the education system while shuttering Islamic seminaries (*medrese*), and transform the Ministry of Sharia and Charitable Foundations into a Ministry of Religious Affairs (MRA or Diyanet İsleri Bakanlığı) under the supervision of the prime minister. Along with the adoption of the Swiss civil code in 1926, these actions curtailed the political, economic, and judicial functions of the Turkish religious authorities (ulema) and left them with a largely toothless social mandate within a secular and modern nation.

Ataturk and the early republican elite did not eliminate the existing ulema, however; they reappropriated and repurposed them for their nation-building project (Aktürk 2015; Lord 2018). As a consequence—although the state clipped the political, economic, and judicial talons of the religious elites—the Turkish ulema, through the MRA, found themselves in a position to regulate the standards for religious practices and norms in the country. Because this institution provided the means to regulate religious behavior, it became an arena of contestation, as existing religious elites competed for the right to oversee the officially sanctioned and state-funded spiritual guidance of the nation. When state elites gave the MRA the ability to educate and train future religious leaders (i.e., imams) through the state's Imam Hatip Okullari (minister and preacher schools), those within the walls of the MRA were further able to consolidate their ability to establish the norms of religious practice in Turkey.

Religious groups who clearly fell outside the lines of sanctioned practice experienced the wrath of the state. Sufi dervish lodges, for example, who could not easily hide their distinct and necessarily communal practices from the state, found themselves at the hard end of the state's regulatory stick. Other communities, however, such as the Naqshbandi and Kadiri Sunni-Sufi orders, were able to maintain their communities and practices more easily and discreetly through their mosques (Yavuz 2003). Thus, despite the efforts to standardize and regulate religious practices within the Turkish Republic, varieties of practice and doctrine persisted across religious communities. Relations between the state and these communities varied in important ways, however. While state and political elites often acted with antagonism toward public displays of what they deemed as excessive or nonnormative religious devotion, they also granted those practicing their faith in ways sanctioned by the state social favor and acceptance that other communities rarely, if ever, realized. These disparities among the practices of religious communities and their consequences created differences in the perceptions of state-religion relations even within members of the Sunni Muslim community, which comprised 85 percent of the Turkish population. As a result, the level of tension between religious communities and the state rarely abated, especially during the initial single-party period prior to the initiation of multiparty politics in the mid-1940s.

Following the Second World War, democratization came to Turkey, and democracy and multiparty politics constituted a referendum of sorts on the relation between the state and religion. While it is important to emphasize that the initial two-party contest was not solely or even primarily divided by a secular-religious cleavage, it would also be false to completely overlook this dynamic (Sunar and Toprak 1983; Wuthrich 2015). Even though the leaders of both major parties in the 1950s came from the same secular, elite social circles as the previous administration, the segment of Turkish religious society whose norms had put them outside the status quo undoubtedly hailed the coming of democratization as an opportunity to redefine their community's status relative to the state. The new Democrat Party (DP) leadership was not particularly religious, but their social liberalization approach represented a break from the authoritarian single-party arrangement that had been problematic for communities whose practices were in tension with state-established republican norms.

When the DP won the election in 1950, the members of devout communities mostly supported the transition and assumed that democracy would provide a social "correction" in support of their preferences. Of course, some groups miscalculated the extent to which democratization would promote religion in society and topple the previous social status quo. The most famous miscalculation came from members of the Ticani sect, who, shortly after the DP took power, began to deface statues and busts of Ataturk in public spaces. Their religious community leader, Kemal Pilavoğlu, was arrested and placed under house arrest. The DP subsequently passed a number of laws protecting the memory of Ataturk and establishing increasingly harsh penalties for defamatory behavior (Karpat 1959; Zürcher 2004). Thus, while the new government did indeed reduce the restrictions on some religious practices (such as allowing the call to prayer to be recited in Arabic rather than Turkish), they continued to ensure that religious political mobilization and religious leaders were kept at a distance from elite politics or policy decision-making.

Following a junior officers' coup in May 1960, opportunities for religious communities to be politically active shifted again. The 1961 constitution increased political rights for individuals and groups, showed greater tolerance for ideological politics, and ushered in proportional representation. By the end of the 1960s, some religious leaders and political elites saw the opportunity to mobilize voters and advocate policies under an explicitly Islamist banner. Necmettin Erbakan and others, with the encouragement and blessing of the Naqshbandi sheik Mehmet Zahit Kotku, established the National Order Party (Milli Nizam Partisi) (Çakır 1990; Lord 2018; Yavuz 2003). After another military intervention in 1971, the National Order Party was banned, so its cadre renamed themselves and became the National Salvation Party (MSP, Milli Selamet Partisi). The MSP ostensibly gave organized religion a politically active presence; however, this appearance of unity among members of conservative religious communities was very brief. Internal politics and distinct approaches led to the rapid fragmentation of the party after it entered parliament in 1973. By the general election of 1977, religious communities such as the Nurcus and other Kadiri sects had left the MSP to the Naqshbandis and redirected their votes to more conventional conservative parties that operated as a (much stronger) rival to the less powerful religious party, the MSP (Yavuz 2003).

The 1980 military coup initiated a new political "fruit basket upset" that ultimately overturned the seats of the established political elites and simultaneously elevated the functional role of religion in society. The military had not taken this tack out of religious conviction but as a functional antidote to the prevailing disorder in Turkey at the time. From the perspective of the military, what is often referred to as the "Turkish-Islamic synthesis" was an incorporation of religion into officially sanctioned social norms through state education (Kaplan 2006). This was an attempt to co-opt the most beneficial elements of Islam to re-instill unity and social order after a protracted period of ideologically driven fratricide. The security-oriented 1982 constitution left no doubt in the mind of anyone in Turkey as to who was in charge. Nonetheless, for those operating under the officially sanctioned Islam of the state and the MRA, the grounds were favorably set for the activities of religious communities within their local contexts. Furthermore, Turkey's economic policy under the leadership of Turgut Özal brought money into the heartland of religiously conservative Turkey. At this time, religious individuals and communities increasingly found that they were awash in economic capital that could be reinvested for personal or religious purposes (Tuğal 2009; Yavuz 2003; Yıldırım 2016).

As Turkey and its religious communities and individuals continued to develop economically, the potential for further economic and political power led some religious communities to become more involved with politics in an effort to stabilize or further advance their social, political, and economic gains. By the mid-1990s, Erbakan's Welfare Party—the newest manifestation of the string of Islamist parties that he tied to what he called the "National View" (*Milli Görüş*) movement—managed to produce an electoral victory at the national level, winning a slim plurality in 1995 and the lead seat for Erbakan in a coalition government in 1996. A year into Erbakan's term, the military, buttressed by the media and the social mobilization of supporters of the traditional secular order in Turkey, produced an ultimatum that ultimately forced Erbakan out of office.

This setback, directly and indirectly, led to the rise of Recep Tayyip Erdoğan, the mayor of Istanbul and one of the bright young leaders of Erbakan's party. The party that Erdoğan and dissenters from Erbakan's National View movement founded, the Justice and Development Party, offered a fusion of Islamist politics and the conservative and economically liberal center right in Turkey. While it absorbed the ideological space of the collapsing center-right parties, its leadership had strong credentials in Islamist and religious-conservative politics. For many of the individuals in religious communities long in tension with the Turkish state, rule by the Justice and Development Party (AKP, Adalet ve Kalkınma Partisi) has come to represent new opportunities and possibilities both for their religious communities and for personal prosperity (Tuğal 2009).

The overview of the Turkish state's relationship with religious society points out several things that are beneficial to keep in mind. The state's countenance toward religious society in Turkey varied with time and showed different patterns of punishment and support to different communities; additionally, despite a clear effort to do so, the state was not able to establish social norms that were adopted by all. The attitude of religious communities toward the Turkish state was distinctly different during the single-party period than during the era of multiparty politics. It is safe to say that many devout Sunnis in Turkey were supportive of democratization when liberalization operated to benefit them in the 1940s and 1950s. Similar groups would likely be less supportive of social liberalization policies under President Recep Tayyip Erdoğan, as Cihan Tuğal (2009) has observed in the changes in political attitudes of Islamists toward the Turkish state pre- and post-AKP rule.

Not all religious communities responded in the same way to the changes in state behavior and policies. Depending on how different communities related to the status quo, the responses of their members could be very different. To the extent that one's religious community was largely unaffected by state policies, the division in attitudes and political preferences could be explained by other factors, social or functional (Meeker 2002). Even in the current period, as the antagonism between President Erdoğan and the Gülen community plays out as an international spectacle, different religious communities have different responses to current politics in the country.

Finally, to the extent that the state has tried to impose a standard of religious practice in Turkey, centralized and coordinated through the Ministry of Religious Affairs, groups outside the sanctioned norm continue to exist and even thrive. The Naqshbandi, Nurcu, and Kadiri orders continue to thrive and, in some ways, have come to represent the orthodox manifestations of Sunni Islam to a large proportion of Turkish society. These groups, even when the state responded with a heavy hand toward unsanctioned practices, found a way to maintain their networks. They have also shown an ability to persist by appropriating the means and opportunities provided to religious society, such as operating through state-run mosques and securing positions in the MRA, although their ability to do this has fluctuated.

While the general picture of religious communities' interactions with the Turkish state presents a beneficial portrait of the dynamics, it is useful to clarify these patterns further by examining a particular set of religious communities, the Naqshbandis: What is the nature of these communities? And how do they orient themselves to politics and the Turkish state?

Being Naqshbandi Differently

Naqshbandis are a Sufi order in Turkey whose members adhere to the Sunni orthodoxy of the Hanafi school of jurisprudence, which is the predominant Sunni interpretation in Turkey among Turks. Their focus on social activism and renewal differentiates these orders from many other orders in which one's internal state, the disciplining of desire (*nefs*), is the predominant focus. Distinct from non-Sufi orthodox Sunni groups, however, all Naqshbandi groups in Turkey incorporate rituals that place the leader, the sheikh, at the physical and spiritual center of their religious practices, as they see these sheikhs as the physical manifestation of the continuance of a long spiritual chain (*silsile*). For initiated members, this involves participating in the ritual of *rabıta*, the meditation of the sheikh, who transfers spiritual light on those circled or circling around him. The assumption is that as the sheikh takes up a central position in the midst of the followers of the order, he is able to transfer the divine light to them. Often as he does so, members perform the *zikir*, a ritualized practice of repeatedly reciting the names of God, together (Yükleyen 2010). Many other Sufi groups require a lodge (*tekke*) to perform their rituals, but Naqshbandis do not and can perform most of their duties in mosques or informal gathering spaces. This is one of the reasons why these groups were able to thrive even when the early republican elites moved to close the venues of other Sufi and heterodox communities.

At this point, it is helpful to return to the classic practice of distinguishing between religious groups based on their level of tension with their social environment (Johnson 1963, 543; Stark and Finke 2000, 143). A group's level of tension with society can be generated by a variety of different factors. One of the most obvious ways to generate tension is through unique, identifiable physical characteristics—such as manner of dress—that may come through participation in an exclusive religious community. Members might wear distinct garments that physically demonstrate their association with the group. Tension might also occur through behaviors that ultimately cause members of a religious community to opt out of socially normative practices or engage in behaviors that clarify their association with a group. These include such manners as socially distancing themselves from women, specific worship rituals, and the use of particular words in speech. The demands of group membership might be time consuming, and the very act of participation might pull the individual members out of society at large.

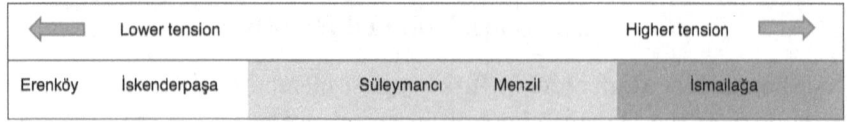

Figure 2.1. Relative Levels of Tension with Society among Various Naqshbandi Communities

Exclusivity, attitudes to the systems and technology of the world around them, and the level of private practices of rituals beyond what is conventionally associated with the faith would also indicate the relative level of tension of a group with society at large. Of the Naqshbandi groups discussed in this chapter, their overall level of tension with society is roughly reflected in figure 2.1.

A prime example of a community with a high level of tension would be the İsmailağa community, which has chosen to distinguish itself from the norms of attire that are common in the metropolis of Istanbul, where the main community resides. The baggy pants (*şalvar*), long robes (*cübbe*), and turbans (*sarık*) worn by the men clearly differentiate them from even other religious conservatives in their urban environment. The women shroud themselves in the *çarşaf*, a black, head-to-toe overgarment that covers all but the face or eyes. In this sense, even this group members' physical presentation of themselves, whether men or women, demonstrates a rejection of the environment around them and their connection to their religious community (Çakır 1990). Among all the Naqshbandi groups, the İsmailağa community exhibits the highest tension with modern Turkish society and its norms.

The Naqshbandi community associated with Erenköy's Zihnipaşa Mosque, following in the tradition of Sheikh Mahmud Sami Ramazanoğlu, would be a prominent example of a Naqshbandi group in relatively low tension with the society around them (although the İskenderpaşa Mosque community would also be similar in this regard). Although it adheres to the classic practices of the Naqshbandi, the Zihnipaşa Mosque's community, through the initial priorities and focus on elite outreach of Sheikh Ramazanoğlu, has catered to and welcomed the economic movers and shakers in Turkish society by targeting the spiritual welfare of the social upper echelon. Therefore, this group, composed of prominent business executives, journalists, and academics, sees its role as applying Islamic ethics while engaging fully with the social and economic world around them (Çakır 1990; Yavuz 2003).

The İskenderpaşa mosque community descends from the tradition of one of the most famous Naqshbandi sheikhs in twentieth-century Turkey,

Mehmet Zahit Kotku, and also exhibits a community largely accepting of modern realities. It also has a diverse group of members, including business executives and highly educated professionals. It is not surprising, then, that this community, along with the Erenköy community, have been known to be extremely well funded, to publish flashy periodicals, and to operate high-profile media outlets (Çakır 1990). For these groups, also, women, though still fulfilling traditional roles, are considered an active part of the community, and the group's gender-related social interactions are only moderately more conservative than the average norms in Turkey's urban environment (Turam 2007).

In the middle ranges of tension with society, we have the Menzil and Süleymancı Naqshbandi groups. While these groups exhibit similarly moderate ranges of tension with their environment, the source of each group's tension comprises very different features from its counterpart's. The followers of Süleyman Hilmi Tunahan—believed by his followers to be the last sheikh on the golden chain (*altın silsile*) of sheikhs, those within a divinely appointed lineage who have carried the message of God from the time of the Prophet Mohammed to the present day (Çakır 1990)—the Süleymancılar are disseminated throughout Turkey and have thriving communities within the Turkish diaspora in Europe. Their famous Koran courses and schools bring them into contact with people from every province in Turkey. While they engage actively with the society around them, those strongly affiliated with the group exhibit expectations, behaviors, and a level of discipline that pull them out of broader society and ensure that their main ties are with the group (Hart 2013; Yükleyen 2010). As Hart (2013) observes, the group's outward differences often lead nonmembers of their local environments to refer to the community derogatively as a *tarikat*, which simply means "order" but in popular parlance conveys the meaning of "cult."

The Menzil community, often referred to as Menzilciler, derive their name from their community and village's remote location next to a bus stop on a dusty road between Adıyaman and Urfa. The name of the village, Menzil, is an old name for "stop," or *durak*, in modern Turkish, and the name simply affirmed the village's proximity to this stop in the middle of nowhere in southeastern Anatolia. Although people came from all over to partake in the healing and reformative powers of Sheikh Mehmet Reşit Erol and his descendants and its community now has branches in Ankara, Istanbul, and elsewhere, it has maintained the reputation of having a more peripheral social status and profile. The group has notably reached out to alcoholics and social outcasts, and though they do not rely on strict discipline in the same way that groups such as the Süleymancı do, their social profile has kept them from being as mainstreamed and integrated with the upper echelon of society as members of the İskenderpaşa or Erenköy communities.

Level of tension, however, is not the only dimension along which these various Naqshbandi communities should be distinguished. Another important delineation comes in the terminology that meaningfully separates *cemaat* from *tarikat*. While both terms are often used pejoratively in common parlance in Turkey—the former representing something like "sect" in English while the latter conveys something like "cult"—they literally mean "community" and "order," respectively. Thus, those in Turkey who are not fond of the Naqshbandis and their social activities might refer to all of them as a *tarikat*. Because of the nature of the laws against Sufi orders (i.e., *tarikatlar*) in the early years of the republic, the term *tarikat* popularly connotes the ideas of being antistate and clandestine. But all the groups have some elements of being a tarikat, in its essential meaning, in that there is a hierarchical ring of members around a sheikh, living or deceased.

Academically, the terms have been the most helpfully distinguished regarding the level to which the community is focused on self-development and self-attainment of its individual members versus social outreach to expand and recruit to enlarge the community. In other words, a cemaat is much more focused on group growth and recruiting and expanding the reach of the group—it is more outwardly focused as a community. A tarikat, while it is engaged in civic activities, is more focused on the order, the sheikh, and one's personal development—it is more inwardly focused and exclusive. A cemaat operates more like a religious social movement while a tarikat behaves more like a club. Based on this cemaat–tarikat dimension, we place these Naqshbandi groups in a slightly different order than the level-of-tension dimension above (see fig. 2.2).

There are many more Naqshbandi communities in Turkey than those discussed in this chapter, especially in the predominantly Kurdish areas of Turkey, but these are generally tarikats in that they do not often actively recruit members to their group, adding to their exclusivity and operating more as a group identity marker than an expanding movement. Although there are many Naqshbandis in the tarikat category, as we are defining it here, they do not generate much outside attention because of their inward focus. The Naqshbandi communities that have received attention despite

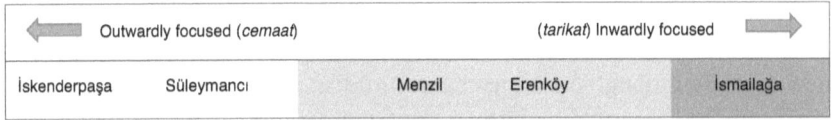

Figure 2.2. Naqshbandi Communities Relative to Inward-Outward Focus

their exclusivity have generally done so because of their peculiarities and their connection to major metropolitan areas, such as Istanbul. The Erenköy and İsmailağa communities receive so much attention because they reside on the extreme ends of the urban social scene, at the most elite and most peripheral, respectively. The Erenköy community is famous for the groups' well-heeled members, while the İsmailağa are notable for their rejection of worldly consumption and goods and their peculiar attire, which appears religious and rural, despite the group residing in the center of one of the largest cities in the world. The tight-knit social community and more distinct markers of dress and appearance of the members of İsmailağa could be usefully compared to some Amish communities in the United States, except that İsmailağa members reject consumption and not the use of technology, per se. They certainly have concerns about how technology is being used, but this does not result in more dramatic levels of abstinence from technology as practiced by some Amish communities (Hülür 1999).

The Menzil community has registered broader interest in Turkey particularly after the important changes in socioeconomic development and global market forces starting in the 1980s. Its missions to wayward Turkish populations struggling with substance abuse have brought many urbanites on buses to Menzil and have in turn established linkages and eventually local branches and outreach centers in the big cities (Çakır 1990; Konuralp 2006). The group and the community's sheikhs, all descending from the Erol family, have not been averse to expanding the community's reach. However, unlike the İskenderpaşa and Süleymancı communities, they use no flashy media to recruit new members; rather, expansion has developed naturally from what is believed to be their miraculous reformations of the lost, downtrodden, and ill.

The İskenderpaşa and Süleymancı communities are much more geared for social outreach and recruitment as envisioned by our conceptualization of the term *cemaat*. The İskenderpaşa community, especially under the leadership of Mehmed Zahit Kotku, sees their mission as reaching out to bring the light of Islam's message to contemporary modern society. They are an active and outward-reaching community committed to effecting change through direct involvement in the world around them. The group energetically seeks new recruits among small merchants, students, and urban professionals. Very early in the republic's history, the followers of Süleyman Hilmi Tunahan began to offer and provide Koran courses to those who wanted to recite the holy text correctly in Arabic. Through these beneficial courses that catered to the interests of devout Muslims and those seeking avenues for greater spirituality throughout Turkey, the Süleymancıs were able to form inroads in many local communities. Once the posture of the state toward religious communities softened in the late 1940s and early 1950s, the group was able to offer Koran courses without government interference. While the group has found even more success in opening mosques, religious schools, and Koran courses to the diaspora in Europe, they have still used these religious courses to establish members in every corner of Turkey. The Süleymancıs actively seek to bring in new membership and are also well known for the strict hierarchy and discipline among members (Çakır 1990; Hart 2013).

It is important at this point to reassert that, although distinctions exist between these groups, their levels of tension with society, and the extent to which they are outwardly or inwardly focused, the devout members of these groups are engaged in the same or similar frequency of spiritual practices in ways that would normally accord them identical ratings of religiosity according to standard survey questions. For those associated with any of these groups, their chances of being rated devout on perceptions and practices of personal piety would also be high. All the groups also operate from a religious doctrine that assumes social activism. Even though recruitment emphasis varies—some like to go out and find members, others prefer to be found—there is a sense of social responsibility inherent to the doctrine of all groups, even the İsmailağa community. Therefore, from the perspective of religious beliefs and doctrine, we would expect that their approaches and orientations toward politics would be similar if the source of their political outlook was, in fact, the core essentials of their beliefs and doctrine.

The Nature or the Nurture of Political Approaches of Naqshbandis?

How do members of these different Naqshbandi communities approach politics in Turkey? Do they largely take a similar approach and outlook, or do these vary from group to group? In other words, does the broader Naqshbandi affiliation, religious understanding, and level of piety naturally guide these groups to a similar attitude toward Turkish politics, or do their communal affiliations nurture their approaches to politics? If we look at these communities' patterns of political behavior over the last decades of democratic politics in Turkey, we see notable differences, from complete silence and aversion to Islamist political party formation.

For most of its history, the İsmailağa community has remained very quiet and ambivalent about involvement in the regular affairs of politics in Turkey. Çakır (1990) noted that active engagement in political activities has been seen as grounds for distancing a member from the group's more exclusive practices. In 2015, one of the leaders of the community, Ahmet Mahmut Ünlü (Cübbeli Ahmet), proclaimed, "Politics is none of our business. Our sole duty is to explain religion to the people" (Aviv 2018). Some reports in Turkey have alleged links between the İsmailağa community and the Justice and Development Party (AKP) government and President Recep Tayyip Erdoğan, but such political activity by the leaders remains mostly behind the scenes or expressed in formal visits (Aviv 2018; Piricky 2012). Writing in the periodicals addressed to their community, the leaders of the group who are the would-be successors to the elderly sheikh Mahmut Ustaosmanoğlu have taken both critical and supportive stances toward the ruling AKP. Most of the actions of the leaders of the organization concerning the current government have tended toward seeking favor or protection for the group, not broadly influencing the policies of the government (Aviv 2018). In general, it seems that their actions, silent or public, have not had as their aim to shape the political policy of the day but to protect the interests of their community within the current environment. This is consistent with the actions we would anticipate from a group that understands that it resides on the margins of society. Its political goal is survival, which can be facilitated by staying away from politics and generally avoiding trouble. Sometimes the group will seek nonpolitical alliances with the state that might ensure protection for their group, whose position in society places them in a more peripheral and vulnerable position.

The political orientation of the Menzil community and its leadership has been the subject of much speculation, an orientation that highlights their long-held strategy of contingent support for external political actors rather than taking political action themselves. While journalists and scholars have debated the political preferences of the Menzil community, the founding sheikh, Mehmet Reşit Erol, clearly indicated his desire to distance himself from political activities (Çakır 1990), and until recently, current leadership has maintained this position (Akyeşilmen and Özcan 2014). Following the fallout in the late 2010s between the government and the Gülen community, some members of the Menzil group have become more visibly active in politics.[1] Çakır (1990) speculates that the fame of the Menzil community has allowed some members of the group an opportunity to promise support to various parties as leverage for personal and group benefits. Of all the Naqshbandi communities, the Menzil community has drawn the most attention from far-right Turkish nationalist politicians and activists, and many observers have commented on these ties (Akyeşilmen and Özcan 2014; Çakır 1990; Konuralp 2006).

However uncertain the positions of the group appear to have been, it seems clear that the combination of their ambiguous posture toward specific political parties and strong pro-state stance was an intentional strategy to leave open the possibility of gaining from the existing governing status quo. This group has always been identified as pro-state, which is undoubtedly why it gained support from the Turkish right. The community has remained vague enough to court the larger right-leaning governing parties to ensure that those in power will sponsor, support, or at least not sanction or punish the community. One ethnographic study (Kılıç 2017) of the group effectively points out the tangible benefits successive national governments have conferred on the village of Menzil compared to other villages of similar size and composition in the area. The paved asphalt roads, the medical clinic, and the village infrastructure that support the shops and restaurants in the town offer a stark contrast to the infrastructure of other villages in the area (Kılıç 2017). If governments did not feel as if they were benefiting from the Menzil community (by their votes and pro-state and status quo positions), it would be easy to leave the Menzil community and their visitors to their own devices and treat the community like any other village.

Now, under the extended rule of the AKP government, the group has begun to feel more comfortable in identifying itself with the government party. This tendency to support the status quo should not be seen as new, but their explicit public actions of support certainly are. Many have noted that this group appears to be filling the void that emerged with the purge of the Gülen movement. They have managed to secure ministerial positions in the AKP government (e.g., in the Ministry of Health), and they have taken a visible pro-AKP position to place their members in state agencies. The Turkish state, under the long tenure of Erdoğan, has appeared to see the benefit of an alliance between AKP and the Menzil community for the potential mobilization the latter's members might provide. Once again, more marginal groups like the Menzil community operate to stay clear of politics due to their marginal position in society, but when the opportunity to link with the state allows them resources and protection without explicitly entering public politics, their orientation shifts.

Pragmatic support for parties in government or with governing potential also seems to be the political approach and strategy of the Erenköy community. Though this community famously includes in its ranks many members who are active in economic and social life, it has never taken on group-level political activism: politically engaged individuals have divided their support among a variety of mainstream political parties. At the height of Naqshbandi political activism led by the İskenderpaşa community in the early 1970s, one of the prominent members of the community, Tahir Büyükkörükçü, ran on the National Salvation Party's ticket from Konya and became a member of parliament. That appeared to be enough of a taste of politics and political activism for the group: since the 1980s, their members have continued to maintain a differentiated approach that appears to mostly favor the status quo. Just as members of their community find themselves in a variety of favorable positions in elite sectors of the economy and society, they have appeared to find benefit in cultivating linkages with mainstream political elites from different parties. Even though most studies of Naqshbandi communities have examined these groups' political activities and orientations, scholars have had surprisingly little to say about the socially and economically elite Erenköy community. It was known that individuals in the group generally supported Turgut Özal and the Motherland Party in 1983 in the first election following military rule, but by the time that the options for mainstream political party representation greatly expanded in 1987, it was clear that the group's vote was fragmenting, especially among parties on the right (Çakır 1990). Yavuz (2003) suggests that the group's integration into social and economic life, especially since the 1990s, has led them to have little reason to be actively involved in politics at the group level.

Up to this point, the general patterned approach to politics in Turkey by Naqshbandi communities has been rather passive, intentionally ambiguous as to party preferences, and . . . well, boring. Each of the communities we've described, although better known and larger than many other Naqshbandi communities, could fit into the category of being a religious order (i.e., tarikat), inwardly focused and not seeking members but hoping to be sought after. Although these three communities—the Erenköy, the İsmailağa, and the Menzil—maintain different positions regarding their relative level of tension in society, their individual approaches to democratic politics suggests that they do not represent a sufficient number of voters to leverage a community agenda. The primary focus of these communities has not been to change the political system but to socially survive it and perhaps even thrive. This general disposition strongly mirrors the political approach of the numerous Naqshbandi orders (tarikats) in the Kurdish-populated southeastern provinces. The mentality is to support those political actors who are willing to see the community as a potential ally (usually through their block of votes) and provide them a measure of support in government. The Kurdish orders have had the double challenge of having to divide this strategy between local support and national support, which requires choosing between very different kinds of political parties.

On the other hand, Naqshbandi communities who have taken a broader outward community focus and worked to forge connections with society at large for the purpose of recruitment and growth (i.e., a cemaat structure) have taken a much more active attitude toward working for political change within the existing framework. Their approach to democratic politics is not simply to protect themselves or to make sure that they receive their piece of the pie from the state but to use their members' political influence as a group to push Turkey toward policy that fits the more ideal national society they envision. Ironically, because both groups actively struggle to recruit the masses in Turkey toward their versions of Naqshbandi Sunni Islam, they have often found themselves at cross-purposes and as competitors with one another within the system.

In the late 1960s, particularly after Necmettin Erbakan entered parliament as an independent in 1969, Mehmet Zahit Kotku, the beloved sheikh of the İskenderpaşa community, encouraged Erbakan and others to create a party that would be the political voice of the community. Kotku and Erbakan assumed not only that they could bring the other Naqshbandi, Kadiri, and Nur communities under their political umbrella but that they represented a large number of Turkish citizens and would have the electoral votes to make political change and potentially govern Turkey. While they never brought the Süleymancı community on board, they did initially receive buy-in from many of the other Naqshbandi communities and the Nurcus (Yavuz 2003). The support translated to an initial 11.8 percent of the vote and a fourth-place finish in 1973. That was probably not the level of social support that Kotku and others were expecting, but the broad coalition of religious communities, even among the Naqshbandis, started breaking down from there. When Kotku passed away in 1982, leaving the mantle of leadership to his son-in-law Esad Coşan, Erbakan broke away and began operating autonomously from the authority of the İskenderpaşa leadership. The break between Erbakan and Coşan was public, but many within the İskenderpaşa community still found that Erbakan's political movement best represented their views. Their support, however, became more contingent when the directives coming from the community largely took a secondary position relative to Erbakan's vision (Çakır 1990).

The Süleymancı community has also been involved with politics, but its members have often found themselves, until the current AKP period, actively supporting a rival party (usually a more successful rival) to Erbakan's parties, and they have done so by fielding candidates in elections for these parties from the top echelons of the community leadership. They have not formed their own political movement, but they have tried to be an active contributor to existing parties willing to work with them (usually on the right). Although their history of having members of their top leadership running as political candidates (e.g., Kemal Kaçar and the Denizolgun brothers) indicates their belief that their social movement has mass appeal and represents a large swath of society, warranting their place in political office, members of the group have been careful to mostly appeal to society through collaboration with the major parties of Turkey's political center right—a calculated but cautious approach to electoral politics.

One important distinction between the Süleymancı community and the İskenderpaşa community is that the Süleymancıs have built a large brick-and-mortar network of schools and gained approval for their religious outreach through this extensive organizational investment. These schools exist at the pleasure of the government, which has made it clear from time to time that these material holdings for their spiritual work can be taken away. The state's religious schools are the main competitors of the Süleymancıs in the provision of spiritual education, and the degrees issued by state educational institutions have become the requisite background for official positions in the mosques run by MRA. As a result, a significant focus of Süleymancı public pronouncements is discrediting the quality of education in the state schools and questioning the authority of the decision makers in the MRA who come from these schools (Ozgur 2012). Under the

AKP government, the number of state-sponsored religious schools and Koran courses in the mosques has increased, and the Süleymancıs as a group have distanced themselves from the AKP. Nonetheless, due to the lack of a rival party occupying the center right, group members and leaders only reluctantly voice their distaste with AKP rule.[2]

The Süleymancı and İskenderpaşa communities have both shown a measure of political action that distinguishes these groups from the noninterventionist politics of the other Naqshbandi communities, but their chosen approach and their objectives differ. The İskenderpaşa community ultimately pushed for and inspired a new party that could meaningfully influence state behavior and policy. The Süleymancıs, however, tried to leverage their social influence by running publicly as candidates under the banner of preexisting conservative, status quo parties. The Süleymancıs also tried to shape religiously relevant state institutions to further their social reach and recruitment possibilities. Although differences can be seen between these two communities in terms of levels of conservatism and group discipline, which also lead to differences in the level of tension between the communities and society at large, both communities feel that their level of engagement with people in Turkey translates into the possibility that the community or their leaders can expect to represent a large enough segment of the population to shape the national political environment toward some aspirational good.

Although it would be interesting to have access to survey data that asked questions of these communities about their support for democracy or alternative regimes (such data are very unlikely to ever materialize), if we follow their political behaviors, such questions might be the wrong ones to ask. Although many, if not all, of these Naqshbandi communities and their members give credence to the idea of a state guided by Islam—even if they admit that such an ideal would be unlikely to come to fruition any time soon, if ever, and only through gradual social transformation—they have all made their peace with democratic processes. The individuals in these groups in Turkey do not openly disparage democracy, but the opportunities and benefits of democracy seen by the individuals in these communities look very different in different communities. Some groups with stronger ties to mainstream society tend to see democracy as a system that allows them to mobilize people for positive change. Others recognize the benefits to their communities of such democratic principles as pluralism, freedom for all, and the ability to use the electoral process to find protection and

Attitudes of the Devout | 51

Lower tension					Higher tension	
Erenköy	İskenderpaşa	Süleymancı		Menzil		İsmailağa
Outwardly focused (cemaat)				(tarikat) Inwardly focused		
İskenderpaşa	Süleymancı		Menzil		Erenköy	İsmailağa
Direct party politics	Calculated, limited, and cautious political action		1970s–2016 ambiguous passive support, but explicit gov't support post-2016		Fragmented political support and action in mainstream politics	Quietism and ambiguous support for existing parties

Figure 2.3. Patterns of Political Involvement

accountability from their representatives to the state. Whether these communities would seek to alter the current state of democratic politics in the direction of more or less democratization or more or less provision for pluralism of ideas is likely to differ. In other words, it is not their ideology or level of piety that guides these groups' members on questions of how to approach politics but their unique status within society, the existing political opportunities, and the posture of the state in relation to religion and their community.

If we map out the general practices of these communities during the relatively open period between the 1960 coup and the AKP's rise to power in 2002, we can see the general pattern depicted in figure 2.3.

Looking at it from this perspective, it might be useful to consider how Stark and Finke (2000) theorize that religious markets in societies are distributed in niches relative to their level of tension with society at large. In such a framework, the Erenköy community, characterized by a low level of tension with society, would find itself at about the midpoint on the curve at the convergence of moderate and conservative, with İskenderpaşa next to it on the right within the large conservative niche. The Süleymancı community would be in the conservative niche but even further to the right than the İskenderpaşa. The consequences and associations of being involved with the Menzil community would put it at the border of conservative and strict, and the İsmailağa community would be solidly in the strict niche. Placed in such a way, there seems to be a relationship between being located in the conservative niche and increased likelihood of political action. As the tension or marginality of the religious community increases, the Naqshbandi communities discussed show decreased engagement with democratic politics and operate with very different goals and approaches. The Erenköy community, operating the farthest to the left and closest to the center, seems to be the most geared toward political action within and in support of the status quo.³

A Season for Politics?

The discussion of the political orientations of these Naqshbandis as presented above treats these strategies as static. This, of course, represents an attempt to capture a general portrait of major outlooks without accounting for political change. As discussed earlier in this chapter, however, the Turkish Republic's state-level policy and posture toward religion in the public sphere has changed in important ways over its short history. These groups' orientations toward the state as openings and closures occur are very instructive. Even though the groups' relative levels of tension with their social environments have not drastically changed, the relative levels of tension or distance from the state have, and we would do well to attend to the changes in orientations that have occurred over time in the Naqshbandi communities experiencing these contextual instabilities.

During the early decades of the republic, neither the closure of the religious schools nor the shuttering and state appropriation of the dervish lodges caused the Naqshbandi communities to dissipate; they maintained their activities and practices in private, outside the direct gaze of the state. As Yavuz (2003) points out, Naqshbandi practices were such that the zikir and rabıta could be performed privately, and state-owned mosques often offered suitable places that could be used for both formal (state-sanctioned) Sunni practices and as "cover" for informal (unsanctioned) Sufi activities. Many Naqshbandi members took civil service jobs with the state through the MRA, providing further cover for their activities (Yavuz 2003).

The heavy-handed posture of the state led to different responses by Naqshbandi communities around the country. Finding themselves shut out of official society in a new secular state after centuries of being a part of the diverse Islamic religious environment of the Ottoman Empire, most of these communities chose to keep a low profile, but others chose to revolt. Persisting and integrating remained the generally preferred path, especially after the initial years. In the first decade following the establishment of the republic, however, there were two notable uprisings attributed to Naqshbandi sheikhs at the extreme eastern and western corners of the country: the Sheikh Said revolt (1925) and the Menemen rebellion (1930).[4] Other minor rebellions occurred as well, but for the most part, Naqshbandi sheikhs maintained their communities quietly without arousing the ire of the state.

Distinct from the other groups and their leaders, Süleyman Hilmi Tunahan's focus on religious education for the community and outward expansion led him and his followers to try to capitalize on the existing opportunities provided by the creation of the MRA. Tunahan himself received certification to be a *vaiz* (a state-appointed imam who is allowed to write his own sermons), and he encouraged his trainees to seek official certification to teach as state-approved imams at mosques. Tunahan and his community continued to offer courses on reciting the Koran correctly in Arabic even when it was not permitted, but such instruction was hard for the state to crack down on because communities saw such activities as filling an existing gap caused by the closure of private seminaries (madrasas) and the lack of state provision for instruction in this area. Taking advantage of this need—the training of imams to fill positions in the state-run mosques—those having received Koran instruction in Tunahan's community were often able to pass the exams and be appointed as state imam. As these imams were sent out to fill posts, this created linkages with the Süleymancı community throughout much of the country.

As the first wave of religious liberalization occurred in Turkey in the mid- to late 1940s, the Süleymancıs were best equipped to take advantage of the policy changes. In 1946, the Koran courses were officially legalized, which led to their rapid expansion; by 1966 there were three thousand Süleymancı Koranic seminaries (Yükleyen 2008). Many within Turkey saw the creation of state-run schools for religious clergy in 1951 as a further example of the pro-religious policy of the state, but from the perspective of the Süleymancıs, this was evidence of a tightening of state control over religious norms. The creation of official state schools that provided certifications for postings within the MRA and to the official state-run mosques was a way for the state to more fully regulate who was—and was not—providing religious instruction. In 1965, the heavy blow was dealt: the official state schools were designated the sole granting body of the education required to receive posts in the MRA. Following the 1971 military incursion into politics, most of the remaining members of the Süleymancı community in the MRA were removed, and many of the Süleymancı Koran schools were appropriated by the state (Çakır 1990; Yükleyen 2008). Over the course of twenty-five years, the opportunity for the Süleymancıs to grow their community through state-sanctioned mechanisms had gone from boom to bust.

The cadre associated with Necmettin Erbakan and his National Salvation Party (MSP), which was strongly dominated by the İskenderpaşa community, supported the new policies and state-run schools (Ozgur 2012). Thus, the activist political outlook toward democratic politics by these two communities led them, ironically, to enter the arena of political competition in effect to attempt to cancel out one another's aims at least as much as they intended to provide an alternative to the primarily secular and material concerns of the other political elites. The Süleymancıs actively supported the largest mainstream conservative party, led by Süleyman Demirel—a not very religious politician who nonetheless lent a sympathetic ear to the devout in Turkey—while the İskenderpaşa community and many of the other Naqshbandis supported Erbakan and the MSP. At least at some level, this well-known political division and the orientation to politics of the members of these communities could be understood as a battle for the spoils of state—that is, the MRA—and the ability to use this institution as a vehicle to shape the religious standards and norms in society through official sanction. This early schism also explains the increasingly cold relations between the Süleymancı community and the AKP government.

Although the language of attack by members of the Süleymancı community in critique of the state-run religious clergy schools used words such as *apostasy* and *atheism*, this battle was not ideological but clearly communal. It was during this time also that the Süleymancıs seized the opportunity to provide religious instruction to citizens moving to Europe as guest workers, a context the Turkish state was less interested in regulating and less equipped to do so until the 1980s (Yükleyen 2010). During the AKP period, but before the political struggle between the AKP and the Gülen movement surfaced, Süleymancıs found themselves in a peculiar situation. They faced a formidable challenger to their Islamic educational activities, the Gülen movement, which threatened to undermine their existing influence through their supporters' increased penetration into state bureaucracy. This situation left Süleymancıs alienated from the ruling party and, in effect, from the political sphere, due to the lack of alternative center-right conservative parties in parliament. The post-2016 purge against the Gülen movement has helped the Süleymancıs return to their original strategies of calculated but cautious political involvement.

In the Turkish context, democratization clearly brought welcome changes to religious communities, particularly devout ones (Sunar and Toprak 1983;

White 2002). Without question, the transition to multiparty elections and democracy was a political improvement for these communities. For this reason, voter turnout—from remote villages to urban centers—was exceptionally high (Wuthrich 2015). There were no extended public debates by clerics about whether democracy was appropriate for Muslim communities. In the 1950s, all parties were largely led by elites from the single-party period, but the opportunity to enter a context where politicians were beholden to voters, including the devout, was seen as a positive development. Voting for the opposition party in 1950 by these devout communities served to protest the state's posture toward religion during the single-party period. Other communities voted for their party of choice based on other—usually material or social-group—considerations, but devout communities operating with greater tension in their environment voted strongly for political change on religious grounds. During this period, the general tendency of Naqshbandi groups toward this political opening was to form alliances with the existing competitors. In this environment, while the state and MRA appeared to have opened space to them, it was notably the Süleymancı leadership, Tunahan and Kaçar, who actively became involved in party activities through Osman Bölükbaşı's Nation Party in 1957.

Following the 1960 coup and the drafting of the 1961 constitution that created much broader space for ideology within the Turkish political system, it took a few years for any of these communities to fully realize or trust the opportunity presented to them. As discussed above, it was the communities who were the most linked with and engaged with society that believed that active involvement with politics was the way to go. Their links to the society around them led their members to believe that they could mobilize social support to make meaningful political change. İskenderpaşa's strong hand in initiating the movement led by Erbakan occurred simultaneously with the Süleymancı community's attempts to enter politics to retain the institutional gains that it had acquired over the previous decade.

As discussed earlier, following the 1980 coup, the military's approach to social solidarity through a Turkish-Islamic synthesis created a role for religion in an otherwise more restrictive environment. Conservative religious communities such as the Naqshbandis continued to find allies, but the fragmented political party system that developed and the rivalries between many of the communities meant that religious political activism was somewhat subdued and fragmented. An exception was Erbakan's Welfare Party, which was trying to break away from the old ties to İskenderpaşa and reinvent itself in the new environment. The party was still very happy to receive Naqshbandi support, but its links to any particular community became far more contingent, giving Erbakan the free hand that he wanted to innovate politically and bring in other communities and segments of society under the party's umbrella.

It was ultimately the subsequent generation of this political movement, led by Recep Tayyip Erdoğan, that had the most success in bringing together the broadest range of religious communities and groups, along with other segments of society, under the banner of the Justice and Development Party, created in 2001. For the first time in decades, many members within İskenderpaşa and the Süleymancıs were voting for the same party, along with many of the Nur communities and supporters of Fethullah Gülen, and even the very strict communities in a high degree of tension with existing society (Tuğal 2009). More conservative and strict religious communities saw in Erdoğan's leadership a democratic system that would not shut them out from the public sphere and through whom they might spiritually and materially prosper without fearing state-directed repercussions associated with their higher levels of tension with society. Support for this strong governing party paid off at the national and local level for many of these communities. Whether truly accurate or not, the AKP represented responsive government to the communities that had been marginalized and that had experienced ongoing tension with the state in previous decades. Now more than ever before, members of these devout communities believed that they had opportunities to work within the bureaucratic system without being flagged and removed for their religious activities and associations.

Although the AKP has not heavily altered the state through the passage of religious legislation, they have liberalized policy toward religious public expression and validated religious identities that have been viewed with suspicion by many in Turkish society. Thus, while many external observers of Turkey might have anticipated that such support by religious communities would have been tied to highly conservative Islamist leadership or policy change, the inclusion of these communities has, nonetheless, led to economic prosperity and social validation for their members that has appeared revolutionary in comparison to the previous status quo. Thus, while the rights and freedoms of many within Turkey have seemed to whither quite dramatically as Erdoğan has acted to consolidate his authority over the Turkish political system, it is unlikely that many within these Naqshbandi communities might opt for political liberalization of under Erdoğan's rule. Some members of these communities have been willing to voice criticism of current government policies, but this is done very carefully, and usually there is another prominent member of the same community indicating support (Aviv 2018; Piricky 2012). Thus, unlike the enthusiasm that was generated among these Naqshbandi communities in the 1940s, 1950s, and 1960s about the prospect of democratization and the political liberalization of the state, members of the same groups have displayed far more ambivalence toward liberalization or deviation from a status quo with Erdoğan at the helm in the current context. Ideology has not changed; the communities' relationships with the state and, to a lesser extent, society have, however.

Thus, complex and dynamic social and political tradeoffs appear to drive the political outlooks of devout individual members of these communities. While religion does condition their political perspectives, these patterns appear to be primarily shaped by the relational influences of religion rather than simply the degree of individuals' orthodoxy or religiosity.

Conclusion: How Communities in Context Nurture Contingent Political Attitudes

By tracing historical changes in political power, religious freedom, and tension with society of well-known communities under the umbrella of the broader Naqshbandi order in Turkey, this chapter highlights how political orientations and outlooks are shaped by religion in ways not easily attributable to doctrine. Rather, these general orientations and approaches to politics and the outlooks that inform broader political preferences are shaped by the implications stemming from communal association. To the extent that a religious community desires to operate with greater exclusivity of membership and higher tension with the environment around them, their political outlook will be different from members of a community that is highly connected and integrated with society. It will also differ from those missionary communities who are seeking to draw in more members—even when their respective essential tenets of faith do not substantially differ (Hülür 1999). Furthermore, these differences in degrees of tension with the environment do not, in and of themselves, predict that a community at a certain position in society will or will not support democracy or economic redistribution, for example. Communities positioned both in the center or at the margins in society may show support for democracy but for different reasons and with different desired outcomes. Furthermore, the chapter highlights how the same group will perceive politics very differently based on the changing political climate in Turkey over time.

This analysis suggests that we may need to reframe our approach to interpreting the influence of religion in public opinion surveys, which generally measure broad political, social, and economic attitudes. These surveys are extremely helpful in our understanding of how people see and interpret their social and political contexts, but as the discussion above shows, their views are context-based and changeable. Attitudes and associations need to be unpacked, and we need to acknowledge that there is a time stamp on any linkage between attitudes and outlooks and how religion is influencing these. To provide another context as illustration, it is highly unlikely that anyone would have predicted that the US president Donald Trump would have received the level of support that he has from the class of religious voters called Evangelicals. His divorces, marital infidelities, millions of dollars coming from his gambling and casino empire, base treatment of women, and completely unchecked arrogance would seem to make him the last possible candidate supported by this segment of voters, especially if we are working from the substance of doctrine. It is also unlikely that such a candidate would be supported by the same class of voters in the future. Context is important, and the patterns of views that develop, which could be seen as influenced by religion, are often influenced by the dynamics of state and society within which members of a community feel they are operating.

We could also compare these dynamics to the changing political involvement of Salafi groups in Egypt after the Arab uprisings. Like the Naqshbandis in Turkey, they house many different shades of political outlooks within their broader community. Salafis were largely known for their political quietism during the Mubarak era, and their activities centered on proselytizing, charity, and religious education (Al-Anani and Malik 2013). Thus, their involvement and success in electoral politics took observers of Egyptian politics by surprise. Most remarkably, Salafis formed several parties, three of which won seats in parliament. What appeared to be a homogenous group to outside observers came to demonstrate not doctrinal but political diversity in short order.

The social and political context is extremely important in determining the political approach of individuals and groups. In the Turkish case, because the normative approach of the state for most of Turkey's history has prioritized nominal Muslim identity and secularism in the public sphere, conservative groups that have had the ear and sympathy of many within society have taken a more active approach toward popular politics, including participation in elections and other political activities that are bolstered by public support. Those individuals from groups that are more marginal have tended toward quietism in political activity or sought protectors for themselves as they were less popular with society in general.

In Iran, the script is arguably flipped but in logical ways. The normative approach by the Islamic republic is an Islamic state order. Political engagement that seeks to garner public support for change does not come from people dramatically more radical than the state's status quo or those who have rejected Islam altogether but from moderates just to the left of center. For example, the Green Movement was led by a reform candidate who had been the last prime minister of the Islamic state and a relative of the supreme leader, Ayatollah Khamenei (Ansari 2010; Parsa 2016). The logic of the Green Movement was the collective action of individuals who had not abandoned the faith but who wanted to actively move the normative position of the state toward less regulation of religion and more civil freedoms (Bayat 2013). The regulation of the state, of course, also ensures that no one too far to the left or the right of the state-imposed Islamic center can engage in political contests, and mosques are all led by state-appointed imams and run through the guidance of the supreme leader himself; these imams are weekly enjoined to "preach" the regime's political propaganda on top of the spiritual content of the message. Thus, if one falls outside of the moderate or conservative circles relative to the normative social position of the Islamic republican regime, one is only left with quietism or the radical antisystem actions that were on display at the end of 2017 and 2019. Context constrains the options for political action and shapes one's religious outlook, and the social-political context is never completely static as depicted by our analysis of Naqshbandi communities in Turkey. At the same time, context matters in patterned and predictable ways, a dynamic we will discuss further in chapter 4.

Cross-national surveys of political and social attitudes in the Middle East and North Africa have greatly enhanced our understanding of this region, but they will be of greater benefit if they attend to the dynamics and nuances discussed above when measuring associations in the data between religion and public opinion. In the chapters that follow, we attempt to build on the existing research on public opinion and religion in the region and construct a new framework for measuring and working with the data at hand, primarily through the waves of the Arab Barometer. A fresh framework for analysis will allow us to tackle anew the complex pattern of associations among religions, politics, and societies. It is to this that we now turn.

Notes

1. From 2002 and until around 2010, the Gülen community—itself a devout religious community that combines fairly orthodox Hanafi Sunni beliefs with some Sufi philosophy and an outwardly focused vision—had been a strong ally of the Justice and Development Party (AKP) government as well as the primary benefactor of political rents. Visible manifestations of a split between the Erdoğan government and Gülen became public beginning in 2013 and culminated with the government explicitly referring to the religious organization as a terrorist group and formally blaming the organization for the attempted coup on July 15, 2016. Following the failed coup attempt, the government imprisoned many ostensible supporters of Gülen in the military and the media and expunged any erstwhile supporter of the group that they could find from government and bureaucratic office.

2. Personal correspondence between one of the authors and an influential group member.

3. Here, we should note that our stylistic representation of these communities does not necessarily imply that we view them as completely isolated groups. These groups are well aware of each other as they pursue different religious-mobilization or political-engagement strategies. It is likely that they watch each other carefully and even engage in informal conversations behind the scenes, given that they share the same mobilization and engagement spaces. The preferences and strategies of these communities are likely also informed by such interactions. It would take additional anthropological research to unfold these interactions and their resulting influence on the religious outlooks of the members of these groups. At the moment, we can argue that our predictions somehow take into account this dynamic, but we cannot separate the unique effect of this endogenous factor.

4. The extent to which these well-known revolts were really Naqshbandi in character is highly debatable. The impetus behind the Sheikh Said rebellion has been the subject of great disagreement. Probably the best composite characterization of the revolt was that the leadership behind the rebellion was motivated by Kurdish nationalism but used Sheikh Said's religious credentials to mobilize the grassroots. Thus, the "purpose" of the rebellion likely appears different depending on what level one chooses to examine. Although Naqshbandi groups were undoubtedly disgruntled about the state's new posture and policy, it is not clear that Sheikh Said would have led a rebellion without instigation from the Kurdish nationalist Azadi organization. The Menemen revolt was characterized by the state as a Naqshbandi rebellion, but the linkages to the revolt remain somewhat contestable.

3

EMPIRICAL FOUNDATIONS OF RELIGIOUS OUTLOOKS

THE PREVIOUS CHAPTERS HAVE HIGHLIGHTED THE LOGIC BEHIND the assertion that individuals within the broad category of what we typically consider and measure as religiously devout in public opinion surveys have reason to form their religious outlooks differently. The reasons for these differences in outlook are, of course, a function of their individual characteristics, and the substance of doctrine also comes into play. However, there is also good reason to believe that, to the extent that religion is influencing individual attitudes and orientations, the relational component of religion—its social and associational components—can be a strong filter in the formation of political attitudes among the devout. This hypothesis predicts two outcomes: (1) diversity in religious outlooks among devout individuals across religious communities in a society and (2) distinct patterns of distributions of these religious outlooks across nations of the same dominant faith as these are, in some measure, reflective of the contingent relationships between individuals' religious communities and their bounded social and political contexts.

The question then becomes how we begin to measure this diversity empirically. The growing body of survey data from the Middle East and North Africa (MENA) can provide evidence for this pluralism. Particularly, the Arab Barometer surveys provide a broad set of religion-related questions through which one can measure nuanced patterns among those who would be considered pious by traditional measures of religiosity. The survey data do not allow the tracing of specific religious communities and their position in society and behavior as shown in the study of Naqshbandi communities in Turkey. Fortunately, Arab Barometer surveys are suitable for portraying with a much broader brush the diversity and patterns across multiple countries. Unfortunately, however, the Arab Barometer is linguistically limited to Arabic-speaking countries, so other notable Muslim-majority countries in the region, such as Turkey and Iran, are not included in this large data set, nor are other Muslim-majority countries such as Pakistan, Uzbekistan, Malaysia, Indonesia, Senegal, Niger, Albania, and Kosovo. To date, the large cross-national surveys conducted in such countries from outside of the Arabic-language community have not provided questions pertaining to religion sufficient to help us measure much beyond the general indexes of religiosity. Despite this current limitation, the analysis of this rich data set from many of the Arabic-speaking countries provides an opportunity to highlight the implications of this diversity of attitudes regarding important issues like preferences for democracy and economic distributive policies. If a diversity of distributions of outlooks and attitudes exists among countries sharing the same language and faith and neighboring one another, it seems reasonable to assume that distinct and diverse conditions would be operating in other countries with different regional, linguistic, and cultural dynamics. To the extent that the existence of various categories of religious outlooks among the devout can be demonstrated empirically, the analysis of survey data should be conducive to showing how state-society relations influence the distributions of these outlooks from country to country, even among this more clustered set of Muslim-majority countries.

This chapter starts to build a model for examining religious outlooks among the devout using the Arab Barometer survey data. Based on the available questions and drawing from social theory, the analysis delineates different categories of potential religious outlooks and then utilizes latent class analysis (LCA) and factor analysis to statistically summon these categories from the data. This categorization and the religious outlook classes constructed in this chapter form the basis for the examination of relationships in the chapters that follow.

Categorizing Measurable Religious Outlooks

Within the broader sociological literature on religion and society, several conceptualizations seem particularly relevant for our task of disaggregating attitude preferences among religious survey participants. Moral cosmology theory is one good starting point to explain religious outlooks and political attitudes (Davis and Robinson 1996, 2006). It asserts that there are two important intradenominational trends that affect political and economic outlooks. The authors argue that within any broader religious faith community, we can distinguish an "orthodox" and a "modernist" trend. The orthodox trend espouses the view that divine authority provides an appropriate social order meant for all members of a society. Davis and Robinson (2006, 169) assert that this outlook regards individuals as "subsumed by a larger community of like-minded believers who are all subject to the laws and greater plan of God." In other words, God's laws are meant for everyone, and all should be held accountable to their adherence. Established moral guidance from religion with its benefits and obligations should apply to everyone in the broader sense. It is assumed that adherence of the individual to the divine order as a whole is of greater benefit than an individual's freedom or personal discretion. Avoiding the loaded orthodox terminology, we refer to this outlook as "religious communitarian" (Benson and Williams 1982; Leege and Welch 1989). It could be argued that these religious communitarians would support religious policy, legislation, and leadership with the understanding that divine authority is intended to be everyone's shared good, be it moral prescriptions or charitable provision for the poor (Davis and Robinson 2006).

Focused on societies in MENA, Bayat's (2007) conceptualization of Islamism overlaps closely with the religious communitarian category emphasized by the moral cosmology approach. In this distinction, Bayat's conception of Islamism fits a religious communitarian position that champions the need for moral authority systematically structuring social order—that is, "Islam is the solution"—and an attendant focus on the poor and downtrodden. Bayat's (2013b, 306) understanding of Islamism distinguishes it from other religious ideologies and outlooks by its "disproportionate" focus on "people's obligations over their rights." What we refer to as religious communitarianism could also be beneficially understood as closely related to Bayat's understanding of Islamism.

To place this in illustrative comparison, if we consider the discussion of Naqshbandi communities in Turkey from chapter 2, we would anticipate that individual members within the İskenderpaşa and Süleymancı communities would be the most likely to hold a religious outlook consistent with our religious communitarian category. These communities are located on the conservative side of the national norm but remain relevant enough to appeal to relatively large segments of society, a position that could encourage them to believe that this combination of popular support and political activism could push the national norm of religious practices further to the right.[1]

Davis and Robinson (2006) point out that many within a faith community have an outlook they deem a "modernist" cosmology, which, in sharp contrast to the religious communitarian outlook, espouses individual choice and responsibility. This modernist understanding "combines support for individual choice and freedom with an expectation of individual responsibility, inclining its adherents to cultural individualism" (Davis and Robinson 2006, 170). Whether it is or is not appropriate to refer to this worldview as modern—as if such an attitude were entirely a recent product of the modern condition—it is reasonable to posit the category of religious individualist. All things being equal, such a position would incline these religious individualists within a faith community toward religious pluralism, autonomous moral decision-making, and its accompanying individual responsibility and tolerance for other views.

We see a close overlap between this concept and Bayat's (2007) "post-Islamist" concept. Bayat's post-Islamism represents an outlook that—while maintaining an allegiance to Islamic values—prioritizes the decision-making power of individuals, pluralism, and tolerance toward other viewpoints. Within many Muslim-majority countries, the individuals who arrive at this outlook appear to be coming from two different types of religious communities or niches. Bayat sees post-Islamism as manifesting itself as both a *condition* and a *project*. Post-Islamism as a project, best represented by the reformists and the Green Movement in Iran in 2009, is primarily focused on the *activism of a movement*, more so than a *category of individual*; nonetheless, the people most clearly associated with such movements correspond most closely to the religious individualists of Davis and Robinson's framework. Or, if we fit the people in these movements into the niches delineated by Stark and Finke (2000), the majority of the members of these movements would fit best in the liberal and moderate niches relative to other communities in their society. We will classify such religious outlooks as religious individualist.

In the Naqshbandi communities in Turkey, the group within which you would likely find the highest numbers of religious individualists would be the Erenköy community. This group's status in society would simultaneously encourage at least some of its members to adopt a religious individualist outlook, while others might adopt a social communitarian position defined below. Because the Erenköy community operates in low tension with society regarding their public behaviors but holds to a more exclusive communal membership, religious individual members could support pluralism and openness to unique communities like their own, or they might emphasize the desire to maintain existing norms in society, from which many of them have benefited. The general engagement of their members in public life and politics, including various political parties, without developing a "group" approach suggests that interest in politics operates outside of intentions to bring religion explicitly into the political sphere, and this is consistent with both the religious individualist and, as we explain in more detail below, the social communitarian perspective.

Bayat (2007) also observes that even some erstwhile Islamists—among them those operating in greatest tension with society and often experiencing state repression and social marginalization—realize that an authoritative reordering of society will never be successfully achieved through activism in the political system or by imposition of their practices, norms, and beliefs. In such cases, the resulting "condition" is referred to as post-Islamism. Those who have arrived at the condition of post-Islamism have concluded they will never beneficially monopolize the public sphere with their religious ideology alone, and their failed attempts through political activism and social mobilization to reorder society under a definitive Islamic framework have led some to reconceptualize or reinvent their position (Bayat 2007). Thus, despite their high level of religious devotion and ardent beliefs, these erstwhile Islamists come to accept a pluralist public sphere with rights for all. In this context, the expectation is still that their religious values are socially relevant and contribute to the political discussion. This combination of political realism and engagement in a pluralistic society is similar to what Ayoob (2009) describes as the "Muslim Democrat."

For obvious reasons, the post-Islamist category just described will bear similarities to the religious individualist category but with this difference: the religious individualist in our conceptualization desires religious practice to be relegated more to the private sphere, while our category of post-Islamism will support a religiously pluralist public sphere, or "Muslimhood," to use White's (2004) expression—that is, religion can and should be in the public sphere while rights and freedoms for various beliefs are also encouraged and protected. These post-Islamists and members of the Islamist / religious communitarian category will often resemble one another in their religious commitment and devotion, but they will differ in the extent to which they are open to others behaving or believing very differently. Religious communitarians have an active desire to see their norms imposed more broadly on society; post-Islamists, on the other hand, have concluded that successfully imposing their religious standards on others in their society is not feasible.

If we return again to the Turkish Naqshbandi communities in chapter 2, historically it would be easy to imagine, based on the general behaviors of the group and its leaders, that many individuals within the İsmailağa community have had a post-Islamist understanding. They might be comfortable with greater religious emphasis in the public sphere, but they might also support and recognize the need for pluralism that would engender tolerance for their more marginal social status. In recent years, as religion has become ascendant in Turkish politics, İsmailağa communities, along with a number of others, might now favor social stability, or what we refer to as social communitarianism, as described below. As the nature of the relationship between specific religious communities and the state has changed under the extended leadership of Erdoğan, the fluctuating social context of the Süleymancı community also might encourage individuals and groups within its community to adopt more of a post-Islamist outlook toward their current Turkish political environment.

As alluded to above, a fourth category describing the relationship between religion and politics might be proposed, which we refer to as social communitarianism. Such an outlook shows a strong preference for existing social norms and an accompanying desire that the ostensibly agreed upon standards for religious practice and social order be adhered to by others. Social communitarians see a need for neither an increased presence of religion in public affairs nor for greater religious pluralism that would upset the existing order. The communitarian impetus emphasizes group adherence to the social status quo more than a divine order. Though social communitarians may be personally very religious, their preference is that social and political dynamics remain as they are and that other members of society also broadly accept the established order and norms. As with the other categories, context plays strongly into the outlook of social communitarians.

One can see elements of social communitarianism in the Menzilci community in Turkey, discussed in chapter 2. Their affiliated members and leaders have had a strong tendency to support the existing order and to consistently benefit from it despite changing political dynamics. Their perspective, especially in relation to the other Naqshbandi groups, has been to adhere to a pro–Turkish state, pro-government position regardless of the governing party in power. As previously discussed, this community and its members have clearly benefited from this approach. Since 2011, after the AKP government consolidated its dominance over the Turkish political system, the İsmailağa community has appeared to shift toward this outlook as well. The Erenköy community also seems to have members that adhere to more of a social communitarian position.

Although we believe that religious outlooks are strongly influenced by one's associational linkages to communities operating in real contexts, it should be noted—as our attempts to overlay our theoretical categories on real communities illustrate—the status of the community in society often leads to different outlook outcomes within the same community. In some cases, the community's status in its environment is ambiguous enough that there can be disagreement and difference on the best way to orient oneself toward politics. One's community's position in society is still an orienting axis that shapes the limited possibilities for one's outlook.

In Turkey, as elsewhere, there is a rich landscape of diverse religious communities. These communities help shape patterns of religious outlooks among individuals that are relational in nature and, thus, prone to change based on the context and social interactions. The fact that we can detect such differences among a network of communities that all come from similar doctrinal backgrounds but differ in their social interaction with the society and the state is a testament to the general applicability of the conceptual classifications presented here.

In any case, these categories of outlooks—religious communitarian, religious individualist, (conditioned) post-Islamist, social communitarian—are commonly obscured in generic measures of religiosity as operationalized by questions in public opinion surveys. The logic behind these categories enables us to consider them as quadrant categorizations of religious respondents along two important attitudinal dimensions. One of these would be a plurality-conformity attitudinal dimension—that is, how much tolerance respondents have toward a plurality of views and beliefs. The other dimension would relate to whether religion should primarily be a public or private phenomenon. A two-dimensional framework would lead to four logical categories as shown in figure 3.1:

Religious individualist: Individuals in this group tend to be more supportive of religious pluralism and less supportive of religious influence in the public sphere. We refer to this group as religious individualist as described by the modernist position in Davis and Robinson's (2006) conceptualization.[2]

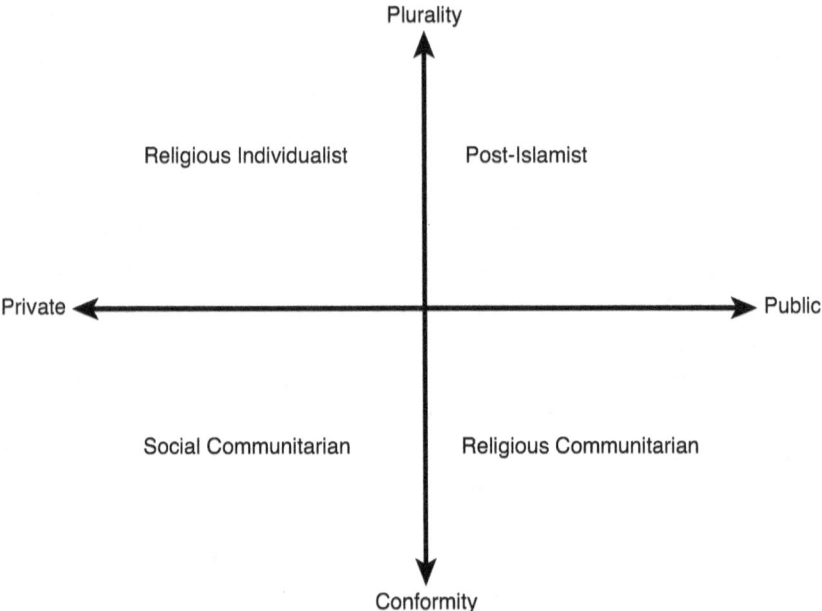

Figure 3.1. Dimensions and Categories of Religious Outlooks

Religious individualism also represents a trend in post-Islamism, which comprises mostly those in the liberal or moderate niches as defined by Stark and Finke (2000).

Social communitarian: This outlook is less supportive of religious pluralism in society and holds strong preferences for social conformity; however, unlike religious communitarians, their directive for stability and order comes from conformity to the norms handed down by the state and social practice and not as much from divine law. Thus, they are also less supportive of changes in religious influence that disrupt stasis in the public sphere. Social communitarians are committed to the conservation of existing social norms and hold a status quo outlook.

Religious communitarian: The individuals in this outlook category are less supportive of religious pluralism in society and more supportive of religious influence in the public sphere. Religious communitarians fit the categories of the so-called orthodox religious communitarians described by Davis and Robinson (2006) or classical Islamism as discussed by Bayat (2007).

Post-Islamist: People in this outlook category tend to be more supportive of both religious pluralism and religious influence in the public sphere.

This group is referred to as post-Islamist, and it fits Bayat's description of erstwhile Islamists who are confronting a condition of post-Islamism. Years of battling with state and social norms have brought about openness to other religious views and positions, but they still believe in a prominent role for religious values and leaders in politics.

In sum, this two-dimensional framework leads to four logical categories: (1) religious individualism, a category in which plurality is valued and religion is private; (2) social communitarianism, a category in which conformity is valued and religion is private; (3) religious communitarianism, a category in which conformity is valued and religion is public; and (4) post-Islamism, a category in which plurality is valued and religion is public.

Data and Latent Class Analysis

The conceptual model developed in the previous section recategorizes religious populations according to their positions along the public-private and conformity-plurality dimensions. Latent class analysis (LCA) and factor analysis enable us to make use of the available survey data conducted in the MENA region for statistical tests of the conceptual model. LCA can link observed variables (e.g., responses to survey items) to latent categorical outcomes that reflect the underlying dimensions of those variables. Specifically, Wave III of the Arab Barometer offers a number of questions on religious perspectives, primarily inquiring about participants' attitudes toward religious pluralism in society and the involvement of religion in the public and political spheres. Prior to reducing our sample according to the procedures noted below, it included over ten thousand Muslim participants from Algeria, Egypt, Iraq, Jordan, Kuwait, Lebanon, Libya, Morocco, Palestine, Sudan, Tunisia, and Yemen. All surveys were designed to be nationally representative at the household level. Although none of the countries in the sample are generally considered full or consolidated democracies, a good deal of variation can be observed in economic and social indicators. Sample sizes for these countries along with various statistics about political and economic trends are presented in table 3.1.[3]

Although all countries included in the analysis are Arab-majority societies, the sample provides variation in several political and economic indicators. The values of three measures of democracy—the polity, Freedom House, and polyarchy scores—show that democracy is a rare commodity in the Arab region, and "Arab exceptionalism" (Stepan and Robertson 2004) continues to

Table 3.1. Primary Indicators for Countries in the Sample

Country	Sample size in AB III	Polity	Freedom House scores	Polyarchy score (V-Dem)	GDP per capita	Human Development Index (rank)	Government regulation of religion
Algeria	1,220	2	3	0.23	5,584	83	6.9
Egypt	1,196	−4	5.5	0.23	3,068	108	7.8
Iraq	1,215	3	5.5	0.26	6,650	121	7.8
Jordan	1,795	−3	5.5	0.30	4,897	80	7.8
Kuwait	1,021	−7	4.5	0.34	50,904	48	7.8
Lebanon	1,200	6	4.5	0.35	9,729	67	4.7
Libya	1,247	−7	6.5	0.38	13,035	94	6.1
Morocco	1,116	−4	4.5	0.41	2,931	126	4.7
Palestine	1,200	NA	5.5	NA	2,783	113	2.2
Sudan	1,200	−4	7	0.48	1,662	167	8.6
Tunisia	1,199	7	3.5	0.60	4,188	96	6.1
Yemen	1,200	3	6	0.61	1,289	160	6.1

Notes: GDP is measured in US dollars and obtained from World Bank (https://data.worldbank.org/indicator/NY.GDP.MKTP.CD). The Human Development Index is obtained from the United Nations Development Programme (http://hdr.undp.org/en/indicators/137506), and higher values indicate lower levels of human development. The polity score is obtained from the Polity 4 data set (http://www.systemicpeace.org/polityproject.html), with higher values showing increased levels of democracy. All macro indicators represent values for the years 2011 or 2012 based on availability. The Freedom House score is the average of political and civil liberties scores as reported by the Freedom House (https://freedomhouse.org/reports/freedom-world/freedom-world-research-methodology). The V-Dem score is the arithmetic average of various indicators related to political participation and inclusion as reported by V-Dem at https://www.v-dem.net/en/.

characterize the region. With the exception of Tunisia and Lebanon, post-uprising Arab political systems are nondemocracies. The Arab region demonstrates significant variation in national wealth and presents a clear division between oil-rich Gulf monarchies and other countries. While our sample includes only Kuwait and Libya from among major oil exporters, the remaining countries vary significantly with respect to GDP per capita and scores on a number of human development indicators. At the lower end of the distribution in economic and human development are Sudan and Yemen. Kuwait and Lebanon are located at the higher end of the distribution, but most countries in the sample are at middle or low levels of economic and human development. Finally, table 3.1 shows that nuances exist in government regulation of religion. In Lebanon, Palestine, and Morocco, government has a less regulatory role in religious affairs, but in other countries, government interference in this area reaches considerable levels. It is not surprising that government will regulate the religious sphere in most MENA countries given the significance of Islam as a social and political force.

The analysis in this chapter does not deal with the effects of national-level indicators that may influence religious outlooks such as GDP or the level of political rights and freedoms. That task is reserved for chapter 4. However, it is important that the sample include participants coming from countries having a range of national indicators for the reliability of the results to be derived from the LCA. The statistics presented in table 3.1 provide a good starting point for the subsequent analysis deriving religious outlooks from responses to survey questions asked in nationally representative samples.

Our theoretical discussion builds on a classification of individuals based on their preferences regarding the role of Islam in public and private spheres and their preferences for pluralism and conformity in social life. From a measurement perspective, then, it is imperative to observe clusters of survey respondents in groups varying along these two dimensions that roughly correspond to our conceptual framework and to observe religious outlooks not only among all respondents (more versus less religious) but also among those individuals who are reasonably pious.

To empirically validate our four religious outlook categories, it will be necessary to observe a match between our conceptual constructs and the clustering of responses to survey questions assessing aspects of religious belief, religious practice, and values. LCA allows the identification of groups of individuals based on their responses to multiple survey questions. As a finite mixture model, LCA estimates underlying class memberships with categorical or continuous variables (Hagenaars and Mccutcheon 2002; Lazarsfeld 1950). It uses information about the frequency of responses to survey questions and partitions these responses into groups (classes) based on similarities and differences as well as assessing the probabilities of group membership for each individual (Blaydes and Linzer 2008). This produces a posterior probability of class membership, which subsequently allows the prediction of which religious outlook a respondent has adopted. The analysis utilizes Stata's GSEM (generalized structural equation modeling) utility to estimate categories of religious outlooks with LCA.[4]

To assess variability among the religious will require selecting only moderately to highly religious individuals from the full set of respondents.

Working with a reduced sample of religious individuals provides a more difficult empirical test. If we can find differences even among the moderately to highly religious, this will be a litmus test for our argument that there is indeed a diversity of views among the religious on both religious pluralism and the role of religion in public life. That there will be heterogeneity in the belief and practice of a particular faith and that this intrafaith heterogeneity will result in different views could be easily established. If empirical analysis points to significant differences and clustering of views among the devout, this supports the validity of applying our proposed conceptual classification to a broad group conventionally classified as religious in previous studies. Thus, by reducing the sample to the moderately to highly religious, we are able to contribute to the field of knowledge by demonstrating the existence and characteristics of nuanced outlooks among the pious.

Three questions from the Arab Barometer (Wave III) survey inquired about frequency of religious practice, including daily prayer, Friday prayer attendance, and Koran readership. The responses were used to create an index of religiosity and to separate the moderately and highly religious individuals from the less religious. For each question the range for responses was from never (1) to always (5). To obtain a subsample consisting only of moderately and highly religious individuals, we dropped respondents whose responses were never (1), rarely (2), or missing for any of these three questions. An analysis using the full sample of respondents provided similar results to this subsample. This could be due to the relatively small number of respondents who report to be less religious across all countries in the full sample. Nonetheless, we believe it is conceptually more valid to use the reduced sample as the basis of our analyses because one of the goals of this study is to specifically demonstrate the existence of variability in religious outlooks among the pious. The results of the LCA estimations for the full sample are provided in appendix A and will be discussed as a comparison group for the religious subsample.

Figure 3.2 shows the distribution of responses in the full sample to the three questions used to select subjects for the subsample of religious subjects. Not surprisingly, the distribution of self-reported religious behavior even in the overall sample has a negative skew for all three items. The data also reveal minor differences among the countries in this measure, which are addressed in the next chapter. For now, the focus of the analysis is on the general patterns across the whole sample. Considering the overall distribution of responses, 74 percent of individuals reported that they prayed daily,

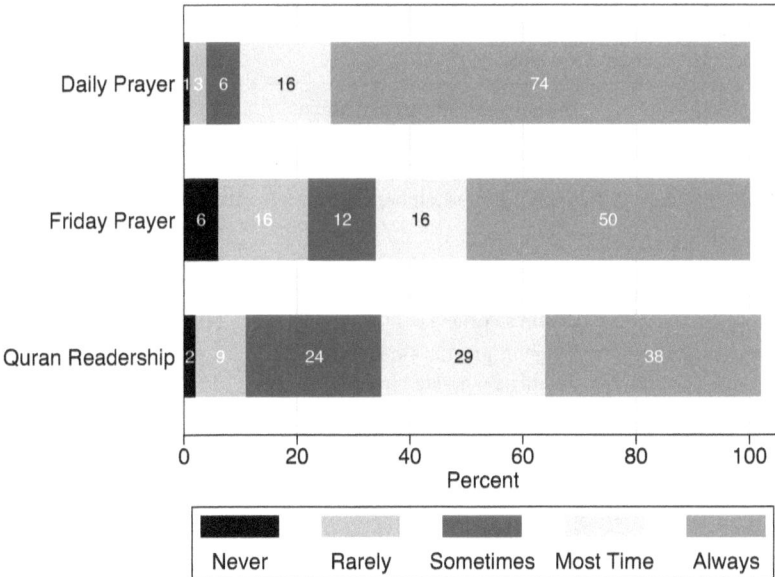

Figure 3.2. Distribution of Responses for Self-Reported Religious Behavior

50 percent attended Friday prayer consistently,[5] and 38 percent reported that they read the Koran daily. In the full sample, 22 percent of the respondents reported that they did not attend Friday prayer, and 11 percent reported that they did not read the Koran daily. As noted, these less religious individuals constituted a small portion of the total respondents and were removed from the analysis sample before running the statistical estimation.

Estimation Results

Once the sample is truncated to include only the respondents who are moderately to highly religious, we look for questions that can be used in the LCA estimation. Wave III of the Arab Barometer includes many items tapping into respondents' views about the role of religion in the public / private sphere and their attitudes toward social conformity / plurality. The main factors determining the selection of these questions were the face validity of the survey items and their availability across the countries. The survey questions employed in LCA estimation are presented in table 3.2.

Before we estimated the LCA to test whether the data supported our fourfold classification of religious outlooks, we ran factor analyses to explore the

Table 3.2. Description of Survey Items Used in LCA Estimation

AB code	LCA code	Variable	Response category
Q6052	LCI2	The government and parliament should enact laws in accordance with Islamic Law	4-point scale of strongly disagree to strongly agree
Q605b2	LCI3	Applying *shari'a* more strictly.	4-point scale of strongly don't support to strongly support
Q6072	LCI4	In a Muslim country, non-Muslims should enjoy less political rights	4-point scale of strongly disagree to strongly agree
Q6064	LCI5	Religious practices are private and should be separated from social and political life	4-point scale of strongly disagree to strongly agree
Q608ab	LCI6	Laws regulating marriage and divorce shall be based on an accurate explanation of the Islamic *shari'a*	3-point scale of absolutely disagree to strongly agree
Q6062	LCI8	Country better off with religious people in public office	4-point scale of strongly disagree to strongly agree
Q6082	LCI9	Difference and variation between Islamic scholars with regard to their interpretation of religious matters is a good thing.	4-point scale of absolutely disagree to strongly agree
Q6087	LCI10	Religious Minorities such as Christians and Shi'a have the right to practice their religion freely.	4-point scale of absolutely disagree to strongly agree
Q605a	LCI11	Which of the following sentences is the closest to your point of view? 1. I prefer a religious political party over a non-religious political party 2. I prefer a non-religious political party over a religious political party 3. I don't agree with either	5-point scale of strongly prefer a religious party to strongly prefer a non-religious party
Q6065	LCI12	Religious institutions should not influence voters	4-point scale of strongly disagree to strongly agree

Source: Arab Barometer Survey.

underlying conceptual dimensions present in the data. To that end, both exploratory and confirmatory factor analyses were utilized. The main idea behind the factor analyses was to find a smaller number of latent factors that explain the interrelationships among manifest or observed variables. Presumably, factor analysis will result in fewer factors than the number of manifest variables. Factor analysis partitions the total variance associated with the interrelationships among a set of manifest variables into common and unique variance components. The goal is to find common factor(s) that explain most of the shared variance and that leave out as little unique variance associated with each variable as possible. This method allows researchers to see the common patterns that cover a good degree of overlap across responses to survey items. Factor loadings are used as measures of contribution to common factors by manifest variables. Exploratory factor analysis does not limit the number of common factors, and there could be as many factors as manifest variables. Confirmatory factor analysis is driven by theory and assumes a certain number of factors according to the theoretical expectations a researcher may have.

Using exploratory factor analysis our model of the data returns four dimensions, but the factor loadings across different dimensions do not provide much guidance about the dimensionality of the survey responses in measuring religious outlooks. The first dimension, which could be defined as "preferences about Islamic law," is determined by the responses to three questions that ask about the views concerning the law. Other factors, however, do not represent consistent patterns, and the survey items asking about rights, pluralism, and religion / state relations randomly explain the remaining three factors. Therefore, it is preferable to run confirmatory factor analysis of two factors. This second technique is driven by our theoretical expectation that proposes two dimensions, public / private and plurality / conformity, in classification of religious outlooks. Confirmatory factor analysis allows parsing of the underlying dimensions according to the responses to survey questions that measure various aspects of religiosity.

The results of the confirmatory factor analysis (table 3.3) lend some support to a two-dimensional scenario in conceptualization of religious views. Of the four items loading strongly on the second factor, three items tap respondents' views about tolerance and social preferences about pluralist ideas. These items include the following:

> LCI5: Religious practices are private and should be separated from social and political life.
> LCI9: Difference and variation between Islamic scholars with regard to their interpretation of religious matters is a good thing.
> LCI10: Religious Minorities such as Christians and Shi'a have the right to practice their religion freely.

The question asking the respondents about the influence of religious institutions in voting (LCI12) unexpectedly loads stronger on the second

Table 3.3. Rotated Factor Loadings (Pattern Matrix) and Unique Variances

Variable	Factor 1	Factor 2	Uniqueness
LCI2	0.5665		0.6883
LCI3	0.5950		0.6727
LCI4			0.8859
LCI5		0.3808	0.6942
LCI6	0.3006		0.9100
LCI8	0.5167		0.6608
LCI9	0.3202	0.3453	0.8579
LCI10		0.5104	0.7670
LCI11	0.4912		0.7370
LCI12		0.4078	0.7816

Note: factor loadings smaller than 0.30 are neglected in the table.
Source: Arab Barometer Survey.

dimension. Other items generally deal with the role of religion in the public sphere, and they load strongly on the second factor measuring the public-private dimension in religious preferences. Although informative, these results and factor analysis are not designed to help researchers assess the distribution of individuals across unobserved clusters according to their preferences. Factor analysis demonstrates the correlations between observed responses to various questions according to a smaller number of unobserved dimensions. LCA, on the other hand, allows the classification of survey respondents into different groups according to their likelihood of responses to certain questions and response categories. Since we are interested in different religious outlooks among the respondents—that is, classes of individuals—LCA is a more suitable technique for the analysis of religious outlooks based on survey questions.

Using the questions reported in table 3.2, an LCA model was estimated and resulted in a four-class solution for the respondents selected for the moderately to highly religious subsample. Most of these items have been used as indicators of religious values, adherence to religious principles, public and private religiosity, or Islamist ideology by the scholars of Middle Eastern public opinion (Ciftci 2013; Driessen 2018; Karakoç and Baskan 2012; Tessler, Jamal, and Robbins 2012). While the LCA estimation can provide an empirical distribution of responses to survey questions that sheds light on the feasibility of different classes, it does not guide researchers about how many classes are needed or in allocating individuals to latent clusters. The

Table 3.4. Model-Fit Statistics for Latent Class Analysis Estimations

Sample	Statistics	2 class	3 class	4 class	5 class
Moderately/highly religious	AIC	224,415	219,848	218,255	217,376
Moderately/highly Religious	BIC	224,856	220,514	219,144	218,490
Full sample	AIC	313,898	307,058	304,754	303,680
Full sample	BIC	314,359	307,753	305,684	304,844

Source: Arab Barometer Survey. Akaike information criterion (AIC) and Bayesian information criterion (BIC) provide estimates of the error in prediction. They are two commonly used methods in model comparison and selection.

choice about the number of classes should be driven by theoretical considerations, and it should be complemented by the empirical patterns obtained in LCA estimation. In the analysis presented below, we chose a four-class specification over alternatives with fewer or more classes primarily based on our theoretical expectations. Supporting these expectations, posterior class probabilities of LCA estimations, percentages of class shares, and additional model-fit statistics confirm that a four-class solution is the best fit for the data in hand. To corroborate this finding, the model-fit statistics from the LCA estimation are shown in table 3.4.

The model-fit statistics show that a four-class solution is superior to two- or three-class solutions. AIC and BIC statistics significantly improve as the number of classes increase until the model switches from a four-class to a five-class solution. At this stage, the models improve only marginally, indicating the feasibility of a four-class solution (Akaike 1973; Kass and Wasserman 1995; Schwartz 1978). Although this pattern is weaker in the full sample estimations, especially between the four- and five-class solutions, the distribution of class probabilities indicates the feasibility of a four-class solution in the larger sample as well. Therefore, in addition to our theoretical rationale, the statistical tests lend empirical support to the feasibility of the fourfold conceptual classification proposed in this study. Specifically, we find that the empirical patterns of responses to the survey questions measuring various preferences about religion justify a four-class solution to religious outlook categories. Individuals are generally distributed along four categories of religious outlooks, which are defined as religious individualist, religious communitarian, post-Islamist, and social communitarian.

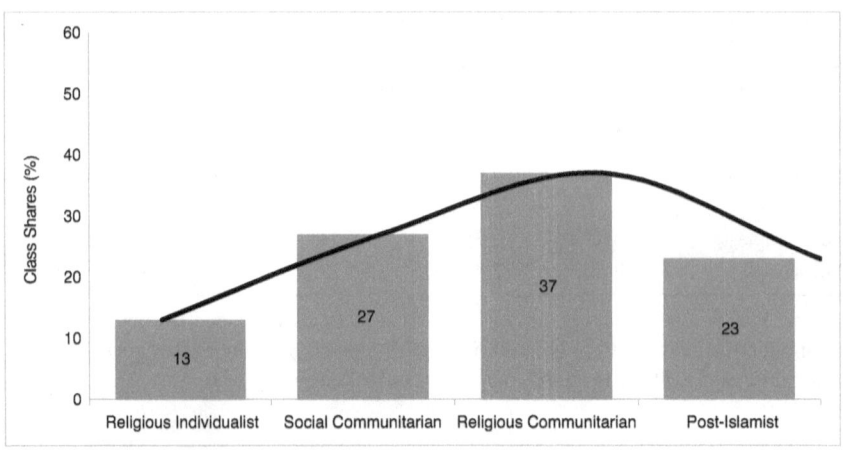

Figure 3.3. Class Shares of Religious Outlooks. The bars show the percentage of each class share according to the LCA estimation. The line shows the smoothed distribution. Source: Arab Barometer, Wave III.

The class shares for the four-class solution are presented in figure 3.3. The distribution of classes has a visible left skew with the largest class shares belonging to religious communitarians (37 percent) and social communitarians (27 percent). Post-Islamists constitute 23 percent of the respondents, and religious individualists the smallest class, with a share of 13 percent based on the LCA estimations of the reduced sample.

The class shares for the religious outlooks are determined according to the distribution of probabilities for each class and across response categories. These posterior probabilities for the response categories of the twelve items are presented in table 3.5. By and large, individuals who prefer a greater role for Islam in social and political life have a higher probability of belonging to the religious communitarian or post-Islamist outlook than the other groups. Post-Islamists also lean favorably toward religious pluralism, a tendency that can be observed even more strongly among the members of the religious individualist outlook: religious individualists have the strongest preferences toward pluralism and also prefer a minimal role for religion in the public sphere. Finally, social communitarians take middle positions with respect to religious pluralism and Islam's role in social and political life. The same classification scheme also prevails in estimations with the full sample, which includes both religious and nonreligious respondents.[6]

Are these patterns in line with certain organizational outlooks among the vast Islamist landscape of religious movements and political parties?

Table 3.5. Distribution of Posterior Probabilities by Religious Outlooks

Variable	Response categories	Religious individualist	Post-Islamist	Religious communitarian	Social communitarian
The government and parliament should enact laws in accordance with Islamic Law.	Strongly disagree	0.28	0.02	0.00	0.05
	Disagree	0.23	0.02	0.05	0.25
	Agree	0.30	0.16	0.62	0.61
	Strongly agree	0.18	0.79	0.33	0.09
Applying shari'a a more strictly.	Strongly don't support	0.22	0.02	0.00	0.05
	Don't support	0.23	0.04	0.04	0.26
	Support	0.31	0.16	0.40	0.58
	Strongly support	0.24	0.78	0.56	0.11
Non-Muslims should have less rights.	Strongly disagree	0.65	0.39	0.08	0.13
	Disagree	0.22	0.25	0.50	0.59
	Agree	0.05	0.18	0.34	0.25
	Strongly agree	0.07	0.19	0.08	0.02
Religious practices are private and should be separated from social and political life.	Strongly disagree	0.03	0.35	0.06	0.07
	Disagree	0.03	0.20	0.47	0.20
	Agree	0.12	0.13	0.42	0.58
	Strongly agree	0.82	0.32	0.05	0.16
Laws regulating marriage and divorce shall be based on an accurate explanation of the Islamic shari'a.	I disagree to a certain extent	0.14	0.02	0.01	0.08
	I agree to a certain extent	0.33	0.12	0.19	0.30
	I absolutely agree	0.52	0.86	0.80	0.62

Table 3.5. (continued)

Variable	Response categories	Religious individualist	Post-Islamist	Religious communitarian	Social communitarian
Country better off with religious people in public office	Strongly disagree	0.66	0.17	0.01	0.16
	Disagree	0.22	0.16	0.31	0.65
	Agree	0.08	0.26	0.61	0.17
	Strongly agree	0.03	0.42	0.07	0.01
Difference and variation between Islamic scholars with regard to their interpretation of religious matters is a good thing.	I absolutely disagree	0.13	0.08	0.06	0.07
	I disagree to a certain extent	0.13	0.09	0.14	0.20
	I agree to a certain extent	0.26	0.23	0.49	0.56
	I strongly agree	0.47	0.60	0.31	0.17
Religious Minorities such as Christians and Shi'a have the right to practice their religion freely.	I absolutely disagree	0.05	0.15	0.11	0.06
	I disagree to a certain extent	0.04	0.11	0.14	0.20
	I agree to a certain extent	0.18	0.22	0.47	0.51
	I strongly agree	0.72	0.53	0.27	0.23
Which of the following sentences is the closest to your point of view? 1. I prefer a religious political party over a non-religious political party 2. I prefer a non-religious political party over a religious political party 3. I don't agree with either	Strongly prefer a non-religious party	0.29	0.04	0.02	0.09

Table 3.5. (continued)

Variable	Response categories	Religious individualist	Post-Islamist	Religious communitarian	Social communitarian
	Prefer a non-religious party	0.26	0.05	0.06	0.31
	I prefer neither	0.27	0.17	0.21	0.23
	I prefer a religious party	0.08	0.17	0.32	0.23
	I strongly prefer a religious party	0.10	0.57	0.39	0.15
Religious institutions should not influence voters.	Strongly disagree	0.03	0.14	0.01	0.06
	Disagree	0.02	0.18	0.23	0.12
	Agree	0.08	0.21	0.67	0.65
	Strongly agree	0.87	0.47	0.09	0.18

Source: Arab Barometer Survey, Wave III.

The answer would be both yes and no. Post-Islamists, for example, would include members of social movements or political parties that prefer a significant role for religion in social and political life. At the same time, this group would prefer to stay within the limits of political systems and try to achieve change toward democratization without drawing the ire of the regime elements, bringing them closer to social communitarian positions. Specifically, members of groups like al-Wasat in Egypt, Ennahda in Tunisia, or the Justice and Development Party in Morocco would be examples of this class. Similarly, the profile of the Islamic Action Front in Jordan, Salafi groups in Egypt, and Parti Islam SeMalaysia (PAS) fits closely with the religious communitarian view, with their preferences leaning toward increasing the role of Islam in the public and social life. We can also find examples conforming to the religious individualist category. For example, the Green Movement in Iran, the youth movements who reconciled their beliefs with a preference for a pluralist order in the Middle East (Bayat 2007), or the anticapitalist Muslims movement in Turkey (Yenigun 2017) exemplify the religious individualist outlook. In Turkey, liberal members of the Justice and Development Party before the consolidation of power by Erdoğan and the authoritarian turn would also closely fit with this outlook.

Notwithstanding these examples, a note of caution is in order. While we can view members belonging to these groups as holding certain religious outlooks, our analysis does not propose a direct correspondence between a specific religious outlook and any particular organization. It is likely that the membership in these organizations will also include some individuals with religious individualist, social communitarian, and religious communitarian outlooks. However, there is likely a greater degree of overlap between members of certain organizations and certain religious outlooks, such as the membership profiles of Salafi groups with a religious communitarian outlook or the new Islamist youth movements with religious individualist views. For now, it would suffice to say that across the landscape of religious organizational membership, the LCA analysis of survey responses confirms the existence of variability in religious outlooks among the pious.

Religiosity and Religious Outlooks

LCA estimations provide strong support for the predictions of our conceptual categorization of religious outlooks. Additional LCA models using different survey items and specifications confirm the robustness of these findings. Therefore, from an empirical standing, we can be quite confident about the existence of different religious outlooks among pious individuals as measured by the questions in the survey. This delineation of religious outlook classes within the population of the survey designated "religious" presents an opportunity for a more nuanced study of the influence of religion on other political and economic attitudes. This provides us with far more analytical tools for our statistical models than the conventional approach, which only uses a single item or an additive index based on self-reported religious behavior for a scaled measurement of religiosity. The additional classification of religious outlooks can help examine, with greater nuance, the relationship between religious considerations and attitudes toward democracy, regime support, economic preferences, gender equality, or other political issues. The ambiguities in the relationship between religion and public attitudes that have been detected by previous quantitative public opinion research in MENA can now be reexamined from a new vantage point by introducing these identifiable religious outlooks to the analysis.

How do these more nuanced proposed conceptual categories empirically compare with conventional measures of religiosity? Do religious outlook categories convincingly unfold the unobserved variance across the

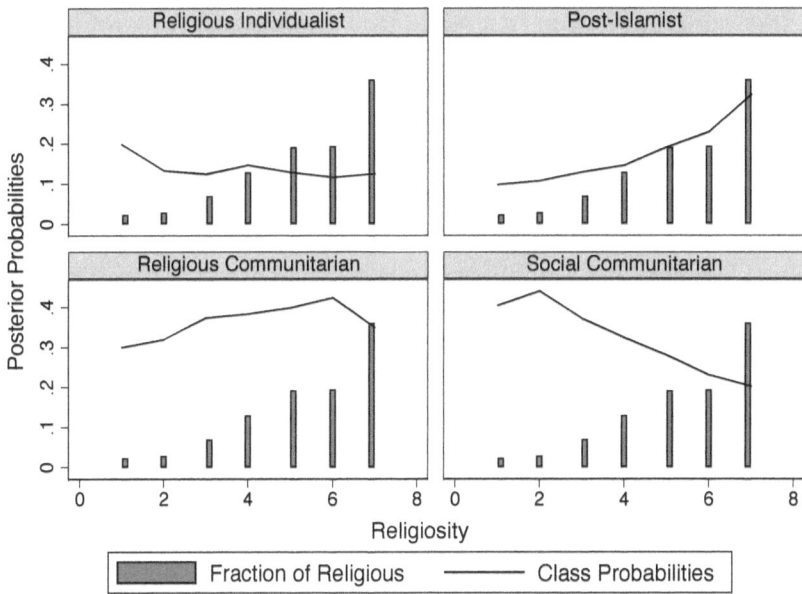

Figure 3.4. Distribution of the Four Religious Outlooks along Religiosity Index. The bars represent fraction of religious individuals in the sample. The lines represent posterior probabilities for each group. Source: Arab Barometer, Wave III.

conventional measures of religiosity? To answer these questions, the analysis utilizes the posterior probabilities from the LCA estimation to explore the associations between our conceptual categories and conventional measures of religiosity. Figure 3.4 maps the distribution of posterior probabilities along the religiosity index.

As discussed above, our baseline measure of religiosity is an additive index of responses to Arab Barometer questions about daily prayer, Friday prayer attendance, and Koran readership, and our analysis uses data only from subjects identified as moderately to highly religious individuals in the surveys. As depicted in figure 3.4, the religious individualist class shows a higher percentage of respondents located at the low end of the religiosity index, yet the distribution of religious individualists is relatively even across all levels of religiosity. Conversely, the probability of belonging to the post-Islamist class consistently increases with religiosity and is highest among the most religious individuals. Religious communitarians are also most likely to be found among those who score highest on the religiosity index; however, the religious communitarian class percentage is high across all levels of religiosity. In fact, while the posterior probability of being a religious individualist is highest at low levels of religiosity, individuals who have low scores on the religiosity index are substantially more likely to be religious communitarians than religious individualists. Finally, social communitarians also have considerable shares across all values of the religiosity index, but there is a relatively consistent negative correlation between religiosity and the probability of an individual belonging to the social communitarian class. Based on these results, the conceptual classification corroborated by the analysis of the survey data using LCA estimation seems to provide insights about the different religious views that one can see among the pious.

Overall, religious communitarians and post-Islamists do tend to be more religious than the other outlook categories, but members of each of the four classes can be found at all levels along the continuum of the religiosity index. These findings provide strong empirical evidence for the utility of religious outlook categories in unmasking the ambiguity present in conventional measures of religiosity. Classifying pious individuals according to their outlooks may provide significant leverage in explaining nuanced patterns in religious behavior and predicting political attitudes and behavior. Rather than relying on measurement strategies that classify individuals as religious or nonreligious, there could be great utility in categorizing individuals according to their social and political preferences within the religious sphere. This strategy should allow researchers to unpack the black boxes that the binary categories of religiosity represent by differentiating among outlooks of pious individuals. Figure 3.5 illustrates this point by depicting the distribution of posterior probabilities generated by the LCA estimation for each religious outlook category across different levels of religious behavior. Each panel shows the likelihood of respondents belonging to different outlooks who engage in daily prayer, read the Koran, and attend the Friday prayer at different frequencies (sometimes, most of the time, and always).

The distribution of posterior probabilities along religious outlooks categories demonstrates several interesting patterns. First, there is significant variance in the probability of belonging to any religious outlook category both within and between indicators of self-reported religious behavior. For each question shown in figure 3.5, the class shares for each outlook category within each frequency level (sometimes, most of the time, always) hold at proportions very close to those of total class shares (see figure 3.3). Religious and social communitarians have the largest class shares across different

Empirical Foundations of Religious Outlooks | 85

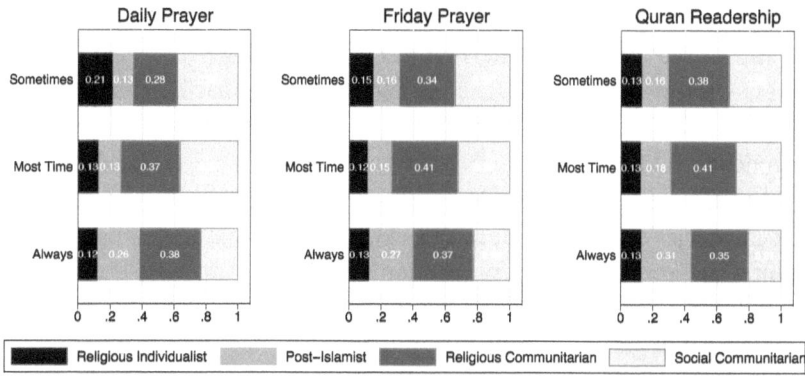

Figure 3.5. Religious Behavior and Religious Outlooks. The stacked bars show the mean posterior probabilities across each response category. Source: Arab Barometer, Wave III.

levels of religious behavior categories, followed by religious individualists and post-Islamists who have smaller class shares.

The analysis comparing religious outlooks and measures of religiosity also points to a second layer of nuance. This layer can be observed within each indicator of religious behavior. The probability of belonging to the religious individualist outlook is almost constant at different frequencies of Friday prayer attendance or Koran readership. Those who pray less frequently on a daily basis are more likely to be religious individualist in their outlooks across different frequencies presented for each item. The posterior probabilities for religious communitarian outlooks are somehow distinct across the three frequency categories for each indicator. Overall, individuals who report they engage in religious behavior most of the time or always are more likely to hold religious communitarian or post-Islamist outlooks. These results corroborate our expectations about the utility of differentiating religious outlooks in measurement of religiosity by confirming further differentiated classifications within the pious.

Robustness Analysis

The robustness of the LCA and factor analysis was tested with the data collected in Wave II of the Arab Barometer surveys. This approach is designed to confirm that the religious outlook categories are not simply an artifact of the sample in hand (Wave III) and that similar results are likely to be obtained even working with different samples of the survey data. Wave II of the Arab Barometer includes Algeria, Egypt, Iraq, Jordan, Lebanon, Palestine

Saudi Arabi, Tunisia, Sudan, and Yemen. The surveys were carried out during and in the immediate aftermath of the Arab Spring. Table 3.6 reports the LCA estimation results. The sample is again restricted to respondents classified as moderately to highly religious for consistency with the current approach.

As the class probabilities demonstrate in table 3.6, similar religious outlook categories capture religious individualist, post-Islamist, religious communitarian, and social communitarian groups. The attitudinal differences between religious individualist and post-Islamist categories are somewhat less visible, but generally, religious individualists have the strongest preferences concerning rights, diversity, and tolerance of other religions. Religious individualists desire a lesser role for religion in the public sphere as opposed to religious communitarians and post-Islamists. However, post-Islamists may be equally pro-rights and pluralism in the religious/public sphere as religious individualists. In most cases, the probabilities for the post-Islamists' affirmative responses concerning a public role for religion swing between the positions of religious individualists and religious communitarians.

The distribution of religious outlook categories across different levels of religiosity from the analysis of Wave II of the Arab Barometer is very similar to the comparable distribution obtained from the analysis of Wave III as shown in figure 3.6. The largest class share is religious communitarian (32 percent), followed by the post-Islamists (30 percent). Religious individualists have a class share of 13 percent in the sample, and the social communitarians comprise a quarter of the respondents. Overall, a higher percentage of respondents is cumulated among the less and moderately religious within the religious individualist class. In contrast, the percentage that belongs to the religious communitarian and post-Islamist classes is larger among highly religious individuals. However, post-Islamists can also be found among the moderately pious. Finally, social communitarians have considerable shares across all categories of religiosity, with a declining pattern at the high end of the religiosity index.

One difference that can be observed in comparison to the estimation results from Wave III of the Arab Barometer is the spike for the highly religious category in the sample surveyed in Wave II. This minor difference results in a clear separation of religious communitarians from religious individualists in LCA estimation. This could be due to the addition of such cases as Saudi Arabia, which contains a disproportionally high percentage of respondents at the higher end of the religiosity continuum.

Table 3.6. LCA Estimation Results for Arab Barometer, Wave II

Variable	Response category	Religious individualist	Post-Islamist	Religious communitarian	Social communitarian
Accept other religious groups as neighbors	Yes	0.91	0.70	0.55	0.87
The government and parliament should enact laws in accordance with Islamic Law.	Strongly disagree	0.24	0.01	0.01	0.04
	Disagree	0.13	0.14	0.03	0.18
	Agree	0.17	0.63	0.17	0.47
	Strongly agree	0.45	0.22	0.79	0.31
When a person changes his religion he should be penalized with death penalty	Strongly disagree	0.61	0.10	0.15	0.43
	Disagree	0.10	0.52	0.17	0.34
	Agree	0.03	0.30	0.19	0.14
	Strongly agree	0.25	0.08	0.49	0.09
Religious practice should be private	Strongly disagree	0.12	0.02	0.30	0.03
	Disagree	0.03	0.37	0.34	0.13
	Agree	0.03	0.60	0.19	0.43
	Strongly agree	0.82	0.01	0.16	0.41
In a Muslim society a number of religious interpretations should be available	Strongly disagree	0.11	0.03	0.16	0.07
	Disagree	0.14	0.15	0.27	0.09
	Agree	0.18	0.66	0.33	0.42
	Strongly agree	0.57	0.16	0.24	0.41

Table 3.6. (continued)

Variable	Response category	Religious individualist	Post-Islamist	Religious communitarian	Social communitarian
Religious minorities have the right to practice their religious ceremonies	Strongly disagree	0.02	0.01	0.14	0.01
	Disagree	0.02	0.11	0.16	0.02
	Agree	0.07	0.61	0.34	0.35
	Strongly agree	0.89	0.27	0.37	0.61
Women should wear modest clothes without needing to wear hijab	Strongly disagree	0.19	0.03	0.31	0.09
	Disagree	0.09	0.34	0.21	0.21
	Agree	0.14	0.56	0.24	0.50
	Strongly agree	0.57	0.06	0.24	0.20
Gender-mixed education should be allowed in universities	Strongly disagree	0.15	0.01	0.33	0.03
	Disagree	0.06	0.32	0.35	0.10
	Agree	0.16	0.63	0.21	0.63
	Strongly agree	0.64	0.03	0.10	0.25
Better if religious people hold public office	Strongly disagree	0.57	0.04	0.08	0.19
	Disagree	0.18	0.50	0.17	0.42
	Agree	0.07	0.44	0.39	0.33
	Strongly agree	0.18	0.02	0.35	0.06
Religious institutions should not influence vote	Strongly disagree	0.05	0.01	0.09	0.01
	Disagree	0.02	0.21	0.23	0.07
	Agree	0.03	0.77	0.38	0.49
	Strongly agree	0.90	0.01	0.30	0.44

Source: Arab Barometer, Wave II.

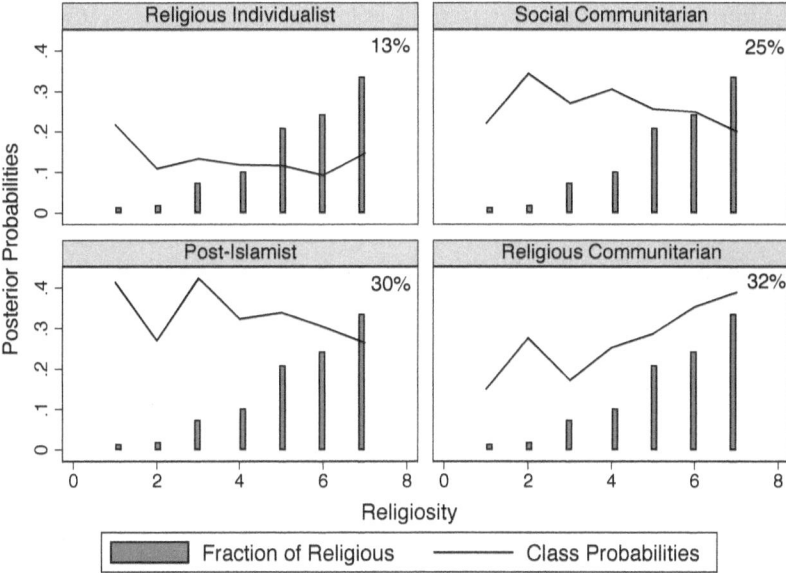

Figure 3.6. Distribution of the Four Religious Outlooks along Religiosity Index. Source: Arab Barometer, Wave II.

Notwithstanding this difference, the additional LCA estimation results confirm the viability of the same four religious outlook categories in the MENA regardless of the survey sample. Furthermore, the changing proportion of religious outlook categories confirms the contention that these outlooks are dynamic and prone to change in different circumstances.

By and large, these results should be taken with a grain of salt due to special conditions surrounding the fieldwork phase of Wave II. This wave was conducted during the Arab uprisings. The survey was conducted in a reliable way; however, it is likely that these responses were primed by the extraordinary social and political conditions of the day. On a positive note, the analysis confirms the existence of different religious outlooks and the nuances among the pious even during times of uncertainty.

Conclusion

The analysis in this chapter reveals significant variation across religious outlook categories in relation to religious behavior. Existing research has used one or several indicators of self-reported religiosity as the sole variable to gauge the influence of religion on attitudes. However, using such a unidimensional continuum ranging from less to more religious masks significant nuances that are observed when we attend to different religious outlook groups among practicing Muslims. We cannot, for example, always assume that individuals located at the low (or high) end of this continuum will engage in similar religious and social behavior. Furthermore, as we previously discussed, these religious outlooks stem from relational influences related to the context of an individual's communal association and that community's interaction with the state and society. Measures of the influence of religiosity are likely to show greater salience in relationship to policy or attitudes that address discreet elements of doctrine—in other words, in analysis that seeks to understand the substantive influence of religion. For most issues of broader social and political concern, however, where the connections to doctrine are less explicit and given to debate and interpretation, the relational influence of religion carries far more weight.[7] In these latter cases, religious outlook categories stemming from variables addressing plurality-conformity and public-private dimensions provide a better basis for analyzing preferences toward political institutions and socioeconomic policy. Thus, it seems beneficial to measure how these outlooks relate to these important questions in Muslim-majority countries.

Now that the analysis has provided the conceptual foundations of these religious outlooks and empirically demonstrated their distribution across a large cross-national sample, the next logical step is to study how these outlooks might operate in differing proportions from one national social context to another. Does the proportion of respondents with such religious outlooks vary to a significant degree from country to country? If so, why? Chapter 4 examines cross-national distributions of these outlooks in an effort to explain their individual and contextual determinants. Building on the analyses presented in this and the next chapter, chapter 5 develops a novel theory that employs our conceptual model to explain support for democracy in the MENA region.

Notes

1. While the İsmailağa community could also be placed in this category, they are positioned further to the right among the religious conservatives, making them a cultlike community that is less likely to appeal to a large group of religious individuals.

2. These could also share preferences with post-Islamists who see post-Islamism as a project (Bayat 2007).

3. Since we explore both the individual- and country-level correlates of religious outlooks in chapter 4, our analysis in this chapter combines all countries and does not utilize survey weights.

4. Stata, a statistical software package, includes generalized structural equation modeling that allows simultaneous equations involving multiple levels of analysis. The maximization of the log-likelihood function that produced our estimates and predictions are rooted in the EM (expectation-maximization) algorithm implemented by GSEM for categorical latent class models.

5. We note that this question has a male-only bias since most respondents who report to attend the Friday prayer are men. Dropping this item from the index construction does not alter the results of the statistical models.

6. These results are presented in the appendix.

7. For example, it is likely that a measure of religiosity would be a salient determinant in attitudes regarding fasting during Ramadan, gambling, or punishment of adultery. When it comes to questions of state distribution of resources or preferences regarding political or social liberalization, however, measures of religion that do not take into account the potential categorical variation of outlooks among the devout would be less helpful.

4

THE INDIVIDUAL AND CONTEXTUAL DETERMINANTS OF MUSLIM RELIGIOUS OUTLOOKS IN MENA

IN CHAPTER 2, THE STUDY OF NAQSHBANDI COMMUNITIES highlighted the fact that members of these groups, who follow a similar doctrine but occupy very different social positions and levels of tension with society, formed different approaches to politics. Individuals from the most marginal groups tended to avoid public engagement with democratic politics, and when opportunities did arise, the members would seek a protective political alliance with either the state or a strong political party for group survival. The members of conservative groups who saw themselves as close enough to the pulse of Turkish society that they could mobilize an influential population of voters for political and policy change actively engaged and coordinated with one another to this end. Furthermore, as the political context within Turkey changed, it also transformed the political approaches of the members of Naqshbandi communities and other religious groups and individuals.

Are Turkey's Naqshbandi cases unique, or do changing social and political contexts interact with one's religious associational preferences to create different religious outlooks? Evidence from the American case strongly suggests that it does (Djupe and Claassen 2018). Devout American white Evangelicals have dramatically different political attitudes than Black Evangelicals. White Evangelicals in the southeastern United States, where their religious norms are still part of the dominant cultural practices, see politics very differently than white Evangelicals in the major urban centers of the Northeast, where they are a very evident minority. In the former contexts, it is quite common to hear white Evangelicals espouse a religious outlook that closely conforms to our categorization of religious communitarian. White Evangelicals within the cultural context of the Northeast are much more likely to adopt a position that supports pluralism and a significant role for religion in the public sphere, a position that could be seen as the Christian correlate to our post-Islamist category. Evidence from both the US and Turkish contexts suggests context matters in shaping individual religious views and preferences. And if one's religious associational preferences interact with context, we would expect that distributions of the religious outlook categories would not simply mirror the aggregates that we presented in chapter 3 but would show different distributions from context to context and over time.

Many might have already suspected that this proposition is true. Numerous examples can be cited in MENA and the broader Muslim world to illustrate how contextual variations affect political expressions of faith. The dynamic posture taken by individuals in communities in response to changing state policies and socioeconomic context can be seen within the same organizations over time as well as across Muslim-majority societies. For example, from 1965 until its democratization period, Indonesia's religious landscape was replete with pluralities in Muslim religious outlooks. A secular-minded military elite aimed to manipulate this rich landscape with a nationalist worldview known as Pancasilla. However, many different groups, including the Sufism-oriented and traditionalist Nahdlatul Ulama, the more progressive Muhammadiyah, and such independent scholars as Nurcholish Madjid, developed highly dynamic interpretations of Islam (Hefner 2011). These groups and individuals do not stick to static interpretations of Islam; rather, they represent many different dynamic and, in most cases, highly pluralistic ideologies against an authoritarian regime to play an instrumental role in Indonesian democratization. During the democratization period, various Islamist parties in Indonesia adjusted their positions to the new reality by running on dynamic policy programs addressing the shifting imperatives of ideology, social diversity, and economic development (Pepinsky, Liddle, and Mujani 2012).

Other notable examples of observed shifts in political attitudes and activism occurred in the Salafi communities in Egypt after the Arab uprisings (Al-Anani and Malik 2013). These formally politically quietist groups came out with differing outlooks concerning the political realm in response to changing political conditions. Not only did Salafis come to represent different outlooks vis-à-vis the Muslim Brothers, but they also revealed significant variation in their political strategy. Even in settings where the state's regulation of religion is dominant and intended to preclude a rich array of religious communities, groups and individuals with different outlooks are likely to emerge. In Saudi Arabia's strictly monopolized religious market, which has been based on the official state-sanctioned Wahhabi interpretation of Islam, communities were formed to present a challenge to the status quo in state-religion relations.[1] Scholars marrying Wahhabi teachings with a Salafi brand of political Islamism formed the opposition movement Sahwa (awakening) to create a schism within what appeared to be a uniform religious landscape (Al-Rasheed, 2006). Even within the Sahwa movement, it was not difficult to see individuals with divergent outlooks, including such influential scholars as Safar al-Hawali and Salman al-Awdah (Dekmeijan, 1994).

While the existence of religious communities with an array of distinct outlooks is easily established, religious preferences might be best measured through individuals' religious outlooks. The outlooks of members of a community cannot simply be imputed from the actions of their community, and a focus on the actions of elites or community-level data may mask potentially important intracommunity heterogeneity in preferences. At the same time, as discussed in the previous chapters, religious outlooks themselves have sociopolitical roots stemming from national contexts that juxtapose one's own religious identity and community with existing dynamics in state-religion relations, compounded by regime types and other identity dynamics, like ethnic and sectarian nationalisms (Hinnebusch 2020). Whether Naqshbandis in Turkey, Nahdlatul Ulama or Muhammadiya in Indonesia, or official clergy and members of the Sahwa movement in Saudi Arabia, the social and political context will have significant sway on the evolution of outlooks within and between religious organizations as well as the manifestations of these outlooks among individuals who are attached to these organizations. Including context in the study of religiosity and religious outlooks matters in two ways. First, this approach illustrates the ways in which the sociopolitical context helps to explain the distribution of membership among types of religious communities. Second and relatedly, it highlights the impact of contextual factors in shaping religious outlooks.

Identifying religious communities and their sociopolitical positioning in society is an important step for explaining distributions of observed religious outlooks. Knowledge of outlooks, in turn, is instrumental for understanding the implications of political context and approaches to state-religion relations. We have already found empirical support for diversity in religious outlook among the devout through our fourfold conceptualization of outlooks in MENA using the data from Wave III of the Arab Barometer. The next logical step would be looking for additional evidence regarding the determinants of religious outlooks. The subsequent analysis investigates the contextual and individual factors insofar as they inform religious worldviews.

In this chapter, again using data from the Arab Barometer, we provide evidence that observed relationships between sociopolitical status and contextual factors and the distribution of religious outlooks in society validate the predictions of our theory. Controlling for the contextual and individual factors, the statistical analyses of Arab Barometer data corroborate the existence of the same four religious outlooks representing worldviews that roughly correspond to types of religious outlooks representing positions within a particular religious landscape. It is hardly surprising that the data demonstrate that states' regulation of religion, political and civil liberties, educational attainment, social trust, and feeling of safety significantly inform religious outlook distributions in MENA. Across Muslim-majority societies, religious communities and devout individuals form their views in relation to social and political context. The individual and contextual determinants of religious outlooks, in turn, have important implications for understanding the role of religion in shaping political attitudes and behavior in MENA.

Individual and Contextual Determinants of Religious Outlooks

As presented in chapter 3, the latent class analysis (LCA) with ten questions from the Arab Barometer, Wave III, supports the feasibility of classifying practicing Muslim survey participants into four groups that emphasize two primary dimensions: attitudes toward religious pluralism and attitudes toward religion's place in politics. To a certain extent, these dimensions contain the conventional conceptualizations along the less-to-more religious continuum. Nonetheless, classification along these dimensions provides greater insight into the nature and extent of piety and introduces nuance about religious preferences.

The four classes generated by LCA conformed to quadrant categories along these two dimensions, which, as described in chapter 3, are religious individualist, social communitarian, religious communitarian, and post-Islamist. To briefly recap, religious individualists tended to be more supportive of religious pluralism and less supportive of religious influence in the public sphere. Social communitarians were both less supportive of religious pluralism in society and less supportive of religious influence in the public sphere. Religious communitarians were less supportive of religious pluralism in society but more supportive of religious influence in the public sphere. Finally, post-Islamists were identified with a class that tended to be more supportive of both religious pluralism and religious influence in the public sphere.

This four-class categorization system provides a good starting point to tackle the individual and contextual determinants of these distinct outlooks. Statistically, a modeling strategy is needed to derive outlook categories while at the same time to assess the likelihood of belonging to a certain outlook based on the values of individual and contextual factors. Latent class regression (LCR) allows us to estimate categories of religious outlooks while assessing various effects associated with these outcomes.[2] For consistency, before running the analysis, the sample was truncated to include only the respondents who reported to be moderately to highly devout. After narrowing the pool of respondents based on the level of religiosity—and dropping the Kuwaiti and Palestinian respondents due to the lack of country covariates needed for the analysis—the variables measuring religiosity were left out of the statistical estimations.[3]

Latent class regression involves two parts. The first part of the model (measurement model) includes the same ten survey questions used to evaluate individuals' views about pluralism and their preferences regarding the presence of religion in the public/political sphere and estimate a four-class solution within this distribution of the devout participants.[4] This part of the process is similar to the one utilized in the LCA estimation in the previous chapter. The second part of the model (structural model) runs a multinomial logit estimation to test the effects of respondents' age, sex, income, social trust, self-assessment of security, and educational attainment along with context-specific, country-level indicators of civil rights and liberties (V-Dem), GDP per capita, and state regulation of religion on these four classes. The LCR estimation uses a one-step procedure to simultaneously estimate the covariates along with the latent class model due to the biased estimates produced by the three-step procedure (Dayton and Macready 1988). This one-step procedure both relaxes the assumption that all individuals share the same prior probability of class membership while allowing the estimation of the relationship

Determinants of Muslim Religious Outlooks in MENA | 97

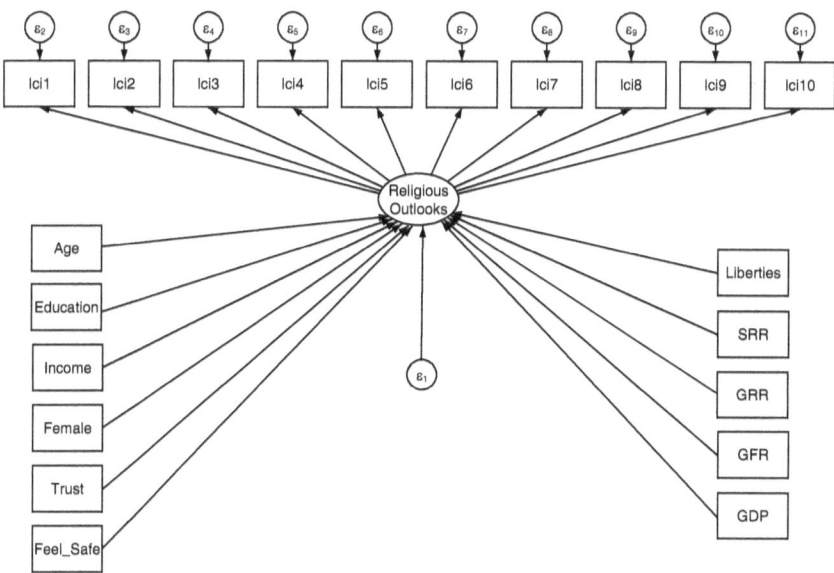

Figure 4.1. Multinomial Latent Class Regression (Individual and Contextual Determinants of Religious Outlooks). Religious outlooks include religious individualist, post-Islamist, religious communitarian, and social communitarian categories. Variable descriptions for lci1-lci10 and independent variables can be found in table 3.2 and in chapter 4.

the covariates in the model share with the probability of class membership (Bolck, Croon and Hagenaars 2004; Linzer and Lewis 2011). In other words, in one step, the model both estimates class membership based on certain items and assesses the likelihood of belonging to a certain class according to the covariates included in the model. Applied to the current analysis, the model presented in figure 4.1 estimates both statistical clusterings, representing religious outlook categories and their relations with specific covariates that are related to these outlooks.

The model includes covariates for both individual and contextual characteristics. At the individual level, the baseline model includes respondents' education, harmonized cross-nationally (on a seven-point scale), age, household income, and sex. Of these variables, age is a continuous variable while household income is measured along a five-point scale with larger values showing high income. The models use a dichotomous measure of sex where female respondents are coded as 1 and males are recorded as 0. Since we argue that religious outlooks are shaped by the social relations one engages in, the model also includes a variable asking respondents if they trust most people (value of 1) or not (0). This variable is named *social trust*, following the conventional approach in existing studies. Subjective assessments of feelings of security are measured with an item asking the respondents whether they currently feel that their personal safety and security, as well as their family's, are ensured. The responses to this item range from absolutely not ensured (1) to fully ensured (4).

There are many contextual factors that could shape religious outlooks in a given country. The nature of secular institutions, the role of religion in the constitution, the state's involvement in the religious market, government policies about religious freedom, economic and human development, and regime type can be cited among these factors. Muslim-majority societies represent significant diversity in state-religion relations, socioeconomic background, and political institutions. In countries like Tunisia and pre-2007 Turkey, governments have imposed a highly strict version of French style *laïcité* that gives significant leverage to the state to control the religious landscape. In these countries, religious actors and the states have engaged in a constant struggle for control of the public sphere and politics, where exclusionary and repressive policies are not uncommon. An even higher degree of control over religious markets is exerted in cases like Saudi Arabia and Iran, where governments favor official interpretations of Islam and sanction and punish actions deviating from the regulated religious norms.

Religious actors and individuals are likely to respond differently to the context of state-society relations. For example, in Iran, the religious opposition has employed highly pluralistic and democratic outlooks or reverted to violence to counter the state's monopolization of religion (Ayoob 2009; Bayat 2007; Kazamipur and Rezaei 2003). In Saudi Arabia, manifest protest to the regime's status quo has often come from groups like the Sahwis pushing for "purer" and stricter implementations of religious guidance (Ayoob 2009; Okruhlik 2002). The state's posture to such individuals and groups on either side of the regulated norms, in tandem with the level of political freedom and economic development, may similarly influence the preferences and outlooks of religious individuals and give way to distinct religious communities.

The posture of the state can also manifest itself in distinct ways in various regions of a country, and this is particularly evident in federal systems like Malaysia and Pakistan. In these cases, the posture of the local state government and regional social norms have a significant influence on the formation and distribution of religious outlooks in various regions. In Malaysia, the social tension between conservative religious communities and the federal state in Malay Muslim-dominant provinces like Kelantan and Terengganu on the eastern side of the peninsula is much lower than it is in Sabah and Sarawak on the island or those on the western coast. In Kelantan and Terengganu, Islamist political activity through the Islamist party PAS has historically demonstrated strong pressure for social conformity to religious norms and religion in the public sphere (religious communitarianism), while those affiliated with the branches of the same Islamist party in pluralist areas have adopted an outlook that is more pluralist and pro-religion in the public sphere (post-Islamist) (Yong Liow 2004; Wuthrich and Ciftci 2020). Thus we should note that while the countries included in the Arab Barometer survey are smaller and unitary states, we should recognize that states' and societies' interaction with religious communities, the resulting tension dynamic (or lack of it), and the shaping of religious outlooks can vary in important ways at the subnational level. Here too, we anticipate, as in Malaysia, that the subnational dynamics and distributions of outlooks are generally predictable but that a unitary assessment of such countries would bring back confusing results.

With our survey data from the Arab Barometer (Wave III), to test the relationship between state posture toward religion and the distribution of religious outlooks, we utilized the political equality and civil liberties index from the Varieties of Democracy project, GDP per capita, and three indicators of state-religion relations from the Religion and the State (RAS) data set (Fox 2012). These indicators were chosen based on their theoretical relevance insofar as these factors may shape how individuals view religion and its functions for personal and social life. The models test these three indicators of state-religion relations to measure state regulation of religion in aggregate and the extent to which government policies utilize regulation (sticks) or favoritism (carrots) to influence their citizenry. The first measure, state regulation of religion (SRR) is an index summarizing the interactions of the state with the religious landscape. In MENA, states differ in the way they regulate religion, ranging from complete endorsement of a specific religious interpretation or group to recognition and support of a variety of interpretations. The following category definitions for SRR are taken from the codebook for the RAS data set.[5] In the sample under investigation, this variable contains categories ranging from 6 (cooperation) to 13 (religious state):

> **Cooperation:** The state fails to endorse a particular religion, but certain religions benefit from state support (Lebanon).

Preferred religion: The state does not officially endorse a religion; one religion serves unofficially as the state's religion, receiving unique recognition or benefits; minority religions all receive similar treatment to each other (Sudan).

Active state religion: The state actively supports religion, but the religion is not mandatory, and the state does not dominate the official religion's institutions (Algeria, Iraq, and Morocco).

State controlled religion: The state both supports a religion and substantially controls its institutions but has a positive attitude toward this religion (Egypt, Jordan, Libya, Tunisia, Yemen).

Religious state: Religion is mandatory for members of the official religion (Kuwait).

A second indicator from the RAS data set is government regulation of religion (GRR). This RAS measure ranks nations according to government practices that regulate the selection, practice, and profession of religion through official laws, policies, or administrative actions. This indicator is qualitatively different from the SRR to the extent that it captures how governments use policy to regulate the religious market, whereas the former is a summary measure of long-term trends in state-religion relations. For example, the symbiotic relation between the Saudi regime and the Wahhabi clergy would squarely put this country into the category of a religious state based on the SRR. The government's prosecution and co-optation of opposition Islamists (e.g., Sahwa) would be best captured by the GRR indicator. This second variable is coded from the International Religious Freedom Report (2002), and within our sample it ranges from 2.2 (lowest regulation) to 8.6 (highest government regulation). Finally, government favoritism of religion (GFR) captures the extent of privileges and government support for specific religious groups. This index ranges from 2 (least favoritism) to 9.3 (most favoritism).

An indicator of democracy from the Varieties of Democracy (V-Dem) project that provides a nuanced operationalization of democracy is utilized to assess the regime type. Equality before the law and individual liberty index (v2xcl_rol) captures various dimensions of rule of law and civil liberties. As described in the *V-Dem Codebook*, this index tackles the following questions: "To what extent are laws transparent and rigorously enforced and public administration impartial, and to what extent do citizens enjoy access to justice, secure property rights, freedom from forced labor, freedom of movement, physical integrity rights, and freedom of religion?" (Coppedge et al. 2016, 55). This indicator is selected over alternative measures of democracy including polity scores due to its multidimensional nature spanning legal and civil areas. This index captures distinct areas, including impartial public administration, transparent laws, access to justice, property rights, freedom from torture, freedom from political killings, freedom of religion, and freedom of domestic movement. As such, it measures rule of law in a country and civil liberties in areas that are directly relevant to individuals' daily life.[6] The status of freedom in a country is likely to shape religious outlooks. In an authoritarian regime where criticism of religion is prohibited and individuals are not free to abstain from religious practice, individuals may take hostile or conformist views of religion, such as in Iran. Where freedoms and rights flourish, a multiplicity of religious outlooks could be the norm, and one view may not necessarily dominate the others.

The World Bank measure of GDP per capita is included to account for the overall level of economic development in the baseline models. While GDP certainly does not capture all aspects of social and economic modernization, it nonetheless provides a good proxy for socioeconomic development. Research suggests that existential security is more likely at high levels of development. Consequently, religion's role in coping with hardships through provision of social services or psychological mechanisms will be less prevalent in wealthy countries (Gaskins, Golder, and Siegel 2013a; Inglehart and Norris 2004). This approach has implications for the extent, nature, and effect of religious outlooks, especially the religious communitarian outlook. Together, these macro indicators allow us to account for the most important contextual factors that may influence religious outlooks. Table 4.1 shows the summary statistics for all variables included in the baseline models.

Statistical Analysis

To reiterate, latent class regression is a technique that is suitable for simultaneously estimating various outlook patterns present in the data and the relation of covariates to these patterns (i.e., latent classes). Before presenting the discussion of the results associated with the covariates of the structural model, we examine the latent classes produced by the analysis. To that end, first a base model including individual-level predictors and country fixed effects is run to account for cross-national variation in the prediction of religious outlook categories. The posterior distribution of class shares for the response categories from the measurement model largely confirms our expectations about the preferences of religious outlooks and cross-national

Table 4.1. Summary Statistics (Mean) for the Variables in the Baseline Models

Country	Income	Age	Sex	Trust	Safety	ECL	SRR	GRR	GFR	GDP	Polity
Algeria	2.4	38.3	1.5	0.2	2.7	0.5	11	6.9	9.3	5325	2
Egypt	2.0	39.4	1.5	0.2	2.0	0.4	12	7.8	8.8	3110	−4
Iraq	2.3	35.5	1.5	0.4	2.6	0.4	11	7.8	9.3	5790	3
Jordan	2.0	38.1	1.5	0.2	3.2	0.7	12	7.8	9	4618	−3
Kuwait	3.1	36.8	1.5	0.5	3.3	N/A	13	7.8	7.2	52198	−7
Lebanon	2.4	37.4	1.5	0.1	1.8	0.6	6	4.7	6.2	9793	6
Libya	2.6	38.1	1.5	0.3	2.4	0.3	12	6.1	9	12029	−7
Morocco	2.2	35.2	1.5	0.1	2.7	0.7	11	4.7	6.3	3146	−4
Palestine	2.2	37.8	1.5	0.3	2.7	0.5	N/A	2.2	7.8	2674	N/A
Sudan	2.1	33.7	1.5	0.3	2.7	0.1	9	8.6	2	1438	−4
Tunisia	2.0	43.6	1.5	0.2	2.5	0.6	12	6.1	8.8	4263	7
Yemen	2.2	35.4	1.5	0.4	2.3	0.3	12	6.1	2	1422	3

Notes: SRR, state regulation of religion (RAS data set) (Fox 2008); GRR, government regulation of religion (RAS data set) (Fox 2008); GFR, government favoritism of religion (RAS data set) (Fox 2008); ECL, equality and civil liberties index (V-Dem, five-year average, Coppedge et al. [2017]); GDP, GDP per capita (World Bank); Polity, polity score (Marshall, Gurr, and Jaggers, 2016). All other variables are from the Arab Barometer data.

variation in the distribution of these outlooks as reported in the appendix (table A4.1). By and large, individuals who prefer a greater role for Islam in social and political life have a larger class probability of belonging to the religious communitarian class than the other classes. While longing for a role for religion in the public domain, post-Islamists also lean favorably toward religious pluralism, a tendency that can be observed even more strongly among the members of the religious individualist class.

Unlike a hypothetical unregulated religious environment that would predict a normal-shaped curve, the Arab Barometer participants are generally operating within regimes that are highly regulating and incentivizing a certain level of normative religious practice. Many of the countries in our sample carry provisions for Islam in their constitutions, and they intervene in religious markets favoring certain interpretations, sects, or groups over others. Notably, a number of these countries have Islamist political parties that have acted as formidable challengers to the nondemocratic regimes within which they operate. These include the Islah Party in Yemen, the Muslim Brothers and their political wing the Freedom and Justice Party in Egypt, the Islamic Action Front in Jordan, Ennahda in Tunisia, and the Justice and Development Party in Morocco. These parties do not necessarily constitute a homogenous bunch, and they differ in their ideology, political strategy, and organizational features across different political systems (Wuthrich and Ciftci 2020). This provides evidence that religious outlooks as observed within these parties will differ by social and political context. In addition, these parties also respond to their conditions in a dynamic fashion over time.

The distributions of religious outlooks are not uniform from country to country. Although the LCR model, at least in part, supports our general theoretical expectations for how these outlooks would distribute themselves within a religious market, significant cross-national variation exists in the sample, and this may also affect the distribution of classes within each country. Figure 4.2 presents the distribution of religious outlooks obtained from this baseline model in the ten countries included in the analysis.

As can be seen from the country distributions, certain outlooks are significantly more or less prevalent in particular country contexts than in the aggregate. For example, a high proportion of respondents fall within the religious individualist class in Egypt, Lebanon, and Tunisia. An understanding of religious markets can help us understand these patterns. Lebanon and Tunisia currently score highest on measures of democracy in the

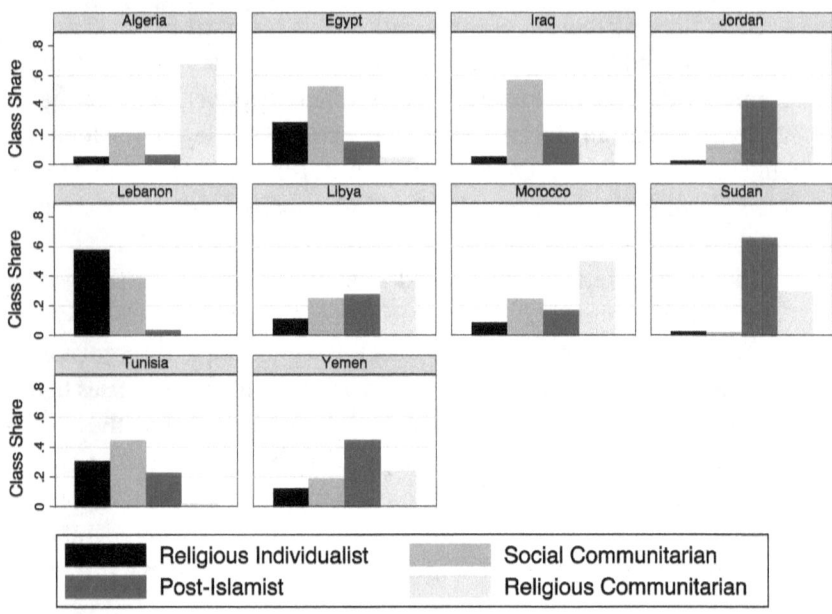

Figure 4.2. Cross-National Variation in Religious Outlooks. Source: Arab Barometer, Wave III.

Arab region and, for different reasons, have the lowest level of state support for a particular religion in the Arab world. In Tunisia, the authoritarian state forcibly imposed a French-style laïcité on society, and strict vigilance against Islamism led to an abundance of religious individualist communities in addition to the social communitarians, who have a strong preference for the status quo. In Lebanon, the danger of the imposition of one religious order and the consequences of prioritizing religion in the public sphere have caused the religious individualist outlook to dominate across a broader range of communities spanning multiple religious niches. Civil war and the consequences of sectarian identities have certainly facilitated the religious individualist perspective among Lebanese citizens. Thus, the social and political context has dramatically suppressed post-Islamist and religious communitarian classes, likely due to the manifest futility of championing a single religious perspective in a multicreedal environment.[7] Thus, as anticipated above, those countries hold the conditions in which we would expect the religious individualist outlook to thrive.

In Jordan, Morocco, and Algeria, a strong clustering is seen in the religious communitarian outlook, with a secondary clustering in the post-Islamist group in the first. With the two monarchies (Jordan and Morocco), you have countries with a relative degree of social liberalism offset by regimes that have nonetheless leaned heavily on the symbolic value of Islam for the legitimation of authority and the nation-building process. Arguably, it is this combination of a liberal public sphere and simultaneous exploitation of Islam for legitimacy that creates a fruitful ground for the religious communitarian outlook. Each of these regimes tinkers with political pluralism yet manages to mostly declaw the Islamist opposition in one way or another. In general, these regimes have either co-opted the Islamists or found ways to limit their influence and redirect their political power and energy to marginal (Jordan) or regulated (Morocco) quarters of the political system.

The secularization and pluralism in the public sphere by regimes that draw heavily from religious symbolism while sending mixed signals regarding political participation by religious organizations set the grounds for many within the moderate and conservative communal niches in these countries to take a religious communitarian position. In Algeria, where anti-regime Islamist political mobilization was halted, resulting in the Algerian Civil War, there may have been a shift away from pluralistic religious orientations toward religious communitarianism among the constituents of the regime opponents. This, in combination with the National Liberation Front (Front de libération nationale, FLN) actively attempting to co-opt and control religious practice in Algeria, may have produced a context in which religious communitarianism could thrive.

In Tunisia, Libya, Iraq, and Egypt, surveys were conducted in a period with the prospect of political liberalism following a history of suppression of religious political mobilization. The liberalization itself, following suppression, encourages an increase in the proportion of religious communitarians and post-Islamists, but the unstable environment may create a dynamic that leads to preferences for the status quo (Shamaileh 2019). This should be especially evident in some of these countries as they followed paths from authoritarianism to liberalization and vice versa in the past. The high proportion of social communitarians representing preferences for the status quo in Iraq, Egypt, and Tunisia may be a result of this dynamic. These patterns point out the contingent dynamic that generates the outlooks in the first place. It is unlikely that such outlook distributions for these countries, particularly Egypt, Libya, and Iraq, would remain stable across survey waves, an issue we pursue further in the subsequent analysis. It is likely that distributions across all countries would manifest some difference from wave to wave, but certainly in countries where the nature of the regime itself is a moving target, communities across the religious niches in society are likely to shift in their formations of religious outlooks.

Of course, these interpretations of observed patterns of distribution across countries considering religious economic theory and the assumptions of how religious niches might translate into religious outlooks remain descriptive. To provide empirical evidence corroborating the linkage between various outlooks and their social/contextual roots, it will be appropriate to run LCR with individual and contextual correlates of religious outlooks. To reiterate, individual correlates include age, education, gender, income, social trust, and perceptions of safety in one's context, whereas contextual determinants include the equality and civil liberties index from V-Dem, three indicators of state-religion relations from the RAS data set, and the World Bank's GDP per capita measure.

The results from the latent class regression are presented in table 4.2. A discussion is already provided about the rationale regarding the religious outlook categories. The results from the measurement model from the LCR are presented in the appendix and are similar to the results from the latent class analysis. The discussion at this point focuses on the structural model with individual and contextual covariates. The structural model uses multinomial logit to account for the categorical nature of the outlooks obtained from the measurement component. The coefficients from multinomial logit estimations in table 4.2 show the propensity of individuals with various characteristics within specific contexts belonging to each religious outlook class. The reference category for these models is the social communitarian outlook. While all models presented in table 4.2 include all individual-level variables as well as GDP per capita and the equality and civil liberty index, three measures of state-religion relations are also separately included in the subsequent models.

In these models we see a number of associations that distinguish outlook types from one another and fit into the overall predictions of what type of individuals would most likely be found in each outlook category in accordance with our theoretical expectations. For example, educational attainment increases the probability of an individual possessing a religious individualist outlook relative to the social communitarian class, but it does not differentiate the religious communitarians and post-Islamists from the social communitarians at a statistically significant level (except in one model). This pattern fits the proposition that moderate levels of educational attainment support the social communitarian outlook, which in turn

Table 4.2. Latent Class Regression Analysis of Individual and Contextual Determinants of Religious Outlooks

	Religious individualist		Post-Islamist			Religious communitarian		
	Model 1		Model 2			Model 3		
Age	0.018***	0.019***	0.020***	0.013***	0.0058	0.010**	0.0072*	-0.00031	0.0026
	(0.00)	(0.00)	(0.00)	(0.00)	(0.00)	(0.00)	(0.00)	(0.00)	(0.00)
Education	0.14***	0.14***	0.13***	0.034	0.039	0.091**	0.054	-0.070*	-0.026
	(0.03)	(0.03)	(0.03)	(0.03)	(0.04)	(0.03)	(0.03)	(0.03)	(0.03)
Income	-0.090	-0.21**	-0.20**	-0.030	-0.15**	-0.21***	-0.13*	0.038	-0.0059
	(0.05)	(0.07)	(0.07)	(0.06)	(0.05)	(0.05)	(0.05)	(0.05)	(0.05)
Sex (female)	-0.12	0.045	0.0021	-0.11	0.023	0.015	-0.023	0.15	0.14
	(0.08)	(0.10)	(0.10)	(0.10)	(0.08)	(0.08)	(0.09)	(0.09)	(0.08)
Social trust	-0.26*	-0.15	-0.096	0.40***	0.41***	0.46***	0.26*	0.18	0.23*
	(0.11)	(0.14)	(0.15)	(0.11)	(0.09)	(0.09)	(0.10)	(0.10)	(0.10)
Feel safe	-0.75***	-0.52***	-0.58***	0.17*	0.38***	0.41***	0.032	0.47***	0.49***
	(0.06)	(0.08)	(0.09)	(0.08)	(0.09)	(0.10)	(0.07)	(0.04)	(0.05)
Equality / civil liberty	0.12	-0.074	-0.074	-0.81	-1.04***	-0.27	1.09**	-0.38	0.23
	(0.26)	(0.38)	(0.38)	(0.43)	(0.30)	(0.34)	(0.41)	(0.62)	(0.45)
GDP per capita	-0.00*	-0.00	0.00***	-0.00***	-0.00***	-0.00	0.00***	-0.00	-0.00
	(0.00)	(0.00)	(0.00)	(0.00)	(0.00)	(0.00)	(0.00)	(0.00)	(0.00)

Table 4.2. (*continued*)

	Religious individualist			Post-Islamist			Religious communitarian		
	Model 1			**Model 2**			**Model 3**		
State regulation of religion	−0.31***			−0.51***			1.57***		
	(0.03)			(0.05)			(0.22)		
Government regulation of religion		−0.30***			0.23***			0.14**	
		(0.06)			(0.04)			(0.05)	
Government favoritism of religion			−0.19***			−0.21***			−0.14***
			(0.04)			(0.03)			(0.03)
Constant	3.41***	1.55**	−0.13	5.93***	−2.05***	0.12	−20.8***	−1.75***	−0.42
	(0.40)	(0.51)	(0.32)	(0.73)	(0.42)	(0.28)	(2.70)	(0.43)	(0.29)
Observations	8,115	8,115	8,115	8,115	8,115	8,115	8,115	8,115	8,115

Note: Standard errors are in parentheses; * $p < 0.1$, ** $p < 0.05$, *** $p < 0.01$. Social communitarian is the reference category.
Source: Arab Barometer, Wave III.

supports the status quo. However, specialized education (whether secular or religious) leads individuals to pursue their own designs (for autonomy or exclusive communal affiliation) that countervail the status quo.

The results concerning education and the likelihood of belonging to specific outlook categories do not correspond with those trends seen for the income variable. Relative to the social communitarian benchmark, all three outlooks are more likely to have a lower income, particularly the religious individualists and post-Islamists. Such an outcome fits squarely with the theoretical predictions for the social communitarians adhering most carefully to (and presumably benefiting from) accepted social norms. Our theoretical model proposes that social communitarians would gain the most from social favorability, while the trade-offs by religious individualists (for autonomy) and post-Islamists (for club goods) would result in consequences to decreased social favorability. This is exactly what is implied by the results. The models also show that religious individualists, relative to the reference category, also tend to be older. Finally, no statistically significant difference emerges between men and women in terms of belonging to each religious outlook class. This is a surprising finding as the previous research has well established a religiously inspired gender gap or some sort of ambivalence in gendered dynamics of civic participation (Ciftci and Bernick 2015) and democratic orientations (Tessler 2002).

The relationship between religious outlooks and social trust and perceptions of personal safety and security is significant in some models and needs further discussion. The default anticipation of a stable, unregulated religious economy might be that the distinguishing pattern of trust and security would position the social communitarians (often the largest population contingent) as more secure and trusting than those on the margins—that is, the religious individualists and post-Islamists. The results do show that religious individualists are significantly less secure and somehow less trusting (model 1) than the other outlooks, as would be expected. However, the post-Islamists and the religious communitarians are more trusting and feel more secure relative to the reference category.

Why might this be? There is good reason to believe that people who are in social categories that represent the highest number of citizens in society feel the most comfortable in their social context. Most of the post-Islamists participating in the survey are not a marginal social contingent but represent a large segment of the population along with religious communitarians. The supporters of the status quo or social communitarians may perceive that they represent norms in society that are under significant pressure to change—that is, "the good old days" are fading away at their expense—and this would create a lack of trust in those around them and feelings of insecurity. Furthermore, the practices and involvement in religious communities by religious communitarians and post-Islamists and the social networks that they often pursue would also incline them toward higher levels of trust and security with society, if not the state.

The results also point to an interesting variation related to the effects of contextual variables. No consistent statistical relationship emerges between equality/civil liberties and the likelihood of belonging to any outlook class. Regarding the relationship between GDP per capita and religious outlook, there is some evidence of a negative correlation between GDP per capita and the probability of adopting a post-Islamist outlook. Such a result may be due to the tendency of pluralistically inclined Islamist organizations to rely on social services to increase support for their groups. Islamist social service provision is a well-established trend in a number of polities in MENA (Brooke 2019; Wickham 2002). It should be noted that this result is not consistent across all models.

State-religion relations, however, appear to be a significant and perhaps more consistent and pervasive contextual determinant of religious outlooks. The religious individualist outlook, not surprisingly, is negatively associated with high levels of overall state regulation of religion as well as government regulation and favoritism of religion. Reflecting on the carrot/stick elements of religious regulation, however, some nuances emerge in the tendencies regarding religious communitarians and post-Islamists. Higher government favorability toward a dominant religion decreases the likelihood of belonging to religious communitarian and post-Islamist categories, while legal and restrictive regulation of religion increases the probability of association with these religious outlooks. This pattern provides some support for the findings of Grzymala-Busse (2015) and Buckley (2016). Both religious communitarians and post-Islamists comprise individuals who tend to favor Islam being more active in the public sphere, and as this literature points out, in countries where religious communities are already in an advantageous position regarding state policy, there can be a lot to lose for religious authorities if they remain active in the political sphere. In such favorable contexts, the distribution of post-Islamism, which emphasizes pluralism along with an active role for Islam in politics, would most likely be less. Conversely, consistent with Buckley's (2016) argument, it is where the state employs a heavy normative

Determinants of Muslim Religious Outlooks in MENA | 111

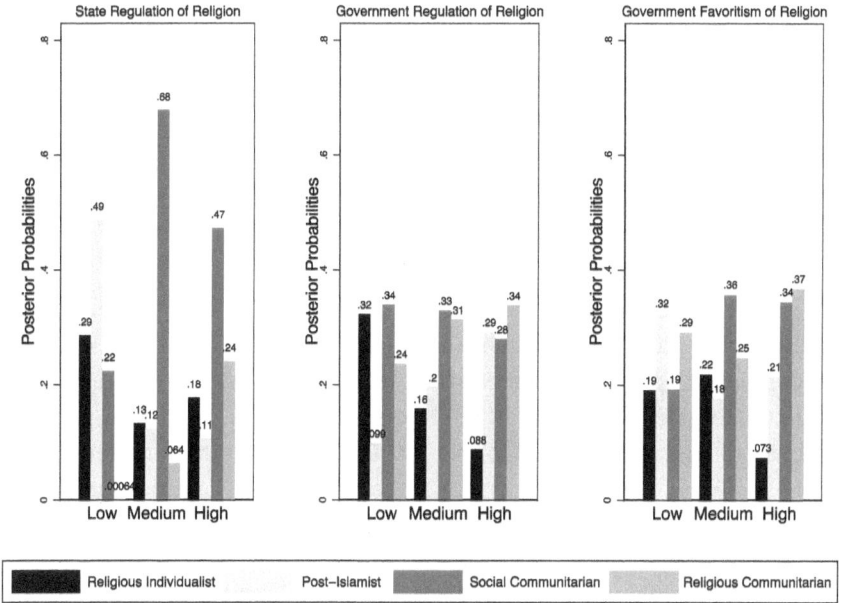

Figure 4.3. State-Religion Relations and Religious Outlooks. The bars represent posterior probabilities for each outlook category. The x-axis shows the level of each state-religion relation. Sources: RAS data set and Arab Barometer, Wave III.

hand in regulating its religious preferences in the public sphere that an outlook for public and political action by religious authorities is more likely to develop in higher proportions.

To further shed light on these patterns, the posterior class probabilities from the LCR estimation are presented across several determinants of religious outlook categories. Figure 4.3 shows the probability of belonging to each religious outlook class at low, medium, and high levels of three measures of state-religion relations. The first noticeable pattern concerns the decreasing proportion of the religious individualist class as the scale moves from low to high levels of state/government involvement in religion. This proportion is less than 10 percent (0.073) in high levels of government favoritism of religion. The opposite pattern is observed for the probability of belonging to the religious communitarian outlook for state and government regulation of religion. The probability of belonging to the religious communitarian outlook is nominally zero in countries with a low level of state regulation of religion, but it gradually increases from 6 percent at the medium level to 24 percent at high levels of state regulation of religion. Post-Islamists appear to peak at the middle level of state regulation of religion. These results show that the state's intervention in the religious landscape will likely suppress the religious individualist class membership due to a lack of avenues for representation of this outlook. To the extent that state intervention into the religious market benefits certain religious groups, individuals will increasingly lean toward the religious communitarian outlook. This is because, in most cases, there will be an overlap between organizational membership to a group favored by the state and the religious communitarian outlook.

In the alternative measures of state-religion relations (government regulation and favoritism of religion), regulatory intervention in the religious sphere creates opposite effects on the distribution of the religious individualist and religious communitarian outlooks. Favoritism also has a negative effect on religious individualism and post-Islamism as seen in the decreasing proportions of class memberships at higher levels of this metric, but it has a mixed, yet largely positive, effect on religious communitarianism. More interestingly, the probability of belonging to the post-Islamist category is sometimes similar to that of the religious individualist outlook (in models using the SRR and GFR), but sometimes its distribution resembles that of religious communitarians (in models using the GRR). In settings where government favoritism of certain religious groups is lowest, the post-Islamist outlook is more prevalent (32 percent) relative to cases where government favoritism is widespread. As expected, the probability of belonging to the social communitarian group does not change significantly according to the condition of the state-religion relations.

The results of the LCR help us understand the effects of individual-level determinants of religious outlooks. Figures 4.4 through 4.6 present the distribution of posterior probabilities for each outlook category for each individual determinant. The figures show the class probabilities (line) for each outlook category along the proportions of different categories of survey responses to questions about education, feeling of safety, and personal trust (bars). Figure 4.4 demonstrates the class probabilities for each religious outlook along the levels of self-reported educational attainment. Not surprisingly, a larger proportion of religious individualists are highly educated whereas religious communitarians are more likely to be among the less educated. Going back to the distribution of outlook groups across ten countries (figure 4.2), membership in the religious individualist class appears to be the highest in Egypt, Tunisia, and Lebanon, the three countries with relatively high levels of educational attainment at the aggregate levels. On the flip side, the religious

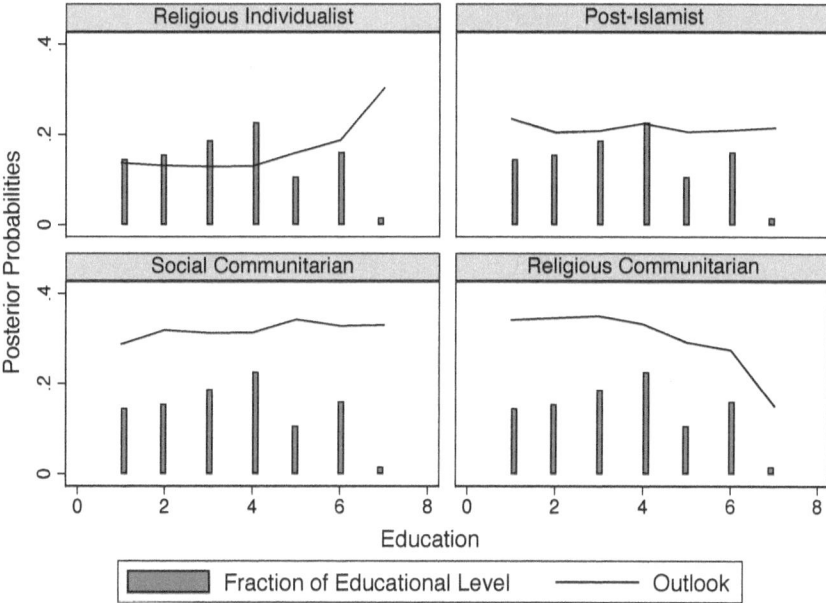

Figure 4.4. Education and Religious Outlooks. The bars represent the proportion of respondents at each educational attainment level. The line represents the likelihood of belonging to specific outlook categories. Source: Arab Barometer, Wave III.

communitarian class has high levels of membership in Sudan, Yemen, and Morocco, countries with less impressive educational statistics. The relationship between education and these religious outlooks appears to be driven by behavior at the highest levels of educational attainment. A change in education from illiterate to possessing an elementary school education is not associated with a meaningful increase in the probability of being a religious individualist or decrease in being a religious communitarian, yet postsecondary education appears to be associated with substantial changes in the posterior probabilities associated with these religious outlooks. These results, once again, are consistent with the overall distribution of religious outlook categories in the countries included in the sample. Finally, social communitarians and post-Islamists are uniformly distributed across different levels of education.

Class probabilities for perceptions of safety and social trust also corroborate our expectations about how interpersonal trust and feelings about security may make membership in the post-Islamist and religious communitarian outlooks more likely. For example, the religious individualist

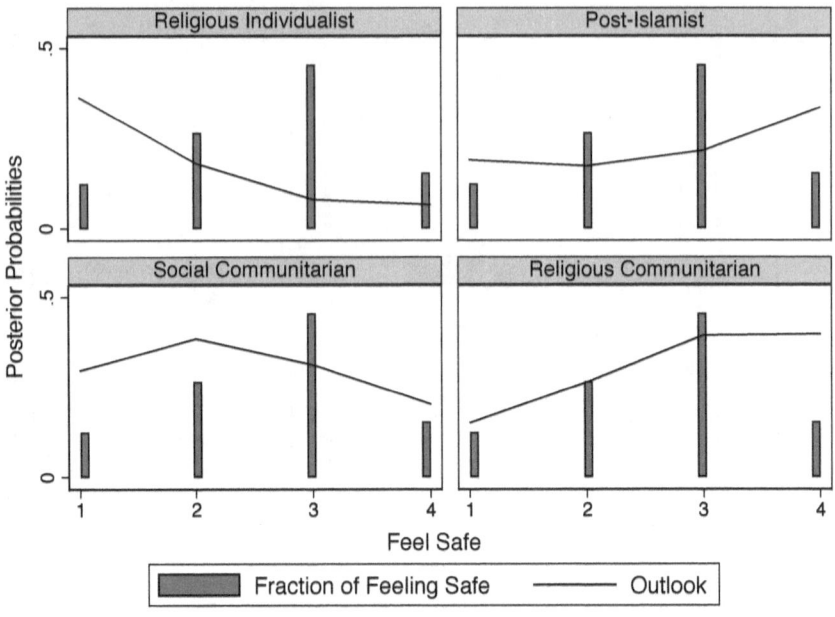

Figure 4.5. Feeling of Safety and Religious Outlooks. Source: Arab Barometer, Wave III.

outlook is less widespread among those individuals who feel safe in their environment. In contrast, the likelihood of being a post-Islamist or religious communitarian increases with the perception of increased safety (figure 4.5). A similar pattern, although less visible, can also be seen in the distribution of these class shares between less trusting and more trusting individuals (figure 4.6).[8] Mapping these results to the distribution of outlook categories in the sample, it can be argued that religious individualist class membership is the lowest in conflict-ridden, unstable countries, such as Sudan and Iraq. Although a consistent pattern is not seen in all countries, in general where security and presumably trust are lacking, membership in the religious individualist outlook suffers.

Implications for Diverse Distributions of Outlooks across Contexts

In the end, the empirical analyses presented in this chapter substantiate the proposition that there are significant variations in the distributions of religious outlook classes and that the patterns of their variation are not entirely random but stem from contextual social, political, and economic

Determinants of Muslim Religious Outlooks in MENA | 115

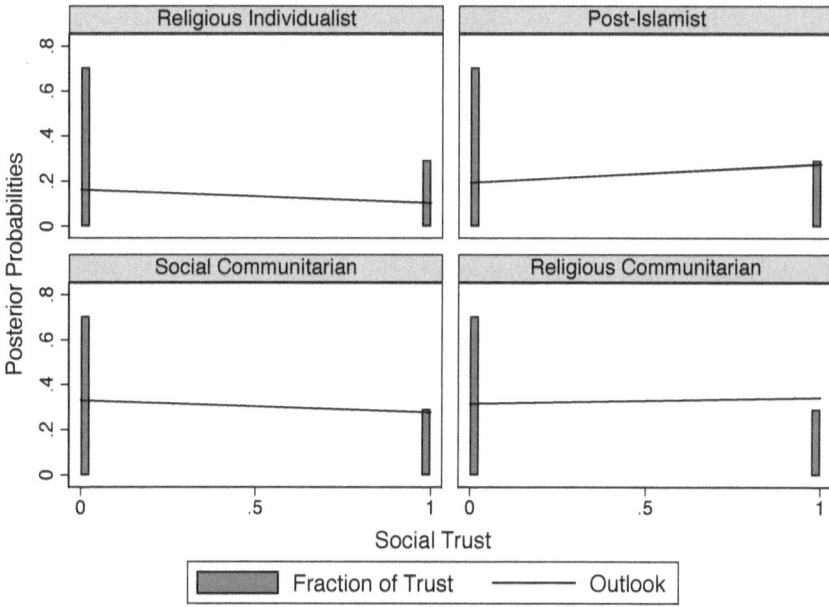

Figure 4.6. Trust and Religious Outlooks. Source: Arab Barometer, Wave III.

factors in predictable ways. Democratic regimes appear to be characterized by high levels of religious individualism among pious Muslims, mixed regimes appear to be dominated by religious communitarians, and highly authoritarian states have relatively high levels of religious communitarians, post-Islamists, and social communitarians and low levels of religious individualists. Regimes with high levels of religious regulation support the religious communitarians and social communitarians at the expense of the religious individualists in particular. Where moderate political pluralism occurs with state regulation of religion, the post-Islamist outlook appears to have greater traction. In addition, wealthier countries generally appear to produce fewer post-Islamists, perhaps due to the reliance of pluralistic Islamist organizations on the provision of social services for recruitment and proselytization. These results are significant to the extent that they help us unmask the huge variation that is hidden beneath a single religiosity category. The analysis illustrates how different outlooks represent different manifestations of religiosity with potentially important implications.

Furthermore, the results imply that we need to consider how a state's involvement in the religious landscape may give way to increased membership in certain outlook groups, such as social and religious communitarians, and suppress others, such as religious individualists. If data were available, for example, it would not have been surprising to find contrasting patterns in the distribution of religious individualist and religious communitarian outlooks in Turkey against those in Iran. Much of the literature on Iran would lead us to suspect that state-society dynamics have generated relatively large numbers of religious individualists and religious communitarians (Bayat 2007; Tezcür and Azadarmaki 2008). Based on what we know about the way that politics plays out in the federal system in Malaysia, the context of local politics within its federal states would lead us to believe that distributions of outlooks would likely show a distinct pattern across regions and differing social dynamics from state to state (Chin 1997; He et al. 2018). While the results from the ten countries included in the analysis also help demonstrate these contrasts in the sample, similar relevant patterns would be expected in other parts of MENA and in other Muslim-majority countries more broadly.

In the general literature on politics in the Middle East and opposition parties, the question of Islamist political party moderation has engendered a great deal of discussion. As such, scholars have largely focused on contexts where some space for independent social mobilization has been tolerated. Not surprisingly, the question of whether moderate Islamist political groups should be included in their respective countries' political landscapes gains a high degree of salience in these contexts. It is primarily within these countries of study and their moderate, ambiguous, and semiauthoritarian spaces that Islamists and post-Islamists occupy the most ground. In most cases, the nexus of state-religion relations will be more complex than the stylistic pattern presented here. A recent study examines this complexity where, in addition to state-religion relations and the resulting Islamist party ideologies, the social base of parties (urban vs. rural) plays a prominent role in coalition building across political parties in North Africa (Buehler 2018). In these cases, individuals with different religious outlooks will calculate these other factors in their actions.

In the end, as our empirical analyses suggest, it is not likely that the aggressive regulation of the public sphere will decrease the potency of religious communitarians (i.e., politically participatory Islamists); if anything, the opposite might be true. Where the state tries to establish limitations to practice, it may stimulate religious communitarian attitudes where these individuals believe that their preferences represent a potentially large block of society. It should be stated that there is often an endogenous element in play: the growth of a large number of individuals with communitarian preferences for the expansion of religious norms in society also pushes some states to increase regulation to control this population of the devout that threatens the status quo. Concerning the post-Islamist class, as Ciftci, Wuthrich, and Shamaileh (2019) have already pointed out, members of this outlook class show a strong level of support for democracy, much like religious individualists. Thus, in country contexts where regime exertions on the public sphere have truncated the number of religious individualists, it is the post-Islamists within the religious economy that offer the greatest amount of support for democratic institutions.

Although this examination provides a glimpse into the contextual and individual-level factors that influence the adoption of these religious outlooks, there is significant room for further examination of the determinants of religious outlooks. For example, it will be important to examine how significant political events and temporal changes may influence religious outlooks in the MENA societies. In chapter 6, we focus on this question in the context of the Arab uprisings, but other areas of study on this subject remain wide open. For example, future studies of Islamic religious outlooks may incorporate substate contextual factors that likely play a substantial role in shaping the views of individuals. Our communities and social environments affect our religious preferences and views, and such social determinants should be further explored.

Notes

1. It must be acknowledged that the influence of Wahhabi scholars has been waning for some time. Nevertheless, they continue to hold a state-sanctioned comparative advantage over religious doctrine in the kingdom.

2. We use the generalized structural equation modeling (GSEM) from the Stata software package. The maximization of the log-likelihood function that produced our estimates and predictions in rooted in the EM algorithm implemented by GSEM for categorical latent class models.

3. To reiterate, we use three questions tapping frequency of religious practice, including daily prayer, Friday prayer attendance, and listening to or reading the Koran. Responses to these questions range from 1 (never) to 5 (always). We drop all respondents whose responses are never (1) and rarely (2) to obtain a sample of 10, 245 moderately and highly religious individuals. The sample size may be further reduced in some estimations due to nonavailability of contextual variables.

4. See table 3.2 for a description of these items.

5. The details about this dataset and a codebook can be found at https://www.thearda.com/ras/about/.

6. In alternative specifications, we use polity scores from the year 2012. We take five yearly averages for cases where the Arab uprisings made appropriation of a score more difficult for the year 2012. The results of these alternative specifications do not differ from the estimation results reported here.

7. It should be noted, however, that membership levels in these religious outlooks should not be viewed as static. Changes in the political landscape, whether abrupt or occurring over time, may shift the religious outlooks of individuals and class membership levels throughout societies. A more robust discussion of temporal changes in religious outlooks is presented in chapter 6.

8. We do not detect a significant difference in the distribution of class shares between low- and high-income individuals.

5

ISLAM AND SUPPORT FOR DEMOCRACY

> Satan sends his agents to seduce people and the greatest in rank among them is the one best at producing *fitna*.
>
> The Prophet Muhammad, according to Sahih Muslim (52:61)

RELIGIOUS TERMINOLOGY, UTILIZED PRECISELY BECAUSE IT RESONATES strongly with devout members of the faith, can be appropriated and applied for different political purposes and interpretations. In fact, the same religious term has often been employed by holders of different religious outlooks to advance diverse political perspectives.[1] For example, the term *fitna* has historically played a central role in discussions of political contestation in the Islamic world. Among those whose native language is not Arabic, their initial exposure to the word likely came during their exploration of early Islamic history and the civil strife that beset the Muslim *umma*, the global Muslim community, during the Rashidun and Umayyad caliphates. In particular, the focus of such readings was likely the civil war that ostensibly produced the Sunni-Shia divide within Islam. While there is no consensus regarding the meaning of the word *fitna*, it is most fundamentally tied to the concept of a trial or tribulation, and its early usages were often apolitical and applicable both to individuals and communities (Mallat 2015). The Koran itself contains usages of the term that span a wide array of meanings and contexts. Perhaps for this reason, its definitional fluidity can be observed within and between various sects and schools of jurisprudence. Nevertheless, it rapidly became synonymous with the inherently social concepts of discord, sedition, and oppression in popular parlance and is largely used to describe conditions and behaviors within and directed at communities.

"Fitna is worse than killing," according to the Koran (2:191), yet it is unclear what exactly constitutes this central notion of Islamic political theory.[2] The context for the chapter-opening verse indicates that it is the oppression of the Muslim community that is "worse than murder," yet both the Koran and hadith contain numerous discussions of fitna that are no less dire and tied to a variety of other implied definitions, including sedition, discord, and division. The amorphous, religious, and politicized nature of the term has produced a struggle over its appropriate application, further complicating attempts to delineate its boundaries (Mallat 2015).

During the early stages of the 2011 Syrian uprising, President Bashar Al-Assad had characterized the revolutionary fervor throughout Syria as the product of both legitimate grievances and conspiratorial forces attempting to produce fitna, using the term to imply anarchy and sedition (Abbas 2014). While some in the opposition adopted a similar definition, they saw the subsequent actions of the regime and its allies, such as Hezbollah, as being the primary potential causes of sectarian fitna (Saouli 2019, 80).[3] For many others, the Assad family's repression was responsible for all forms of fitna observed in Syria, including the sectarian strife that enveloped the country.[4] For an individual seeking autonomy of movement, action, or expression, government interventions that limit freedom may be perceived as producing fitna or as fitna itself. From the perspective of a government supporter, an individual who seeks such autonomy may be the one sowing the seeds of fitna. As such, the term has become a tool used by political actors in the Arab-Muslim world to present their opponents in a negative light.

Yet fitna is not simply relegated to discussions of battles over the institutions of a political community. A new Islamic social movement that forms around heterodox interpretations of the Koran and hadith may also be thought of as purveyors of fitna. In such a case, this heterodox movement may be perceived as bringing about divisions within the Muslim community. However, the members of that heterodox Islamic movement may perceive the source of fitna to be the social or institutional pressure they face to disband and assimilate. For the religious individualist, it may be any undue intrusion by others into his or her manner of practice, yet for communitarians the term may be firmly associated with challenges to a perceived consensus. Those seeking the construction of a pious society may see the absence of religion from the public sphere as constituting fitna, but for others, it may refer to the attempts to coerce citizens into expressing piety in a particular way.

Devout believers with differing religious outlooks, even when adhering to the same religious school of thought and set of foundational tenets, may perceive the term to be primarily associated with opposing sides of a political struggle. Thus, for devout believers, either authoritarian rule or democratization may be characterized as fitna, and each side of that struggle can find sources of support for their point of view. An individual's religious outlook and associated social preferences helps shape his or her view of what constitutes fitna at the level of the community, and this has the potential to play a fundamental role in influencing their political preferences. The differences in various religious outlooks are presumably justified with a similar logic that underlies an individual's adoption of a given outlook and its relation to political preferences.

The first fitna led to the division of the umma into various communities resulting in doctrinal, social, and political cleavages. Such divisions have become the norm rather than exception and continue today in Muslim communities around the world. Its historical legacy and ideological flexibility highlight once again just how much more careful conceptualizations matter in understanding political attitudes among Muslims, who have often been taken to hold a monolithic worldview (Ciftci 2021). The conceptualization and measurement of religious outlooks presented in preceding chapters provided empirical and theoretical support for the contention that these religious outlooks exist and can be characterized by the social preferences associated with them. However, conceptualizing and categorizing the role that individuals envision religion to play in society are not simply exercises meant to provide greater descriptive rigor or clarity. The role that others play in influencing the quality of a one's religious experience has the potential to fundamentally shape one's social, political, and economic preferences (Gaskins, Golder, and Siegel 2013a; Gaskins, Golder, and Siegel 2013b). As discussed in previous chapters, theories of religion and democracy that focus exclusively on the intensity of an individual's faith or adherence to a fundamentalist set of beliefs (the substantive influence of religion), while often insightful, neglect the effect that the social dimensions (the relational influence) of religious belief have on political preferences. Such unidimensional approaches to religiosity cannot convincingly conclude whether religion is a private matter (the perspective of religious individualists, for example) or an inherently social undertaking that requires the participation of others. This approach also cannot explain the extent to which the religious contributions of others enhance an individual's own experience.

Given the heterogeneity in beliefs regarding the role that religion should play in organizing the social order, diversity among the pious regarding how religion shapes their political preferences should also be observed.

Preferences can be shaped by either substantive or relational religious influences. The broader the implications of the object of consideration, the higher the likelihood that the social context of an individual's religious practice will come into play. Preferences regarding specific policies—like regulation of gambling—might be informed largely by doctrine and predicted by the level of one's adherence to her or his faith. At the broader relational level, however, preferences for sociopolitical arrangements are varied across the nationally dominant faith community and clustered in religious outlooks. Therefore, it is anticipated that these outlooks would influence beliefs regarding such a broad and critical issue as the appropriateness and suitability of democratic governance in their own state.

While earlier chapters provided a theoretically and empirically driven alternative to religiosity, this chapter focuses on connecting this conceptualization to preferences regarding regime type. In particular, the analysis focuses broadly on social preferences across two dimensions, religious homogeneity and the provision of religious public goods, and connects these to preferences concerning regime type. To structure this theory, a parsimonious formalization of the theoretical framework is provided (see appendix B for proofs). Although the model presented herein is simple, it presents a novel lens from which to view the effects of religious outlooks and, more broadly, social preferences on attitudes toward democracy. The theory is subsequently tested on data drawn from Wave III of the Arab Barometer, and the analysis finds that members of the outlook classes associated with preferences for social conformity, religious communitarians and social communitarians, were generally less supportive of democracy than religious individualists and post-Islamists. In addition, pious Muslims who prefer that individuals contribute to the religious public good were more likely to support democracy for extrinsic rather than intrinsic reasons. The analyses provide little evidence to support the contention that there is a linear relationship between religiosity and support for democracy and no evidence that Islamic piety reduces the probability of supporting democracy in the Arab world. In fact, the analysis, while not focused on levels of piety itself, finds a significant nonlinear and generally positive relationship between Islamic religiosity and support for democracy in the Arab world.

A Theory of Islamic Religious Outlooks and Support for Democracy

In this section, the theoretical linkages between piety and politics are explored systematically through the analysis of a parsimonious behavioral formal model to evaluate the religious mechanisms that could potentially shape political preferences. Three potential religious sources of support for versus antagonism toward democracy are explored: the ideological position of an individual, support for religion's presence in the public sphere, and preferences for religious homogeneity. While each of these factors has the potential to influence an individual's attitude toward democracy, one of the core implications of this theoretical model is that a preference for religious homogeneity should share a more consistent relationship with support for authoritarian regimes than the other dimensions of religious preference. This section presents the model, the underlying logic of the model, and its core implications. A more complete examination of the implications of the model are presented in appendix B.

Assume that there are n citizens of a state, indexed by $i = 1, \ldots n$, who choose to locate themselves at some point x_i regarding religious observance, and where no individual, i, can influence the distribution or aggregate level of observance within the state (i.e., the community is sufficiently large that no individual can meaningfully change aggregate levels of religious participation). Thus, within one-dimensional space, individuals commit to a certain level of religious observance. Each individual has a preferred level of religious observance, x_i^*, where she would locate herself absent any other considerations. Deviations from an individual's preferred level of religious observance are modeled using a simple quadratic loss function, $-(x_i - x_i^*)^2$. This component of the individual's utility function is maximized if the individuals practice their faith at the location of their ideal point, which would be the case if other factors did not pull them away from this ideal location.[5] Moreover, deviating from this preferred level of religious observance in either direction decreases an individual's utility at an increasing rate. Thus, the further an individual moves away from this ideal point, the greater the disutility associated with a subsequent shift away from her ideal point. For example, imagine that a pious Muslim prefers to fast during the month of Ramadan but would prefer not to fast on all other days. Were this person to be compelled, for some reason, to fast on Ashura as well, this would move the person away from her ideal amount of fasting, leading the person to experience a loss.[6] If the person was compelled to fast an additional day on top of Ashura, perhaps the day before or after Ashura, the loss experienced would be even greater. Each additional day fasted per year beyond what the individual prefers to fast would be costlier still.

Whether making decisions regarding religious practice or other behaviors, individuals are often faced with trade-offs between acting in accordance with their own beliefs and accommodating other individuals or entities. Within the context of this exploration, it is the influence of a political regime over behavior that is of greatest relevance. The institutions of the state can potentially affect religious practice, and the actors that hold the reins of these institutions often have preferences of their own regarding the religious behavior of others. A political regime, D, can allocate costs, $c \geq 0$, associated with citizens participating in religious observation that deviates from its preferred level x_D. Moreover, regimes need not maintain consistency in the direction of their actions regarding religion. For example, regimes may simultaneously ban or limit the ability of women to wear niqab in public spaces yet also prevent most restaurants from opening before iftar during Ramadan, as is the case in Tunisia. The costs associated with distance from the regime's position are also modeled using a quadratic loss function, $-c(x_i - x_D)^2$. This represents the myriad costs that a regime imposes either directly or indirectly on those who deviate from its preferences. As individuals deviate further from the regime's preferred position, where some cost is allocated, the costs of deviating further grow larger. Such costs may come in the form of restricting access to social services, education, or economic opportunities to the subset of citizens who comply with implicit or explicit religious restrictions or preferred practices or the use of coercion and violent repression to punish deviations from policies regarding religious observance.

The components of an individual's utility function discussed above drive the results that will follow. Thus, a brief discussion of the implications of these components may be appropriate. The first component provides for a cost associated with deviating from an individual's preferred behavior, and the second component provides for the costs associated with deviating from a regime's preferred position. Where the costs of deviating from the regime's preferred point is 0, an individual is free to practice her faith in any manner she chooses. In equilibrium, this will reside at her own ideal point. However, where the cost parameter is greater than 0 and the individual's ideal point does not reside at the location preferred by the regime, an individual incurs a cost for locating herself at her ideal point.[7] Moreover, this does not merely reduce an individual's utility by allocating costs to those located at positions further from the regime. In equilibrium, an individual's religious practice should move away from her ideal location toward the regime's preferred location, and the size of this shift will increase the cost associated with deviating from the individual's own ideal point. Total cost and the equilibrium derived from these two competing optima will be a function of both the individual's distance from her own ideal and from the regime's ideal point.

Figure 5.1 provides a graphical representation of the change in religious behavior in equilibrium as the cost of deviating from the regime's preferred position changes for three representative individuals of varying levels of religiosity. The three dashed horizontal lines that intersect with the curves represent the ideal religious locations of each of these three individuals. The curves represent the location of their actual religious practice as the cost allocated to punishment changes. When the regime imposes no costs on individuals for deviating from their preferred location, individuals locate themselves at their ideal point. As the costs doled out by the regime increase, religious behavior approaches the preferred level of religiosity for the regime, which is denoted by the horizonal solid line at the top of the chart. More importantly, as these costs increase, the gap in the behavior of these individuals decreases, leading to a convergence in behavior among the regime's constituents. This result (weakly) holds for any two individuals in the state. Thus, draconian policies regarding religious behavior, whether aimed at secularization or increasing pious behavior, should produce greater homogeneity in religious practice than when religious regulation is less restrictive. Thus, for example, both the secularization policies of Iran under the Pahlavi dynasty and the religious restrictions imposed by the Islamic regime in the aftermath of the 1979 revolution should produce greater homogeneity in expression than what would appear in a less restrictive environment. While this is a simple point, it lays the foundation for the analysis that follows.[8]

Imagine that there are two potential regimes, $D = d, \sim d$, where d is a liberal democratic regime and $\sim d$ is an authoritarian regime. The preferences of the potential regimes are treated as exogenous within the context of this model since this exploration is not primarily concerned with the regime's behavior. For simplicity, and without loss of generality, it is assumed that a liberal-democratic regime, d, does not allocate costs associated with deviating from its preferred location (and, for the sake of completeness, we can imagine that the ideal point resides at the median). An autocratic

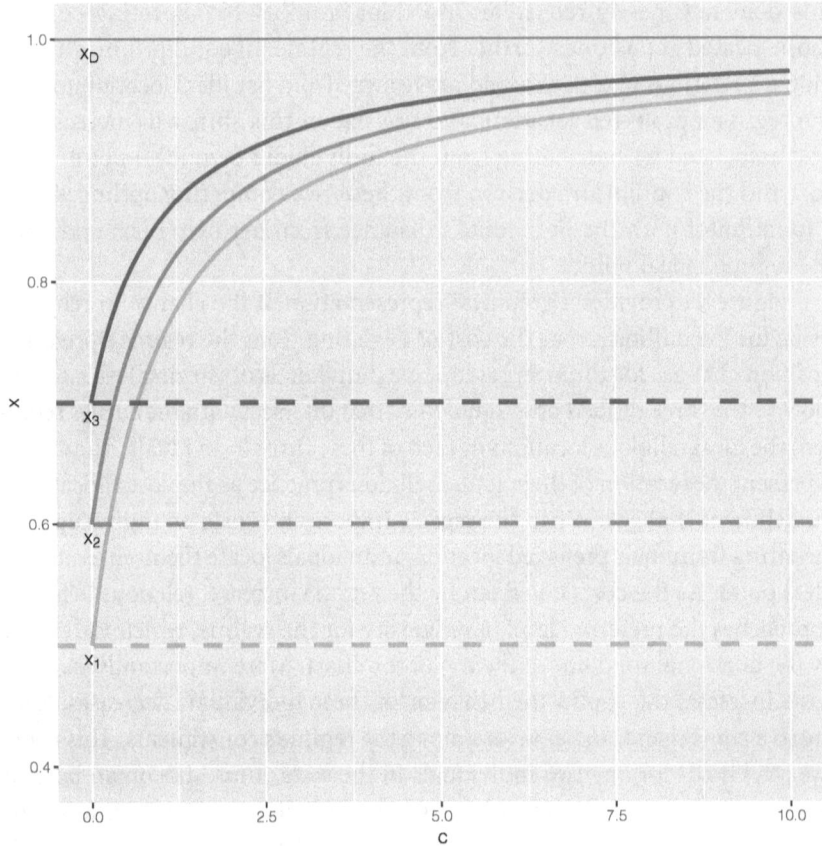

Figure 5.1. Religious Expression and the Cost of Repression. The three dashed horizontal lines represent the ideal religious locations for three hypothetical individuals (x), and x_D represents the preferred position of the regime. The curves represent the location of their actual religious practice along the cost (c).

regime has a preferred level of religious observation that may or may not be located at the median and allocates some cost greater than 0 for deviating from its preferred level of observation, $c_{\sim d} > 0$. Thus, it is assumed that a liberal democracy places lower costs on individuals deviating from the preferred position of the regime than autocracies and normalizes these costs as 0 in relation to the authoritarian alternative. This is not because liberal democracies do not place a cost on deviations from the regime's preferred religious practices but because the costs associated with deviating from the preferred policies of autocrats is assumed to be larger.

As Habermas (2006) and Dreyer (2011) contend, there is no inherent unresolvable tension between individual piety and modern liberal-democratic institutional frameworks. The self-centered utility function presented thus far should lead all individuals, regardless of religious ideological location, to prefer a liberal-democratic regime to an authoritarian regime. Authoritarian restrictions both reduce an individual's overall satisfaction in their practice of religion and produce changes to the practice of their faith. Thus, within a liberal-democratic state, both those who are and are not pious are afforded the opportunity to locate themselves ideologically and religiously in their personal lives closer to their preferred location given its imposition of lower costs for deviating from the median position.

Given liberal democracy's incorporation of freedoms that provide individuals the ability to act according to their own religious preferences at lower costs, why then might some pious Muslims in Islamic societies prefer authoritarian rule?[9] This is arguably because a nonelite individual's preference for autocracy over liberal democracy derives not from preferences related to her own actions but from her preferences regarding the actions of others (Feldman 2003; Feldman and Stenner 1997; Kim and Markus 1999). It is the preferences of individuals to limit the actions of others within certain domains that lead them to support more repressive regime types. While repression can and does occur in democratic contexts, a liberal democracy that incorporates individual rights regarding freedom of speech and religion largely provides for an environment that constrains the actions of others to a lesser extent than an autocracy. For those who benefit socially from a regime that institutionally constrains or promotes the religious behavior of its constituents, there should be a greater tendency to support an undemocratic regime. Not all preferences regarding the actions of others, however, necessarily lead to a preference for a more repressive regime.

The preceding chapters provided a classification of pious Muslims into four categories inspired by social theory. It is reasonable to assume that each of these categories comes bundled with a set of beliefs regarding the role of Islam in society. While the set of beliefs that characterize each type is undeniably large and nuanced, for our purposes, it is the subset of relational (rather than substantive or doctrinal) beliefs regarding the public and social realm that are of relevance to this inquiry. In particular, the previous chapters highlighted the general positions of each category regarding both social or religious cohesion, which is conceptualized as the opposite of a preference for pluralism, and the presence of religion in the public sphere.

Regarding social cohesion, each individual has some degree of preference for uniformity (or antagonism toward pluralism), $a \geq 0$.[10] Without loss of generality, it is assumed that the distribution of ideal religious observance, x_i^*, within the state is symmetric, and, thus, the mean and median levels of religious observance within the state, absent government intervention, fall on the same point, $\bar{x}$.[11] This simplifying assumption is not necessary but is used for ease of exposition so that the reader can conceptualize the distribution of preferences in a state as following a bell curve or a uniform distribution. As the variance of religious observation within the state increases, an individual's utility decreases. This disutility is represented as the variance of the distribution of the behavior of all other individuals within society (x_{-i}) multiplied by the parameter a_i, which represents the strength of an individual's preference for uniformity, $a_i \sigma^2_{x_{-i}}$.[12]

Those possessing a strong preference for social cohesion and conformity implicitly yet necessarily prefer a less pluralistic society. Variance in terms of the religious practices of others negatively affects their own enjoyment of social interactions and threatens the social and political stability of their state. Returning to the example that began this chapter, it may be perceived that it is imperative that fitna be avoided and that the divisions inherent in pluralistic societies are more likely to produce fitna. An autocratic regime's ability to coerce conformity to its preferred religious position through the imposition of costs on deviation provides benefits to those who have a strong preference for social cohesion (Feldman 2003). Thus, when all other variables are held constant, the stronger an individual's preference is for social cohesion and conformity, the lower their support for a liberal-democratic regime should be.

A preference for social cohesion is not the only factor related to the social dimension of piety that is potentially capable of influencing preferences for democracy. As the literature on religion and public goods has repeatedly demonstrated theoretically and empirically, individuals derive utility from the religious contributions of others (Berman 2000; Iannaccone 1992, 1998; Owen and Videras 2007). It is not simply conformity to a norm or social cohesion that produces benefits; the active participation of others provides an atmosphere for some that confers benefits that are both conditional and unconditional. For example, an individual may derive greater utility from attending a religious lesson or prayer when others participate as well (Berman 2000). An individual, however, may also benefit from the payment of *zakat*, or almsgiving, independent of their own pious actions or contributions. Thus, individuals may derive benefits from the religious contributions of others and may prefer a regime type that increases these contributions, whether or not they contribute themselves. Nevertheless, individuals who are religious themselves should generally have a greater preference for others to contribute to the religious public good.

Within the context of the model, the level of interest in religion's presence in the public domain is simply denoted by b, $b \geq 0$. The utility derived from the religious observance of others is assumed to be increasing at a decreasing rate. This is conceptualized as being simply the square root of the sum of the participation of others multiplied by the degree to which an individual prefers that others participate religiously and their own intrinsic level of religiosity, and where the function is increasing in i's ideal level of religiosity and preference for religion in the public sphere (b).[13] The component capturing an individual's preference for religion in the public sphere is noted below.

$$b_i x_i^* \sqrt{\sum_{-i} x_{-i}}$$

Putting these components together, an individual's utility associated with both her or his own religious observance and the religious observance of others can be denoted as follows.[14]

$$U_i = -(x_i - x_i^*)^2 - c(x_i - x_D)^2 - a_i \sigma_{x_{-i}}^2 + b_i x_i^* \sqrt{\sum_{-i} x_{-i}}$$

While religious contributions to the public domain may be achieved through coercion, the opposite is also true—coercion may be used to limit religious contributions to the public domain (Habermas 2006). Thus, democratization may increase the influence of religion within the public domain or reduce it relative to its autocratic alternatives, contingent on the ideological position of both society and the nondemocratic alternatives available. Although preferences over regime type may be driven by considerations related to the religious contributions of others, those preferences are tied to an individual's perception of what viable alternatives to democracy exist (Shamaileh 2019). Therefore, preferences concerning regime type and the presence of religion in the public sphere are mitigated by beliefs regarding the importance of social cohesion. Whereas a stronger preference for uniformity necessarily reduces the utility of democracy, a stronger preference for religion in the public sphere may increase or decrease the perceived utility of democracy. Thus, in equilibrium, when all other variables are held constant, an individual's support for liberal democracy is decreasing in her preference for social cohesion.

Among the four categories of pious Muslims theorized in this book, the two communitarian categories possess a preference for social conformity and antagonism toward religious pluralism. While religious communitarians and social communitarians differ regarding their support for religion in the public sphere, both are opposed to religious pluralism. The other two categories, religious individualists and post-Islamists, also differ as to their views on religion in the public sphere but are both less likely to exhibit strong preferences for social conformity. Therefore, in an autocratic context, we would expect religious individualists and post-Islamists to be more supportive of liberal democracy relative to social and religious communitarians.

Corollary 1

a. Social communitarians should be relatively less supportive of democracy.
b. Religious communitarians should be relatively less supportive of democracy.
c. Post-Islamists should be relatively more supportive of democracy.
d. Religious individualists should be relatively more supportive of democracy.

While an individual's preference for religion in the public sphere may serve as the basis for either supporting or opposing democracy, it also provides an explanation for the divergent reasons individuals express for the regime types they support. Where an individual supports a democratic regime, is it due to the norms and procedural mechanisms underlying democracy or because the tangible products of democracy are viewed favorably by that individual? All individuals derive benefits and costs associated with particular regime types; however, those who derive benefits from the religious participation of others are provided with an extrinsic utility associated with contributions to the religious public good (David and Robinson 2006). The larger the benefits derived from this extrinsic utility, the greater the influence it should exert over an individual's preferences over regime type. Thus, when all other variables are held constant, increasing an individual's preference for religion in the public sphere increases their likelihood of preferring a regime type based on its perceived effect on the contributions of others.

Among pious Muslims, post-Islamists and religious communitarians, both of whom derive benefits from the religious participation of others, should be more likely to support a regime based on extrinsic criteria than religious individualists and social communitarians, who do not derive significant benefits from the religious participation of others. Appendix B provides proofs related to corollaries 1 and 2. The observable implications of both propositions are presented in tabular format in the hypotheses section.

Corollary 2

a. Social communitarians should be less likely to support a regime type for extrinsic reasons.
b. Religious communitarians should be more likely to support a regime type for extrinsic reasons.
c. Post-Islamists should be more likely to support a regime type for extrinsic reasons.
d. Religious individualists should be less likely to support a regime type for extrinsic reasons.

Given that individual piety is associated with increased benefits from religion's presence in the public domain, it trivially follows that devout individuals should be more likely to experience greater satisfaction from the contributions of others to the religious public good. Thus, holding all else equal, piety should generally increase extrinsic support for particular regime types. This relationship, however, should be nonlinear, given that the intrinsic benefits of democracy are larger the further an individual's ideal point is from the potential authoritarian regime's ideal point. Thus, when all other variables are held constant, religiosity should generally increase the likelihood of preferring a particular regime due its effect on the contributions of others until a sufficient level of piety is reached, and this relationship should be nonlinear.

The Scope and Application of the Model

As with any theory, the model presented above provides a simplification of reality rather than a comprehensive framework from which support for democracy can be analyzed. While the basic results should carry into multidimensional space, within the context of the model, the choice of religious observance is a matter of degree and not type. Thus, the model is more readily applicable to contexts where the dominant religious paradigm is more pervasive than where there is greater diversity in distinct religions, yet the results remain largely applicable across a variety of settings.

It must be emphasized that the predictions of the model do not imply that individual levels of religiosity, ideological extremism, and support for the presence of religion in the public sphere are unrelated to political preferences. To the contrary, they can play a substantial role in shaping political opinions and preferences. What is implied by the model is that the effects of individual piety and preferences regarding religion's public presence on support for liberal democracy are dynamic and subject to considerations of both the current context and the alternatives that an individual deems viable. In contrast, a concern for homogeneity in religious practice should produce more consistent results across contexts.

Furthermore, the focus of this particular analysis is on broad religious social preferences rather than the manner in which individuals organize themselves socially. Contexts such as those in Lebanon, where religious identity also shapes the organization of political communities into salient political blocs competing for power, introduce other dynamics and considerations. While the results could be expected to generally hold in such contexts, the political division of Lebanese politics, markets, and society along sectarian lines introduces other considerations for how religion may shape politics. As such, the model is more readily applicable to contexts where sectarian divisions do not play an overriding role in shaping political competition.

Our model does not explicitly incorporate sectarian divisions and other religious cleavages, but it may help explain why there are few political preferences that are consistently associated with the various sects, schools of jurisprudence, and groups within Islam. Much like individual preferences, the relationships these identities share with their preferences over regime type are context specific. As the analysis of the Naqshbandis in Turkey (chapter 2) demonstrated, the effect of context on generating different regime preferences can be observed even among the various communities of the same Sufi order. Although certain social preferences discussed above may be more prevalent among specific groups, schools, or sects than others, the religious outlooks and associated social preferences cut across such divisions. For example, the influence of being Shia on your preference regarding regime should vary across states with disparate distributions of religious identities, such as Iran, Iraq, Syria, and Lebanon, but the deference to authority produced by the adoption of a religious outlook that inspires a preference for religious cohesion should be consistently observed across states. As such, while many of the religious identities discussed in the literature on religion and political preferences may not produce reliable results across contexts, we would expect the religious outlook categories identified here to be more salient predictors of attitudes toward liberal democracy.

Hypotheses

The theory presented above produces testable hypotheses related to an individual's probability of supporting democracy and the potential sources of such support. For this analysis, the social communitarian class is reserved as the reference category. Thus, all predictions are derived from comparisons between social communitarians and members of other groups. Based on the implications of the model as summarized in table 5.1, two sets of hypotheses are presented: the first related to support for democracy and the second related to whether support for democracy derives from intrinsic or extrinsic criteria. In addition to these sets of hypotheses, it is also predicted that religious individuals will be more likely to support democracy for extrinsic rather than intrinsic reasons until crossing a sufficiently high level of piety.

Hypothesis 1.A: Individuals who are religious communitarians should neither be meaningfully more nor less likely to support democracy than individuals who are social communitarians.

Hypothesis 1.B: Individuals who are post-Islamists should be more likely to support democracy than individuals who are social communitarians.

Hypothesis 1.C: Individuals who are religious individualists should be more likely to support democracy than individuals who are social communitarians.

Hypothesis 2.A: Individuals who are religious communitarians should be more likely to express support for democracy based on extrinsic factors than individuals who are social communitarians.

Hypothesis 2.B: Individuals who are post-Islamists should be more likely to express support for democracy based on extrinsic factors than individuals who are social communitarians.

Hypothesis 2.C: Individuals who are religious individualists should neither be meaningfully more nor less likely to express support for democracy based on extrinsic factors than individuals who are social communitarians.[15]

Hypothesis 3: Until an individual reaches a sufficiently high level of piety, piety should be positively correlated with the probability that an individual's support for democracy is due to extrinsic criteria. At sufficiently high levels of piety, there should be a negative correlation between extrinsic support for democracy and piety.

The theory clearly presented the underpinnings from which these hypotheses are derived, yet this analysis also indirectly tests an alternative

Table 5.1. Summary of Core Hypotheses

Theoretical Predictions

		Support for Democracy	
		High	Low
Nature of Support for Regime	Extrinsic	Post-Islamist	Religious communitarian
	Intrinsic	Religious individualist	Social communitarian

Empirical Predictions

Class	Support for Democracy	Extrinsic Support for Democracy
Social communitarian	Reference category	Reference category
Religious communitarian	x (H1a)	+ (H2a)
Post-Islamist	+ (H1b)	+ (H2b)
Religious individualist	+ (H1c)	x (H2c)

Additional Variable

Religiosity	x	+

Note: x, no predicted difference in reference to social communitarian class; +, significant increase in support in reference to social communitarian class.

theoretical paradigm. The literature on Islam and democracy has at times framed the desire for a theocratic autocracy as the offspring of an ideological desire to root the public sphere in a religious tradition and force individuals to contribute to the formation of an Islamic society (Lust 2011). Such theories may imply that those who express support for religion's presence in the public sphere will be less supportive of democracy. Thus, if the theoretical propositions of those who focus on attitudes of individuals related to religion in the public sphere hold, religious communitarians and post-Islamists would be the least likely among pious Muslims to support democracy. While the empirical analysis that follows focuses on testing our own hypotheses, these alternative theoretical predictions are also tested indirectly.

Data and Variables

Data from the third wave of the Arab Barometer was used to test the hypotheses presented above. The sample includes Muslim respondents in Algeria, Egypt, Iraq, Jordan, Kuwait, Lebanon, Libya, Morocco, Palestine, Sudan,

Tunisia, and Yemen and comprises over ten thousand observations. In addition to its broad coverage of the MENA region, one of the primary benefits of using the Arab Barometer is that it contains many questions related to democracy and religion that could be used to help construct the dependent and core independent variables.[16] The analysis in this chapter focuses on the subset of individuals classified as moderately or highly religious as described in chapter 3; however, analyses using the full sample were also conducted.

Dependent variables: The primary dependent variable for this analysis is support for democracy. *Overt support* for democracy is used to measure individual preferences that range from solid support for to noncommitment to democracy (Inglehart and Welzel 2003; Klingemann 1999). Rather than using a single item asking the respondents about their opinion of democratic system, overt support is measured based on differences in responses to two questions:

> I will describe different political systems to you, and I want to ask you about your opinion of each one of them with regard to the country's governance—for each one would you say it is very good, good, bad, or very bad?
> A democratic political system (Q517.1)
> A political system with an authoritarian president (non-democratic) who is indifferent to parliament and elections (Q517.2)

Both questions are recoded to range from very bad (1) to very good (4). The second question was then subtracted from the first one to obtain an index ranging from −3 (weak support) to +3 (strong support).[17] The distribution of this index has a negative skew with 63 percent of the respondents holding very strong preference for democracy (a score larger than 1 on the index).

In addition to overt support for democracy, the determinants of extrinsic support for democracy were also explored. An individual may provide unconditional support for democracy for intrinsic reasons, including her belief in and preference for democratic institutions. At the opposite end, some scholars argue that individuals may support democracy for what it delivers and for its outcomes (i.e., extrinsic support) (Bratton and Mattes 2001). The theoretical model also explained the reasons for individuals supporting or opposing democracy according to their level of piety situated in relational context. To construct the relevant measure, a survey question was used that asked respondents to choose the most important reason for supporting democracy from a list of seven categories including both extrinsic (what democracy delivers) and intrinsic (normative value of democracy for providing freedoms and rights) reasons. *Extrinsic support* was coded as a dichotomous variable that captures whether a respondent listed at least one of the extrinsic factors as being the most important reason for supporting democracy. The question that was used is shown below:

> Which of the following would you say is the most important feature of democracy (Q515)?
>
> *Indicators of Extrinsic Support:*
> Narrowing the gap between the rich and poor
> Providing basic items (food, housing, clothing) to every individual
> Eliminating financial and administrative corruption
>
> *Other Responses*:
> The opportunity to change the government through elections
> Freedom to criticize the government
> Equality of political rights between citizens.
> Other

Independent variables: The main independent variables are the dichotomous measures for class membership obtained through LCA estimation in chapter 3. Dichotomous variables measuring membership in the religious individualist, religious communitarian, and post-Islamist categories were included in the models, and the social communitarian class was reserved as the reference category. LCA produces posterior probabilities of class membership for each of the classes, and class memberships for each individual were designated based on the size of these probabilities. While the posterior probability can also be used to obtain an interval measure, the dichotomous variables approach was used because the theoretical model distinguishes between religious outlook classes and because this approach is commonly used (Blaydes and Linzer 2008; Hagenaars and Mccutcheon 2002; Lazarsfeld 1950). Since a more robust discussion of the use of LCA to categorize an individual's class membership and the posterior probability of her or his class membership can be found in previous chapters, this discussion focuses on the results of the multivariate analysis predicting support for democracy.

For each of the dependent variables, regression analyses were conducted where the religiosity variable was omitted, where it was included, and where both a linear and quadratic term for religiosity were included. The inclusion of the quadratic term allowed for the testing of a nonlinear relationship between religiosity and support for democracy. The variable is an index measuring Islamic religiosity that ranges from 3 (least pious) to 15 (most pious). The measure is discussed in greater detail in chapter 3, and the coding scheme used in that chapter was preserved to maintain consistency. The sample of respondents focused on herein (moderately and highly religious) all have values of religiosity greater than or equal to 9.

The regression models also included variables that are commonly used in analyses of survey data on support for democracy. *Interpersonal trust* is a dichotomous variable taking the value of 1 if respondents believe most other people can be trusted. *Political trust* is an additive index of four items asking the respondents the degree of trust they have in government, elected council, public security, and the army. In addition, a self-reported level of interest in politics (*political interest*) on a scale ranging from not interested (1) to very interested (4) was included in the model. Furthermore, egalitarian gender beliefs, a commonly used indicator of cultural modernization theory by previous studies, is controlled for in the model (Inglehart and Norris 2003). This index ranges between 3 (less egalitarian) and 12 (more egalitarian) and combines responses to three questions measured along a four-point agreement scale: men make better political leaders than women, a married woman can work outside the home, and a university education is more important for males. Additional control variables include the respondents' views about current (four-point scale) and future economic conditions (five-point scale) with higher values showing positive evaluations, gender (female = 1), level of education harmonized across twelve countries (seven-point scale), a proxy for household income, age, and country dummies.

Results and Discussion

Ordinary least square (OLS) regression models were used to examine overt support for democracy, while logistic regression models were specified for the analyses of extrinsic support for democracy. The estimation results that follow were obtained using the data from the subset of the respondents who were at least moderately pious. An analysis of the full sample can be found in the appendix. Since the theoretical model predicts that the effect of religiosity on democratic orientations can be better captured through religious outlook categories rather than a single additive religiosity index, the discussion also presents the models controlling for this conventional measure of religiosity with both linear and quadratic components. Overall, there is significant corroboration of the core implications of the theoretical model, as shown in table 5.2.

The results suggest that different social preferences emanating from religious outlooks can explain democratic orientations better than an essentialist

Table 5.2. Religious Outlooks and Support for Democracy: OLS and Logit Estimations

	Model 1	Model 2	Model 3	Model 4	Model 5	Model 6
	Overt Support			Extrinsic Support		
Religious individualist	0.628***	0.640***	0.641***	0.377***	0.390***	0.391***
	(0.042)	(0.043)	(0.043)	(0.078)	(0.080)	(0.080)
Post-Islamist	0.232***	0.253***	0.266***	0.381***	0.379***	0.394***
	(0.041)	(0.042)	(0.042)	(0.066)	(0.068)	(0.069)
Religious communitarian	0.00659	0.0222	0.0187	0.556***	0.549***	0.545***
	(0.033)	(0.034)	(0.034)	(0.057)	(0.059)	(0.059)
Religiosity		-(0.0007)	0.679***		-0.008	0.791***
		(0.009)	(0.122)		(0.015)	(0.208)
(Religiosity)^2			-0.0267***			-0.0314***
			(0.005)			(0.008)
Personal trust	-0.0372	-0.0249	-0.0213	0.0908	0.0689	0.0729
	(0.029)	(0.030)	(0.030)	(0.051)	(0.052)	(0.052)
Political trust	0.0217***	0.0203***	0.0198***	0.00213	0.00357	0.00295
	(0.005)	(0.005)	(0.005)	(0.008)	(0.008)	(0.008)
Political interest	0.00331	0.000522	0.000244	-0.114***	-0.111***	-0.112***
	(0.015)	(0.015)	(0.015)	(0.024)	(0.024)	(0.024)

	(1)	(2)	(3)	(4)
Egalitarian gender beliefs	0.0734***	0.0753***	0.0727***	
	(0.007)	(0.007)	(0.007)	
Economic perceptions	-0.0588**	-0.0633**	-0.0607**	-0.0216
	(0.020)	(0.020)	(0.020)	(0.012)
				-0.0772*
				(0.033)
Prospective economic perceptions	0.0156	0.0150	0.0149	0.0382
	(0.013)	(0.013)	(0.013)	(0.021)
Age	0.00277**	0.00278**	0.00288**	0.00321
	(0.001)	(0.001)	(0.001)	(0.002)
Female	-0.0579*	-0.0630*	-0.0678*	0.137**
	(0.027)	(0.023)	(0.028)	(0.047)
Education	0.0303***	0.0304***	0.0296**	-0.0659***
	(0.009)	(0.009)	(0.009)	(0.015)
Income	-0.0016	-0.0133	-0.0145	-0.0234
	(0.015)	(0.016)	(0.016)	(0.026)
Country dummies	Yes	Yes	Yes	Yes
Observations	8,469	8,145	8,145	8,855
Adjusted R-squared	0.098	0.099	0.102	

	(5)	(6)
	-0.0274*	-0.0283*
	(0.012)	(0.012)
	-0.0685*	-0.0660
	(0.034)	(0.034)
	0.0375	0.0375
	(0.021)	(0.021)
	0.00345	0.00358*
	(0.002)	(0.002)
	0.132**	0.133**
	(0.048)	(0.048)
	-0.0634***	-0.0646***
	(0.016)	(0.016)
	-0.0205	-0.0219
	(0.027)	(0.027)
	Yes	Yes
	8,507	8,507

Notes: Standard errors are in parentheses; * $p < .05$, ** $p < .01$, *** $p < .001$. Social communitarian is the reference category. Country dummies are presented in the appendix, table A5.1.
Source: Arab Barometer, Wave III.

approach, and this finding is robust to the inclusion of a nonlinear term of religiosity. Models 1–3 provide evidence that religious individualists and post-Islamists are more likely to broadly support democracy (overt support) than social communitarians. While these results lend support to hypotheses 1.B and 1.C, the null hypothesis was not rejected for religious communitarians' support for democracy. This latter finding provides suggestive support for hypothesis 1.A, which proposes no difference between religious communitarians and social communitarians in their democratic orientations. Thus, as the theoretical model predicts, those who have strong preferences for pluralism (religious individualists and post-Islamists) are more supportive of democracy than those who hold strong preferences for social cohesion and conformity (religious communitarians and social communitarians). Furthermore, a descriptive examination of the means by religious outlook for each country corroborates our findings across contexts regarding overt support for democracy. These data can be found in appendix A (figure A5.1).

Marginal effects were calculated to show the substantive differences among the religious outlook groups regarding their level of support for democracy. Figure 5.2 presents the pairwise comparisons for the marginal effects of the religious outlook classes. In substantive terms, religious individualists, the group least likely to prefer social conformist views, hold considerably higher levels of support for democracy compared to post-Islamists, who hold certain pluralist views, and religious and social communitarians, who are most likely to hold conformist views. Post-Islamists, as expected, occupy the middle position between religious individualists and our communitarian classes, but they are located closer to the latter group. This could be seen as an illustration of the theoretical relationship we have proposed regarding Bayat's (2007) Islamist and post-Islamist categories. The proposition that these post-Islamists are erstwhile Islamists (i.e., religious communitarians) that have been conditioned into a shift toward pluralism over time appears to fit the relationships depicted in figure 5.2.

The results regarding the relationship between religious outlooks and extrinsic support for democracy are less clear yet generally descriptively support our theoretical expectations. Religious individualists, post-Islamists, and religious communitarians are all more likely to support democracy for extrinsic reasons than social communitarians. Hypotheses 2.A and 2.B were thus corroborated; however, a substantive difference was not observed between religious outlook groups other than social communitarians in terms of extrinsic support for democracy according to the predicted probabilities

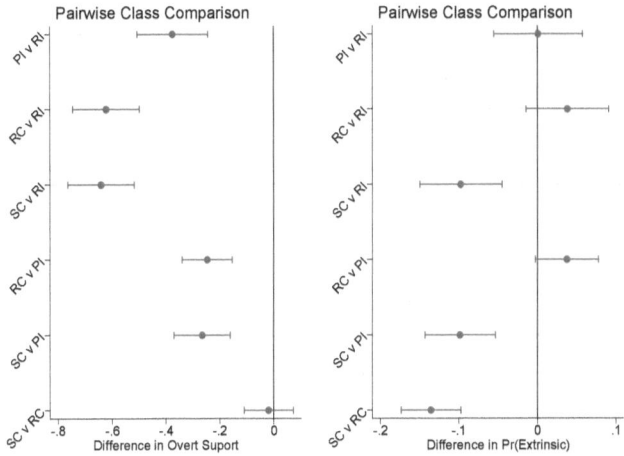

Figure 5.2. Pairwise Marginal Effect and Predicted Probability Comparisons for Religious Outlooks. *RI*, religious individualist; *PI*, post-Islamist; *RC*, religious communitarian; *SC*, social communitarian. The reference group is listed second. The Bonferroni-corrected confidence intervals are at 95 percent level. Source: Arab Barometer Wave III.

in figure 5.2. While this analysis indicates a relationship between religious individualists and extrinsic support for democracy, it should be noted that the results for this relationship are not as robust as the relationship between the other two outlooks and extrinsic support.

The significant correlations of the religious outlook categories remain robust to the addition of the conventional measure of religiosity both linearly and nonlinearly. Interestingly, the analysis finds that religiosity does share a positive nonlinear relationship with both overt and extrinsic support for democracy until reaching a high level of religiosity. Highly religious individuals should, on average, be more likely to support democracy, and the basis of such support is more likely to be extrinsic. Both the marginal effect of religiosity on support for democracy and the predicted probability of extrinsic support are increasing at a decreasing rate until reaching a sufficiently high level of religiosity, and then it begins to decrease (figure 5.3). This result further challenges essentialist conceptualizations of the relationship between religiosity and support for democracy but highlights the potential for absolute levels of religiosity to influence political preferences. Nevertheless, such a relationship may potentially be due to the secularism of the regimes in power in much of the Arab world. The political context matters, and an Arab world dominated by secular authoritarian regimes is likely to produce more favorable attitudes

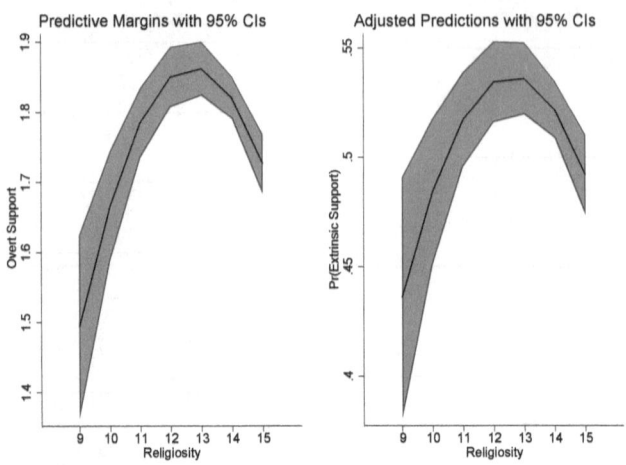

Figure 5.3. Predictions and Predicted Probabilities for Religiosity. The lines represent the predictions for overt support for democracy and the probability of extrinsic support. The gray areas represent the 95 percent confidence intervals. Source: Arab Barometer Wave III.

toward democracy among those who more strongly favor religious policies. This reflects the expressed preferences of many Islamist political parties that have become strong supporters of democratization to escape the ire of the secular authoritarian regimes. While the theoretical model did not directly predict greater support for democracy among the religious, it did predict that extrinsic support would be greater among those who are religious and that such a relationship would be nonlinear. Thus, this analysis corroborates hypothesis 3.

Among the other predictors added to the regression analyses, highly educated individuals, those holding egalitarian gender views, and those with high levels of political trust are more supportive of democracy.[18] Furthermore, the models suggest that the highly educated are less likely to support democracy for extrinsic reasons. On average and when all other variables are held constant, females are less likely to support democracy and more likely to support democracy for extrinsic reasons than males. It should be noted that this result is achieved after controlling for a host of factors, including egalitarian views toward gender. Finally, contrary to the dominant narrative presented regarding youth and support for democracy in the Arab world, when controlling for religious outlook, age is positively correlated with support for democracy.

In addition, analyses were conducted that compared members of the religious outlook classes with those who were coded as possessing a low level of piety. For these regression analyses, respondents were placed into one of five groups: the four religious outlooks previously discussed and a fifth nonpious / low-piety category. The nonpious category was reserved as the reference category. The variable measuring piety was removed due to its relationship to the categorization scheme used. The results of this analysis can be found in table 5.3 and largely corroborate the findings of the primary analysis. Moreover, the results provide evidence that overt support for democracy is greater among religious individualists and possibly post-Islamists (the result verges on significance at the 0.05 level in a two-tailed test) than nonpious Muslims and lower among religious and social communitarians when all other variables are held constant. This result further highlights the relevance of these religious outlooks. Various other robustness checks were conducted, and these analyses can be found in appendix A.

Conclusion

While the literature on Islamic ideology has developed nuanced conceptualizations of the various belief systems adopted by Muslims, few scholars have attempted to explore the relationship between the adoption of these religious paradigms and an individual's political preferences regarding democracy. Studies related to Islam and political preferences have largely focused on the intensity of an individual's piety or adoption of extreme views (Ciftci 2010; Robbins 2015; Tessler 2002; Tessler, Jamal, and Robbins 2012). There is significant added value in theorizing religiosity as entwined with distinct religious outlooks rather than as a binary concept. Furthermore, when controlling for religious outlooks, absolute levels of piety are generally associated with higher rather than lower levels of support for democracy in the Arab world. Contradicting the implications of essentialist theories that locate pluralism firmly outside of the domain of the religious Muslim world (Huntington 1993; Kedourie 1994), the analysis presented in this chapter demonstrated that pious Muslims often adopt outlooks that produce favorable attitudes toward pluralism and democracy.

Social preferences regarding the religious participation of others, a factor underlying different religious outlooks, can be instrumental in explaining orientations toward democracy among pious Muslims. This chapter explored how religious preferences over the social and political realms influence pluralist and conformist ideals and how these ideals, in turn, become the basis for an individual's support for democracy. It is predicted that religious

Table 5.3. Regression Analysis with Nonpious Muslim Category (Full Sample)

	(1) Overt Support	(2) Extrinsic Support
Religious individualist	0.405***	−0.0502
	(0.040)	(0.074)
Post-Islamist	0.0752	−0.0144
	(0.039)	(0.062)
Religious communitarian	−0.145***	0.181***
	(0.030)	(0.053)
Social communitarian	−0.176***	−0.385***
	(0.033)	(0.057)
Personal trust	−0.00415	0.103*
	(0.025)	(0.043)
Political trust	0.0219***	0.00252
	(0.004)	(0.007)
Political interest	0.00574	−0.102***
	(0.012)	(0.020)
Egalitarian gender beliefs	0.0853***	−0.00831
	(0.006)	(0.010)
Economic perceptions	−0.0692***	−0.0787**
	(0.017)	(0.028)
Prospective economic perceptions	0.0108	0.0223
	(0.011)	(0.018)
Age	0.00250**	0.00350*
	(0.001)	(0.001)
Female	−0.0501*	0.164***
	(0.023)	(0.040)
Education	0.0364***	−0.0688***
	(0.007)	(0.013)
Income	−0.0156	−0.0338
	(0.013)	(0.022)
Observations	11,668	12,246
Adjusted R-squared	0.096	

Notes: Standard errors in parentheses; * $p < .05$, ** $p < 0.01$, *** $p < .001$. Religious reference category, nonpious; reference country, Algeria. Piety was excluded as an independent variable due to collinearity with the pious/nonpious categorization scheme. Respondents were first categorized as either pious or nonpious based on the criteria noted in chapter 5, and latent classes for religious outlook were then constructed. Fixed effects are presented in the appendix A, table A5.3.

pluralists (religious individualists and post-Islamists) would generally be more supportive of democracy. The regression analyses corroborated the predictions drawn from the theoretical model, finding significant differences between the groups regarding their support for democracy. These results contribute to the literature on Islam and democracy by providing an answer to the questions that stem from the often-negligible statistical relationship observed between religiosity and support for democracy in many past studies. The analysis demonstrates that this negligibility may be in part due to the differential effects of religious outlooks among pious individuals on regime preferences, as well as the nonlinear and conditional relationship that religiosity shares with preferences regarding regime type.

The analysis presented here provides theoretical and empirical evidence of the relevance of religious outlooks to studies of political attitudes in the Muslim world and contributes to the burgeoning literature on the nuanced relationship between faith, politics, and political preferences (Gaskins, Golder, and Siegel 2013a; Gaskins, Golder, and Siegel 2013b; Huckle and Silva 2020). The findings in this chapter are not meant to provide the last word on how piety influences politics in the Muslim world; they simply skim the surface of the potential value of the conceptualization of religious outlooks that was developed. The next chapter analyzes temporal dynamics by tracing the manifestations of the religious outlook categories over time in two cases, Egypt and Tunisia. In addition, the following two chapters explore the relationship between religious outlooks and different sets of attitudes, including distributive preferences, and highlight the contextual nuances that shape the relationship between political preferences and religious outlooks.

Notes

1. Elements of the argument and the text of this chapter and chapter 3 appear in an earlier article by the authors (Ciftci, Wuthrich, and Shamaileh 2019).

2. Throughout the text, we used the translations provided in the Qur'anic Arabic Corpus at http://corpus.quran.com. We relied on the Sahih International translation as reported at that website.

3. Much of this discussion of fitna was inspired by Adham Saouli's lecture on the subject of the evolution of the term *fitna*, which is the focus of his current book project, at the Arab Center for Research and Policy Studies in Doha, Qatar, in 2020. Although his proposed exploration of the term is of a different nature, the authors found the concept of fitna to be a particularly appropriate one to relate to Islamic religious outlooks. For a thorough

examination of the concept, interested readers should consult his book when it is drafted and published, as it promises to be the authoritative English-language text on fitna.

4. For example, see Humam Hoot's (2018) discussion of the Assad regime and his use of the word *fitna* on his program, which appeared on the Orient Channel.

5. An individual's utility function here captures the relationship between an individual's overall level of satisfaction and the variables believed to influence such satisfaction. In this examination, we focus on the satisfaction derived from religious practice and the religious environment.

6. For Shia Muslims, Ashura is the day of grievance for the martyrdom of Hussein, the son of Ali and grandson of the Prophet Muhammad. Many Sunni Muslims also fast on Ashura, but the fast is not obligatory.

7. For our purposes, we can treat this as a parameter rather than a variable.

8. There are other important implications that will not be discussed in the body of the book. One main implication worthy of discussion is that the greater the costs associated with deviation from the regime's preference, the less expressed preferences should represent actual preferences, and it is those furthest away from the regime's ideal point that should be masking their preferences the most.

9. It should be noted that the framework presented here can be applied to non-Islamic societies as well.

10. We could also allow for a preference for heterogeneity. This would not alter the substantive implications of the model in any way.

11. There exists some point, $\bar{x}^*$, where the mean and median reside absent the imposition of a cost by the government. This distributional assumption is not necessary to produce the results achieved within this chapter but is presented to conceptually simplify the model for the reader using reasonable assumptions regarding the underlying populations. It is easier to see how the distance in religious practice between any two individuals decreases as the cost of deviating from the regime's preference increases if you think of the distribution as being symmetric. The only distributional assumption necessary to support the propositions within this chapter, however, is that there is some distribution with a variance greater than 0. Relaxing these assumptions further leads to the same qualitative conclusions.

12. $-a_i \sigma_{x_{-i}}^2 = -a_i \left(\dfrac{\Sigma_{-i}(x_{-i} - \bar{x})^2}{n-1} \right)$

13. For simplicity, and without loss of generality, it can be assumed that an individual's preference is linearly increasing in preferred level of religious expression, $f(b, x^*) = b_i x_i^*$. The decision to use a square root to capture the effect of aggregate religious participation was also done for the sake of simplicity in this case, but the functional form is likely more appropriate than that of a log transformation.

14. The results of the model are robust to a number of functional form specifications. The specifications presented above identify a simple and reasonable specification of individuals' utility functions. So long as (1) the cost of deviating from the regime's preferred point increases at an increasing rate, (2) some individuals prefer religious homogeneity, and (3) some individuals prefer that religion be present in the public domain, these results should hold. Even if we were to assume some level of dependence between preferences for religion's presence in the public domain and preferences for religious homogeneity, the fundamental qualitative predictions of the model would still hold: authoritarianism is more fundamentally

tied to preferences for uniformity in action than a desire for the public domain to be characterized by a specific set of religious practices. In such a scenario, where perhaps a is treated as an increasing function in b, it would trivially follow that b's effect on preferences for democracy will either depend on the context or the degree to which a preference for religion in the public sphere increases the preference cohesion.

15. Hypotheses 1.A and 2.C make predictions as to the negligibility of the difference between the respective groups compared to social communitarians concerning the relevant dependent variables. Given the lack of any developed standards related to what constitutes a meaningful effect for our dependent variables, testing for equivalence or a negligible effect would be based on arbitrary criteria. Therefore, our analysis will not move beyond testing the null (Limentani et al. 2005; Morikawa and Yoshida 1995; Rainey 2014).

16. We also explored the questions in the Pew Global Attitudes surveys and World Values Surveys. While these surveys include some items that could be used to replicate our analysis, none of these surveys simultaneously provides as many questions directly asking about the role of religion in the public and social sphere and questions about sharia implementation. These kinds of items are necessary for conducting the LCA estimation according to our conceptual and theoretical expectations. Therefore, we prefer the third wave of the Arab Barometer, which provides the most relevant questions in a large sample.

17. Even with this less than ideal measure, the robust findings in our analysis lend support to the implications of our theory. An alternative operationalization was carried out by Inglehart and Welzel (2003), who follow Klingemann (1991), to operationalize "Overt support for democracy" with four items from the World Values Surveys: "Having a democratic political system" (V157), "Democracy may have problems but it's better than any other form of government" (V163), ""Having a strong leader who does not have to bother with parliament and elections" (V154), and "Having the army rule" (V156). They create two indices from these four items and then subtract the second index (V154 + V156) from the first index (V157 + V163). The third wave of the Arab Barometer survey has only three of these items (no question was asked about army rule). Additional analysis using an index constructed with these three items does not alter the results but increases the number of missing values.

18. Recent literature has found greater support for Muslim feminism in Arab societies than Western conceptualizations of feminism (Glas and Alexander 2020; Masoud, Jamal, and Nugent 2016). An examination of the relationship between these religious outlooks and support for Muslim feminism, as well as other variants of feminism, might prove to be fruitful given that these religious outlooks are rooted in social and relational preferences.

6

TEMPORAL CHANGE IN RELIGIOUS OUTLOOKS AND POLITICAL PREFERENCES

AS EMPHASIZED THROUGHOUT THE PREVIOUS CHAPTERS, CATEGORIZing pious individuals into distinct outlooks according to their socioreligious preferences can explain attitudes toward democracy and political preferences in more nuanced ways than examining a single category of religiosity measured along a unidimensional scale of less to more religious. The empirical evidence presented from chapters 3, 4, and 5 strongly supports the relevance and usefulness of a two-dimensional four-class categorization of religious outlooks. This evidence illustrates the significant cross-national variation that exists in the distribution of religious outlooks across countries and highlights the important relationships these religious outlooks have to key political preferences, such as support for democracy.

The observation of these associations prompts an additional, critical question: Next to spatial variation, is there also empirical evidence from the survey data for temporal variation in the distribution of religious outlooks? If outlooks are static within a population, this suggests a measure of determinism in whether a polity is likely to support a successful transition to democracy or some other form of governance. If these outlooks among the devout are formed at some early point in an individual's life and become rigid or fixed, high distributions of social and religious communitarians among the devout would lead to a great deal of pessimism for civil society–inspired political change toward pluralism, for example.

Based on the observations regarding the Naqshbandis in Turkey in chapter 2, however, there is good reason to anticipate that static distributions of religious outlooks should not be expected. While one could posit that distributions of religious communities and the broader religious niches they occupy are less likely to shift dramatically or rapidly, the observed behaviors of members of Naqshbandi groups in Turkey illustrate that members within the same broader Sufi order come to different conclusions about themselves, their community, and their group's relationship to the social and political reality as contexts change over time. To the extent that attitudes and outlooks toward broader political preferences are shaped by the relational, and not primarily substantive, influences of religion, it logically necessitates a focus on dynamics that involve a measure of fluidity. Of course, like any worldview, religious outlooks are unlikely to be either simply a day-to-day perspective or one that is immune to the forces of time and altered circumstances. From such a perspective, attitudes change as these are filtered through shifting opportunities and obstacles for religious individuals in their broader social environment. This was clearly observed to be the case among Turkish Naqshbandis, but is there broader empirical evidence to support that these observations among the Naqshbandis do not just represent an anomaly?

This chapter explores the temporal dynamics of religious outlooks and the change in patterns of attitudes about political preferences. We focus on the cases of Egypt and Tunisia to trace temporal change in the distribution of religious outlook categories and their effects on political attitudes within a given group or country. The analysis also tackles the possibilities for locating the incarnations of certain religious outlooks within Islamist organizations. The evolution of political strategies within the Muslim Brothers and Ennahda during and after the uprisings presents many opportunities for understanding the role religious outlooks play in organizational strategy over time. If, as we anticipate, religious outlooks are influenced by social and political changes, Egypt and Tunisia offer ideal case studies to examine the possibility of temporal change in outlook distributions, given the dramatic ruptures in the political landscape of both of these countries during and after to the Arab uprisings. These changes in outlooks appear to stem from a base of stable attitudes and preferences while also reflecting a gradual adjustment of individual political orientations in response to the dramatic events in their environments.

Egypt and Tunisia are considered among the most significant cases of the Arab uprisings with divergent trajectories in democratization in the postuprising period. Our analyses can benefit from two waves of the Arab Barometer surveys (Waves II and III) to run a series of latent class analyses (LCA) and multivariate regression estimations among population samples taken at different points during the enormous shifts in the social and political environment. The analysis confirms that the distribution of religious outlooks demonstrates considerable variation within Egypt and Tunisia from the start of the protests to the end of the post-protest transition period. More significantly, we observe that such changes are consequential in shifting the preferences of these outlook categories toward democracy.

Arab Uprisings, Islam, and Religious Outlooks

The mass protests that erupted across Arab countries in the spring of 2011 famously took many by surprise (Bayat 2013a; El-Ghobashy 2011). During these unprecedented popular uprisings in late 2010 and throughout 2011, protesters filled the squares and cities of the Arab capitals chanting, "*Aysh, hurriyah, karamah.*"[1] While the initial enthusiasm for democracy ultimately encountered stiff obstruction from the status quo, ideological hijacking, and repression, with parts of the region descending into chaos, the protests are considered to have had significant consequences in shaping the future of Arab polities (Feldman 2020). The uprisings left a mark on virtually every state in the region, but the uptick in political activity during this period produced different imprints in different contexts. The increased mobilization interacted with various historical legacies and institutional, economic, and social environments to produce different results and unique modes of contestation (Brownlee, Masoud, and Reynolds 2015; Gause 2011; Haas and Lesch 2013; Shamaileh 2017).

Islamist organizations, long repressed by the authoritarian regimes (Lust 2011), had generally not taken active roles in protests in these countries during the initial stages of the uprisings, only joining once the protest mobilization had generated sufficient steam (Khatib and Lust 2014). For example, the leaders of the Muslim Brothers were cautious before they threw their weight behind the protesters in Egypt. Similarly, various Egyptian Salafi groups justified their inactivity with their apolitical stance.[2] In contrast, the Islamist organization Ennahda played a central role during the initiation and transition periods in Tunisia. The Ben Ali regime's alienation of all opposition groups and the resulting secular-Islamist rapprochement were the main drivers of Ennahda's activism (Angrist 2013).

Religion, nonetheless, played a crucial role in the mobilization stage and particularly in the postprotest period (Filali-Ansary, 2012; Haas and Lesch 2013; Hoffman and Jamal 2014). Next to traditional liberal and leftist groups, a new generation of liberal-minded young activists who were secular in orientation but who reconciled personal religiosity with universalistic ideas of freedom and democracy, closely exhibiting what Bayat (2007) refers to as post-Islamism, were instrumental in the initial stages of the widespread protests (Zubaida 2012). Where regime change was the ultimate result, however, Islamist organizations—as the best equipped organizations thoroughly embedded in society with the ability to mobilize as political parties—proved to be the most adept at taking advantage of the political vacuum in the aftermath of the protests (Bayat 2013a; Stepan and Linz 2013).

These organizations are not abstract entities; rather, they are created and operated by real people who hold certain preferences. Their members have preferences about state-religion relations and the role of religion in society that form distinct religious outlooks and influence organizational strategy. While it would be difficult to assume that a single religious outlook will shape an organization's ideology or strategy, the distribution of individual religious outlooks within an organization is likely to influence the decisions of these groups. Furthermore, if significant events influence religious outlooks, people who operate within these organizations are likely to want to steer their organization toward those directions compatible with their shifting preferences. Thus, in addition to understanding changing preferences about religion, an analysis of temporal outlooks also has the potential to help us understand religious organizational preference dynamics and how and why they might shift during extraordinary times.

This chapter focuses on the cases of Egypt and Tunisia to explore how the critical moment of the Arab Spring might have shaped the religious outlooks in these countries. The rapidly changing social and political dynamics between 2010 and 2013 and available survey data provide an ideal case to measure the stability or dynamism of religious outlooks and attitudes within a short period. Other scholars have noted the particularly salient impact of such dramatic changes in the external environment on strategic revisions for Islamic and Islamist social movements (Volpi and Clark 2019). Do strategic revisions and considerations of the external environment in short periods also apply to the attitudes of individuals? If a significant component of the influence of religion on attitudes is relational, we should expect that it would.

The religious landscape shows a high degree of diversity in both Egypt and Tunisia, ranging in religious groups from Salafis to Sufis and all manner of organizations and parties from moderate to radical (Claret-Campana and Lampridi-Kemou 2017). As can be seen in the analysis in chapter 4, there are devout individuals who support liberal values and democracy in both countries. Both countries have also differed with regard to state-religion relations.

Tunisia had long implemented a French style laïcité, which Kuru (2009) refers to as "assertive secularism," in which the state suppresses the public manifestations of religion and bans Islamist organizations. Egypt, while ostensibly secular in practice, paid lip service to the Islamic principles in its constitution. Historically, the Egyptian regime has used a combination of carrots and sticks to control numerous religious organizations. Both countries have a long history of institutionalization of religion and have claimed leadership roles in Islamic learning through well-respected schools of Islamic jurisprudence. Al-Azhar in Egypt and Ez-Zitouna in Tunisia have been reputable institutions of Islamic higher education since the early period of Islamic expansion. The primacy of state-religion relations continues to shape the social and political dynamics in Egypt and Tunisia, in addition to their possessing diverse religious landscapes. Both settings, thus, provide many opportunities for studying religious outlooks and their evolution over time.

Religious Landscape in Egypt and Tunisia

In Egypt, the Muslim Brothers (MB) have remained the dominant Islamist organization active in the social and political spheres since the 1950s. The relationship between the regime and the MB has generally been contentious since its founding (El-Ghobashy 2005; Masoud 2014; Mitchell 1993). However, numerous offshoots have split from this organization to form such radical groups as Al-Gama'a al-Islamiyya (Kepel 1985) and moderate groups like Al-Wasat (Wickham 2004). Thus, the MB has historically encompassed religiously conservative and more liberal factions but was unable to keep them under one roof due to ideological disagreements. Presumably, the splits within any organization are indicative of schisms among its members. These schisms can be tied to disagreement about strategy, ideology, and different religious outlooks within the membership body. While greater ideological homogeneity is more likely in marginal and niche groups, it is only natural that a large organization like the MB will look more like a microcosm of the population of the pious in Egypt. Hence, one factor that may lead to splits could be divergent religious outlooks held by its members. In many cases, the divergence can be seen among those with what we classify as post-Islamist and those with religious communitarian outlooks (Wickham 2004, 2013).[3]

In addition to radical and moderate groups, the Egyptian religious scene has witnessed a surge of Saudi-backed Salafi groups since the 1990s (Al-Anani and Malik 2013). The regime in Egypt found strategic value in supporting Salafi groups to balance the rising influence of the MB. Most Salafi leaders were under the influence of Saudi clerics, and they successfully mobilized devout individuals partly through the use of remittances streaming in from Gulf countries (Karakoç, Köse, and Özcan 2017). Salafis have usually taken a politically passive strategy, but as social mobilizers, they have been highly active in neighborhood associations, as well as nationally televised programs since the mid-1990s. There is diversity in religious outlooks between and within Salafi groups, and most Salafis have chosen a peaceful and quietist stance in social and political affairs, but violent jihadi organizations have also emerged within these organizations.[4]

As highlighted in chapter 2, religious communities in high levels of tension with society, often in the strict or ultrastrict niche, have good reason to eschew participation in the political status quo as they cannot mobilize effective numbers for change that would benefit the radical vision of social order espoused by the group. Therefore, outside of a protective alliance with the state or powerful elites, these groups often choose one of two dramatic poles: quietism or revolutionary radical and violent action. Such groups, especially those that choose the latter, are a tiny minority of the devout population and do not meaningfully appear even in representative samples of public opinion surveys. Thus, for our purpose, the focus below is limited primarily to peaceful Salafi groups, especially those who chose to become active in the political realm.

Finally, Egypt has also seen the rise of a new genre of devout youth who have reconciled Islam with pluralistic values and human rights (Bayat 2007). These individuals are not traditional Islamists to the extent that they do not mobilize under the roof of a formal organization. Their devotion is personal, and they are fierce supporters of rights and liberty. Some of these young people were instrumental in the initiation of uprisings. It is evident that individuals who reconcile Islam with pluralistic values will also be among the membership body of other organizations, such as Salafi groups and the MB, and compose a group most often fitting our post-Islamist religious outlook category. This specific group of youth under consideration, however, prefer not to be affiliated with any formal religious political organization, and most of them would fit in our category of religious individualist.

Tunisia under Bourguiba, on the other hand, since independence from France in 1956 followed a militant secularism that has removed religion from the public sphere and repressed religious civil society. The secular regime's closure of al-Zitouna University was intended to undermine the Islamist mobilization that had been instrumental during the independence era. The Tunisian autocracy's posture toward religion was never friendly, and the notable Islamist group Ennahda was officially banned as a political party. Yet despite repressive religious policies, numerous religious groups, including Ennahda and Salafi organizations, survived the regime and flourished after the uprisings because Islam remained entwined in the nation's social fabric despite the strong secularist policies and repression of religion. Like the MB in Egypt, Ennahda used its flexible, informal, organizational advantage and grassroots activities to emerge as the strongest contender in the postuprising environment (Anderson 2011; Bayat 2017; McCarthy 2018).

Tunisian Salafi groups attempted to take advantage of the democratic opening, but at the same time, they had to operate under the strict secularist policies. This environment served the goals of jihadi Salafis, who exploited the system to advance their causes (Cavatorta 2015), but eventually it led to their marginalization due to the common front formed by democratic-leaning actors against jihadi ideology and violence. At first sight, it looks like Tunisian Salafis are more homogenous than their counterparts in Egypt. However, a closer look will demonstrate a diverse group with multiple tendencies.

For example, Merone (2017) argues that Ansar al-Sharia has always held double tendencies. During its emergence in 2011, some of its members envisioned it as a social and political movement that strives to build an appealing national strategy. On the flip side, it had a radical tendency toward violence. The organization swung between these tendencies, but it eventually succumbed to the radical ideology (Merone 2017). Like Ennahda and the MB, Ansar provides a prime example of changing organizational preferences in response to a dramatic shift in the existing environment. Just as the splits within Islamist groups may be indicative of distributions of religious outlooks of their members, these tendencies of Ansar could be sign of a similar inclination in marginal organizations. It is hard to tell if this is the case without in-depth studies of these organizations and their members. However, it is reasonable to assume that within the religious landscape of Tunisia, religious outlooks played a role in changing the ideology and strategies of Ennahda and radical groups like Ansar. Thus, it is to the temporal analysis of religious outlooks in Egypt and Tunisia that we now turn.

How Did the Arab Spring Outcomes Shape Religious Outlooks?

Given the diversity of religious landscapes in Egypt and Tunisia, how are religious outlooks structured in those countries? It is evident that a binary continuum of less to more religious or secular versus Islamist cannot

Table 6.1. Average Religiosity in Egypt and Tunisia (2010–2013)

Country	Wave	Obs.	Mean of Religiosity	Std. Deviation	Min	Max	Std. (0–1) Mean
Egypt	AB-II	1,148	10	1.9	3	12	0.82
Egypt	AB-III	1,126	13.2	1.9	5	15	0.86
Tunisia	AB-II	1,173	7.7	2.7	1	12	0.61
Tunisia	AB-III	1,193	11.8	2.8	2	15	0.75

Notes: The average religiosity is an index of responses to questions about prayer frequency, religious attendance, and Koran readership as reported in the two waves of the Arab Barometer. The scale of religiosity index varies by survey wave and country based on the availability of survey questions asking about religious practices.
Source: Arab Barometer, Waves II and III.

capture the ideology and behavior of pious individuals. As the summary of distributions in table 6.1 demonstrates, both populations exhibit high levels of religiosity, but in general, Egyptian citizens appear to be more pious than Tunisian citizens. The results from Wave III (conducted in the spring of 2013) of the Arab Barometer show the highest average religiosity relative to the other waves at a point when religious political parties in both countries had strong influence in government. This is an interesting empirical observation, but it does not provide any insights about changing outlooks or preferences of religious individuals in either setting.[5] Pious individuals may shift their positions about state, religion, secularism, and democracy while the extent of their piety along a continuum of less to more religious remains unchanged. Thus, we need to examine the available data for changing preferences and distributions of outlooks to fully answer these questions.

The preferences of Islamist and religious groups about various issues do not necessarily overlap with the views implied by our conceptual classification of religious outlooks. It is not our intention, for example, to classify Salafis as equivalent to religious communitarians or to place all Ennahda voters within the post-Islamist category; it is likely that these organizations have membership that includes individuals of both religious outlooks. Not all Tunisian Salafis are religious communitarians, nor can they be characterized with a distinct outlook that captures the violent extremist ideology of some.

Besides the pluralism in religious outlooks among Islamic and Islamist organizations, it is likely that temporal variation will be observed from case to case. For example, Ennahda has shifted its position throughout the post–Arab

Spring transition period in response to the political environment and its strategic interactions with the other actors in the system (McCarthy 2018). There were times when Ennahda resembled a religious conservative movement, but during the transition phase, the party made appeals and took positions that would resonate with post-Islamist and social communitarian outlooks (Boubekeur 2016; Somer 2017; Stepan and Linz 2013). Although these two outlooks should result in conflicting preferences, research suggests that Islamist parties may demonstrate vacillations in their ideology and behavior in responding to the contextual imperatives as exemplified in the strategies of Islamist political parties, including Parti Islam Se-Malaysia (PAS) in Malaysia, Islah in Yemen, and the Justice and Development Party (AKP) in Turkey (Wuthrich and Ciftci 2020). This ambivalent strategy, in effect, proved to be highly instrumental in the success of the Tunisian experiment. Notably, Salafi movements in both Egypt and Tunisia have shown a great deal of flexibility in their ideology and strategy (Al-Anani and Malik, 2013; Cavatorta 2015; Merone 2017).

Examining how the strategies of mainstream religious groups evolve in response to the requirements of the political competition can provide important insights about the changing preferences of religious individuals who may adjust their preferences stemming from religious outlooks. We illustrate this point by first looking at the evolution of MB and Salafi strategies since 2011. At the beginning of the protests in Egypt, neither Salafi groups nor the MB took an active role. However, both groups increased their activism as it became evident that the ancien régime would eventually fall. In the historic free legislative elections in 2011–2012, the political wing of the MB, the Freedom and Justice Party (FJP), won 45 percent of the seats in the lower house and 58 percent of the seats in the upper house. In the presidential elections, the MB candidate Muhammad Morsi narrowly defeated the establishment candidate Ahmed Shafiq to become the first democratically elected head of state in Egypt. In this context, and to the surprise of observers of Egyptian politics, Salafis formed political parties, quickly adapted to the pluralistic environments, and made significant gains in the political arena.

The MB were no foreigners to the intricacies of the political scene. As such, they have maneuvered frequently against the state and have shifted their positions on various issues regarding Islam and politics numerous times. The transformation of the MB—from holding relatively rigid Islamist positions to a reformist stance that aimed to reconcile Islam and democracy—reached a new milestone in the new millennium. In its 2007 party program, the MB increasingly shifted its rhetoric toward "Islamic constitutionalism," which drew on

Islamic doctrine but also promoted such ideas as executive constraint, rule of law, and protection of civil/political rights (Haas and Lesch 2013). These efforts resonate with the expected behavior of individuals holding a post-Islamist outlook. This trend continued with the FJP's emphasis on the "civil state" (*al-dawla al-madanīya*) in the legislative elections; however, the FJP and Morsi shifted their appeals and actions to fit the inclinations of religious communitarians during the presidential elections. This later swing can be explained with the rising appeal of Salafi parties among the pious citizens to the extent that they consistently took religious communitarian positions on various issues. Thus, while advocating relatively liberal policies in one election, when faced with a formidable challenger, the MB did not hesitate to maneuver toward conservative ideology in the next election. This balancing act was clearly demonstrated in Morsi's statements about Israel. On some occasions, Morsi would state assurances about Egyptian commitment to international agreements and recognition of Israel's right to exist as a state. On other occasions, he would vow to free Jerusalem (Nordland 2012), mainly targeting Islamist-leaning voters.[6]

Salafis, too, detached themselves from the protests during the initial stages of the uprisings since, presumably, their ideology was of quietist Sunni doctrine. Some Salafi leaders called for obedience to the Mubarak regime in the face of political instability (Al-Anani and Malik 2013; Haas and Lesch 2013). However, during the transition period, they have significantly shifted their position vis-à-vis political participation. Before the Egyptian uprisings, Salafis concentrated their efforts on preaching (*da'wa*) and other religious activities. They were adept at seizing political opportunities during the transition stage. For example, some Salafi groups have adopted positions that appeal to individuals with religious communitarian outlooks, promoting the strict implementation of sharia and leaning toward social conservative policies, including gender segregation in the public sphere. Some see democracy as *bid'a* (innovation) and view pluralistic institutions with great skepticism (Al-Anani and Malik 2013). Yet they participated in the formal political sphere by forming several parties and engaging in negotiations with multiple actors. These various strategies arguably reflect the influence of the intraorganizational distribution of different religious outlooks within the membership body.

What needs to be examined here is whether these different positions are evidence of a paradigmatic shift in Salafi religious doctrine. According to two observers of Egyptian politics, the answer is no. Al-Anani and Malik (2013, 67) state that "almost all Salafis are looking at the political participation as a means to strengthen the Islamic identity of Egypt, and to assert the Islamic character of the society, which they perceive as a legitimate and noble aspiration. They have, however, remained silent on the acceptance of the concept of political pluralism, which is a fundamental building block of democracy." Thus, their shift in stance toward political participation can be viewed as a strategic adaptation in response to changing political circumstances rather than the immediate evolution of their ideology (Shamaileh 2017).

Just as these religious groups change their positions in responding to the political environment, we can expect pious individuals to adjust their preferences in relation to social cohesion and state-religion relations as context changes. For example, those holding a religious individualist outlook may fully support democracy when elites make concessions to ease transitions. Such a change is likely to be viewed as a move toward a pluralistic system, and this may be highly desirable for religious individualists. Religious communitarians may be threatened by a full swing toward democracy insofar as transition would endanger some of their gains. However, if they can exert a degree of control on posttransition gains by shaping institutional design through democracy, they may take a supportive position. Religious outlooks are likely to influence preferences for democracy, yet the direction of that preference should depend on how they perceive democratic institutions will influence pluralism and contributions to the formation of a more religious public domain.

One can come up with numerous shifting positions for each outlook category contingent on the context. As a result, assessing the empirical evidence about the distribution of religious outlook groups as well as their changing preferences would be the best course of action to examine the temporal change in these outlooks and the related attitudes. In the remainder of this chapter, we present empirical analysis that traces patterns of religious outlooks and shifting political preferences among the religious individuals in Egypt and Tunisia during the extraordinary uprisings and the transition period.

Temporal Variation in Religious Outlooks: Empirical Analysis

We use Waves II and III of the Arab Barometer since these surveys include the necessary items to conduct LCA and multivariate analyses. Wave I was not carried out in Egypt and Tunisia, and Wave IV lacks many of the items used in LCA analysis as well as some of the measures of democratic orientations in the Egyptian surveys. The timing and scope of the fieldwork does not allow the measurement of the change in religious preferences and political attitudes before and after the uprisings. Rather, the data are conducive to providing an evaluation of religious outlooks and their impact on regime preferences at the onset of the protests and comparing these to their counterparts during the early transition period. The Egyptian surveys were conducted in June, and the Tunisian surveys were conducted in September–October 2011 for Wave II. The fieldwork dates for Wave III are reported as March–April 2013 for the Egyptian sample and February 2013 for the Tunisia surveys.

At first sight, it may look like the period between the two waves of Arab Barometer surveys is not long enough to warrant the analysis of shifts in religious outlooks and political preferences. However, significant social and political developments had taken place before or between these dates. In Egypt, some of these developments include the first free legislative and presidential elections since the 1950s, the Morsi presidency, and the tension between the military and the MB on the eve of the military takeover in July 2013. In Tunisia, noteworthy events include the free elections, Ennahda's first electoral plurality, successful coalition building geared toward democratic transition, and several terrorist attacks carried out by new radical groups, including jihadi Salafists, inside Tunisia. Given such significant developments in a short period, were there real shifts in religious outlooks? Before we move on to assess the data, we note that our analysis is by no means suited to observe shifts in religious outlooks at the individual level; nor do we claim to map these shifts onto changes in the ideology of the organizations. In the lack of panel data covering a relatively long period of observations for the same set of subjects and the lack of in-depth analysis of organizations at the time of the uprisings, we can only assess the aggregate change in the membership distribution of religious outlook categories within representative national survey samples.

In LCA estimations, the same set of items are used to rule out any effects associated with the question wording or different survey questions. This strategy results in fewer questions in the LCA analysis; however, it has the advantage of instrument validity in testing our proposition about the temporal change in religious outlooks. Since surveys are not panel data, this approach is the best alternative for controlling the possible effects related to sampling and other survey techniques. Table 6.2 shows the survey questions used in the LCA analysis.

Five items are available in both waves, but the question asking for respondents' views about having neighbors from other religions was not asked in Wave III (Q6021). An alternative item evaluating respondents' views about the rights of non-Muslims in a Muslim-majority country (Q6072) was used. Together, these six questions provide a comparable set of survey items to

Table 6.2. Survey Questions Used in LCA Analysis

Item Description	Arab Barometer Code	Response Scale
The government and parliament should enact laws in accordance with Islamic Law.	Q6052	4-point scale of strongly disagree to strongly agree
Which group you would not like as neighbors (Non-Muslims)?	Q6021 (AB-II)*	Dichotomous response (0-Do not want, 1-Do not object)
Religious minorities should practice freely.	Q6087	4-point scale of absolutely disagree to strongly agree
Religious leaders should not interfere in voters' decisions.	Q6061	4-point scale of strongly disagree to strongly agree
Religious leaders should have influence over government decisions.	Q6063	4-point scale of strongly disagree to strongly agree
Religious practice is private and should be separate from public life.	Q6064	4-point scale of strongly disagree to strongly agree

*Another question (Q6072) substituted for this question in the third wave. This question asks about whether respondents agree with the statement that in a Muslim country, non-Muslims should enjoy fewer rights.
Source: Arab Barometer, Wave III.

classify individuals according to their social, political, and religious preferences. They present a good overview of individuals' opinions about the role of religion in politics, conformity, and plurality in religious affairs.

Figure 6.1 shows the change in class shares over time based on LCA class probabilities among the Egyptian and Tunisian respondents. In Egypt, we see a noticeable decline in the class share of the social communitarian outlook from Wave II to Wave III (between 2011 to 2013). The class shares of religious communitarians, in contrast, jumps from 18 percent to over 30 percent, and those of the religious individualists, from 18 to 28 percent. In Tunisia, the class share of social communitarians drops from 48 to 25 percent, whereas the difference in the class shares of other outlooks increases, but at a smaller rate between the two waves. The largest increase is observed in the class share of religious individualists, which jumps from 20 to 30 percent. According to these results, we can be fairly confident that next to cross-national variation, the data corroborate the temporal variation in the distribution of religious outlooks in Egypt and Tunisia.

We interpret these findings cautiously, because the time span is short and the samples in the two waves are different. Individual propensity toward

Change in Religious Outlooks and Political Preferences | 161

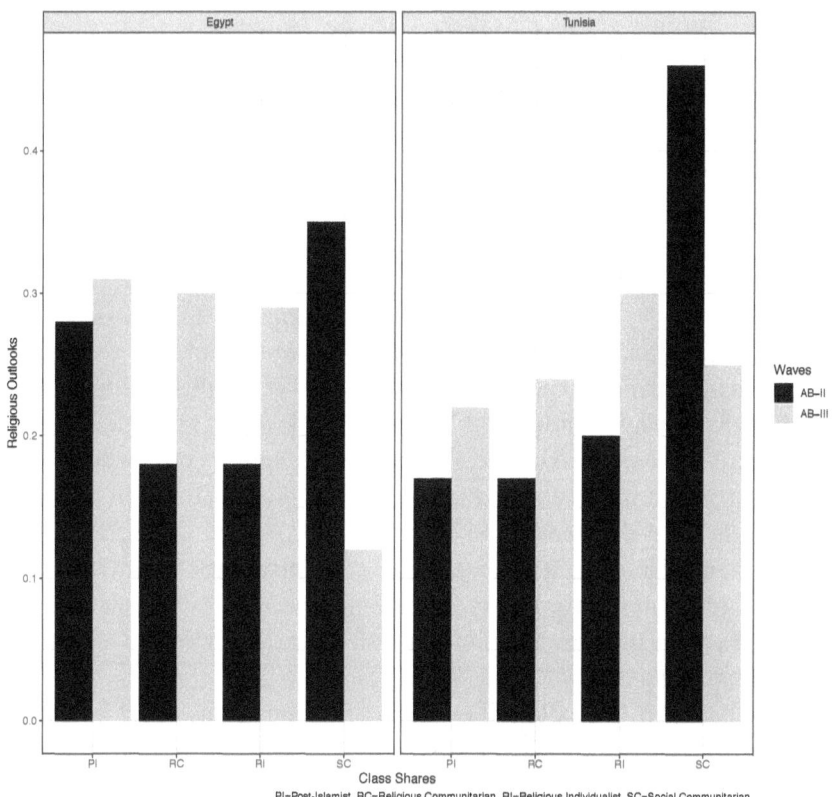

Figure 6.1. Change in Class Shares over Time. The bars show class shares according to the LCA estimations in each wave of the Arab Barometer. *PI*, post-Islamist; *RC*, religious communitarian; *SC*, social communitarian. Source: Arab Barometer.

certain religious outlooks is not likely to change in the short run. However, these changes can occur more swiftly during times of social upheaval and political transitions, such as the Arab uprisings of 2010–2011. This can explain the significant decrease in the share of the social communitarian category in both countries. Uncertainty in the economic and political future of the country, the rapid rise and fall of Salafi groups, and successful coalition building and compromise in the aftermath of terrorist attacks in Tunisia might have been reflected in the reshuffling of individuals who lean toward each of these religious outlook categories. In Egypt, there was disappointment with the whole process. The disillusionment of individuals with the status quo might have led them to search for alternatives to the existing situation. In other words, the sharp decrease in the class share of social communitarians may be due to the public's demand for alternative social / political arrangements against the background of uncertainty and fragile conditions in the aftermath of the protests.

What explains the shift in religious outlooks in contexts like this? Based on the theoretical discussion in chapter 1 and 2, we would argue that as the regime structure of the state entered a period of transition, it changed the calculus of religious communities and their tension dynamic with the state. New opportunities and electoral competition for governing power opened the door to political engagement to groups who would not have considered it previously. Furthermore, the success or failure of Islamist political organizations as they enter the political sphere likely facilitates the recalibration of religious outlooks among individuals from religious communities who see their position in society as adjacent to those groups. Thus, for example, Salafis, whose level of tension with the previous regime removed any real hope of benefit from political engagement, suddenly saw an environment in which the state "moved closer" to them, at least in potential, and this triggered a move in many Salafi members from quietism toward a religious communitarian position.

The change in the political approach of organizations could be understood as the consequence of multiple dynamics during the transition period. First, as mentioned above, reassessments of the level of tension between the individual and their religious communities with the state likely encouraged transformations of religious outlooks. At the same time, many of these Islamist organizations were likely configured by individuals with multiple religious outlooks. For Salafis, prior to a major transition, one would have likely found individuals who were religious communitarian, social communitarian, or even post-Islamist. Among the MB in Egypt and Ennahda in Tunisia, religious communitarians and post-Islamists were evident. Under more stable conditions, the leadership of such organizations adhere to a dominant outlook while the other outlooks stay in a subordinate, dissenting position. When dramatic sociopolitical change occurs, the "outlook balance" in an organization can tip, causing some to shift their outlook to new strategic realities while others maintain their outlook, but their fortunes and influence within the organization may change. New visions of Islamist parties and organizations may not be from new converts to a particular outlook but an internal reconfiguration of an already existing balance of power among differing outlook holders. On some level, both of these dynamics are often at work within organizations experiencing a change in their political environment. As an organization realigns to a dominant outlook and subsequent approach to politics, it can also gain new members or lose others due to the success or failure of the approach and the preferences of individuals in their broader social context.

According to figure 6.1, the class shares of religious communitarians significantly increase from Wave II to Wave III in Egypt, whereas a similar but less pronounced pattern is observed especially among post-Islamists in Tunisia. Given the limitations in Tunisia on post-Islamist mobilization in support of a religious yet pluralistic order prior to the Arab Spring, the revolution may have significantly opened up avenues for recruitment and strengthened the position of moderate Islamic organizations. In Egypt, where such organizations were already afforded significant space to operate, it is likely that we saw little movement toward the post-Islamist position because there was little room for growth in such an outlook. Such shifts in outlooks may have been due to a perception of what was viable for Egypt given the changes in the political environment.

To better understand the shifts in religious outlooks, it is necessary to examine the distribution of probabilities for these outlooks along the religiosity index. We follow our strategy in the previous chapters by creating a religiosity index from self-reported measures of religious behavior. The analysis presented below focuses on moderately to highly religious individuals and drops the less religious individuals from the sample. The responses to these questions are recorded along a four- or five-point scale ranging from the least to most frequent religious practice. All respondents whose responses are coded as "never" and "rarely" are dropped to obtain a sample of moderately and highly religious individuals. Figures 6.2 and 6.3 map the class probabilities along the religiosity index for each wave of the Arab Barometer surveys in Egypt and Tunisia, respectively.

Figure 6.2 shows a nuanced picture about the shifting patterns of class shares between the two waves for Egypt. The level of religiosity is concentrated at the higher end of the distribution of religiosity, and there are relatively few observations at the lower end.[7] There is a significantly lower probability of being a religious individualist at the higher end of the religious distribution in Wave II as opposed to Wave III, where the probability of being a religious individualist remains uniform throughout the distribution but also demonstrates two spikes at the low and high end of the religiosity index. For the social communitarian category, we observe a significant decline in the class share from the second to the third wave. The fluctuating pattern of this group's probability along the religiosity index in Wave II is replaced with a

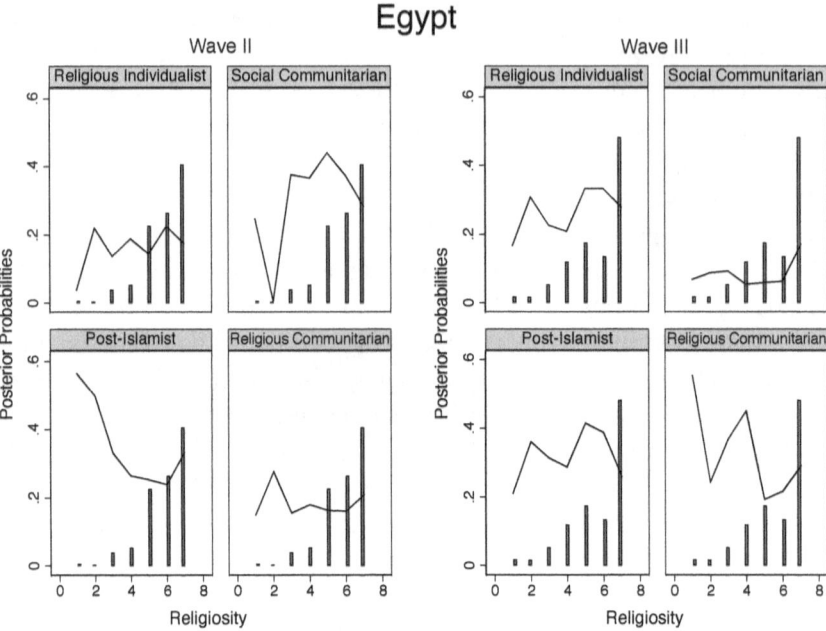

Figure 6.2. Temporal Change in Religiosity and Class Probabilities in Egypt. The bars represent the fraction of religious for all outlooks combined, and the line represents probabilities of class membership for each outlook. Source: Arab Barometer, Waves II and III.

seemingly more consistently decreasing distribution in Wave III. The probability of belonging to the post-Islamist outlook is higher at the low levels of religiosity during Wave II. In contrast, the probability of being a post-Islamist remains high throughout with two spikes at the low and high ends of the religiosity index in Wave III. The distribution of class probabilities for the religious communitarian group is erratic in Wave III, but generally the highest probabilities for membership in this group can be found at the medium to high levels of religiosity. In Wave II, the probability of being a religious communitarian is highest at low and medium levels of religiosity, but in Wave III, religious communitarians can be seen at all levels of piety.

We can explain these shifts when we interpret the changes in different religious outlooks together and in relation to the developments that were unfolding between 2011 and 2014 in Egypt. The transition period was not managed well in Egypt. As the old status quo was shattered, a new normal did not emerge quickly. As a result, the social communitarian outlook declined significantly, and at the same time, it could be seen at all levels of piety, especially with no status quo appearing on the horizon. This argument could also explain the similar distribution of religious communitarians in Wave II but their diverging trajectories in Wave III.

In Tunisia, we see a decreasing trend in the overall probability of being a religious individualist as religiosity increases in Wave II, but the class shares and associated probabilities of this outlook remain quite large among the highly pious in Wave III (fig. 6.3). The share of social communitarians is much larger in Tunisia than it is in Egypt. Figure 6.3 shows that social communitarians are evenly distributed along the religiosity continuum in both waves. The distribution of post-Islamist outlook, on the other hand, remains almost the same between the two waves, yet its share increases slightly from the time of the uprisings to the transition period. Individuals holding the post-Islamist outlook could be either less or more religious, but less religious were more likely to hold this outlook during the uprisings (Wave II). Conversely, during the transition period (Wave III), a relatively large percentage of individuals is cumulated at the low levels of the religiosity index. Finally, religious communitarians are more likely to be found at the moderate to high end of the continuum in Wave II, but one can observe this outlook among the moderately religious in Wave III. However, similar to Egypt, the overall distribution of the religious communitarian outlook demonstrates an erratic pattern in Tunisia for the analysis of Wave III.

What explains the distribution of these patterns in Tunisia? By and large, religious individualists continued to hold a large share of membership within the four religious outlook categories. From the uprisings to the transition period, visible shifts could be observed in the religious individualist and post-Islamist categories in Tunisia. The dynamic coalition-building efforts, several terrorist attacks, radicalization of the youth, and Ennahda's shifting positions could explain this turbulence in the class distribution of the post-Islamist outlook. The somehow decreasing appeal of the social communitarian outlook in Egypt vis-à-vis Tunisia might be indicative of the desire for change during these turbulent times.

Temporal Variation in Religious Outlooks and Support for Democracy

The analysis the Arab Barometer demonstrates that even over a short period, religious outlooks can shift. The data in hand are not panel data and, as such, are not suited to trace the change in religious outlooks of the same individuals

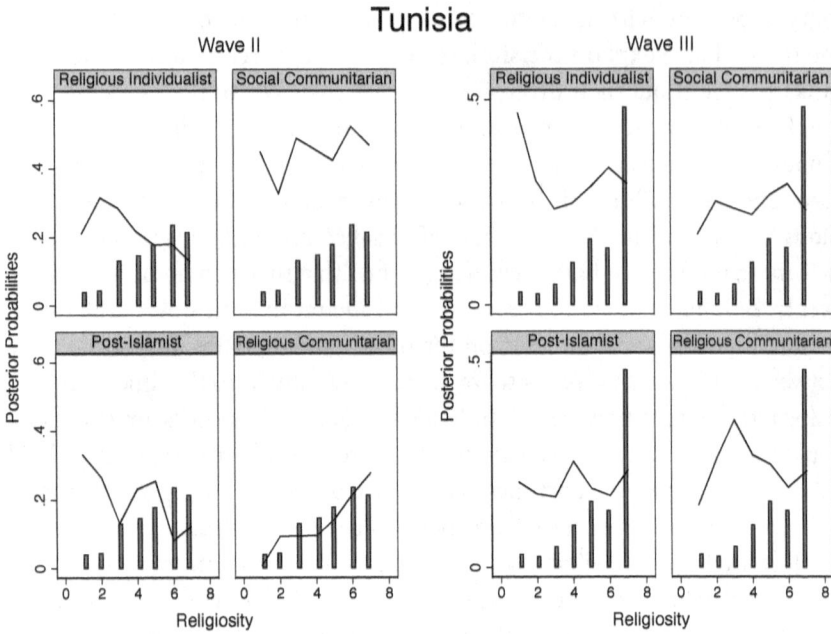

Figure 6.3. Temporal Change in Religiosity and Class Probabilities in Tunisia. The bars represent the fraction of religious and the line represents probabilities of class membership for each outlook. Source: Arab Barometer, Waves II and III.

over time. However, on average, the class share of each religious outlook category and the distribution of these outlooks along the less- to more-religious continuum change over time. What are the implications of these shifts in religious outlooks for political attitudes? Can we expect our theoretical propositions to hold when religious outlooks shift as a result of dramatic events? To answer these questions, the same multivariate models used in chapter 5 are run utilizing the two waves of the Arab Barometer surveys.

The same dependent variable, overt support for democracy (Klingemann 1999; Inglehart and Welzel 2003), is used in the statistical estimations. To reiterate, this item is a subtractive index of two items:

> I will describe different political systems to you, and I want to ask you about your opinion of each one of them with regard to the country's governance—for each one would you say it is very good, good, bad, or very bad?
> A democratic political system (Q517.1)
> A political system with an authoritarian president (non-democratic) who is indifferent to parliament and elections (Q517.2)

Both questions are recoded to range from very bad (1) to very good (4). The resulting subtractive index of overt support for democracy ranges from −3 (weak support for democracy) to +3 (strong support). The distribution of responses along this index presents an interesting pattern. During the uprisings (Wave II), 49 percent of the respondents very strongly support democracy (a score of 3 in the index) in Egypt, whereas this figure drops to 41 percent during the transition period (Wave III). The same figures are 45 and 55 percent in Tunisia. At the lower end of the index (0 to −3), the proportion of nonsupporters increases from 7 to 14 percent in Egypt and from 6 to 12 percent in Tunisia. The loss of enthusiasm for democracy between the two waves may be indicative of the turbulent transition, especially in Egypt. In contrast, the successful management and negotiation of transition in the only success story of the Arab spring, Tunisia, might have increased support for democracy, but skepticism remains in Tunisia as well. Given this aggregate change in support for democracy, does the shift in religious outlooks introduce variation in attitudes toward a democratic system?

Table 6.3 answers this question by reporting the results of the OLS regression estimations. We use the same specification as presented in chapter 5. The models include three dichotomous variables for religious individualist, post-Islamist, and religious communitarian outlooks, and we reserve the social communitarian outlook as the reference category for comparison to the other religious outlooks. In addition, the models control for trust, economic perceptions, and various demographic factors. The results of the analysis show a pattern that suggests that the changing domestic political context led individuals with the same religious outlooks to interpret ideal political preferences differently at different points in the transition. The attitudes toward democracy shift as these individuals in the various outlook categories take stock of developments on the ground.

In the models measuring support for democracy in Egypt in the two survey waves, attitudes to democracy appear to shift primarily by degree, if at all, across the religious outlooks. In 2010 and 2011, all categories show significant support for democracy relative to the social communitarian outlook. This should not be seen as surprising. Social communitarians represent the outlook that most prefers the status quo, which, in the Egyptian case, was a fairly socially liberal authoritarian regime that had long espoused fears that an opening toward democracy would embolden opposition Islamist elements and push Egypt toward a more religious state (Lust 2011). In such a context, we would expect that all the other religious outlook

Table 6.3. Religious Outlooks and Support for Democracy: OLS Regression Results

	Model 1 Egypt, Wave II	Model 2 Egypt, Wave III	Model 3 Tunisia, Wave II	Model 4 Tunisia, Wave III
Religious communitarian	0.24*	0.26	0.40***	0.22
	(0.10)	(0.15)	(0.12)	(0.14)
Post-Islamist	0.33***	1.00***	0.51***	−0.0025
	(0.09)	(0.15)	(0.12)	(0.16)
Religious individualist	0.35***	0.93***	0.21	−0.24
	(0.10)	(0.15)	(0.12)	(0.15)
Personal trust	−0.074	−0.36***	0.0094	−0.27*
	(0.07)	(0.10)	(0.09)	(0.12)
Political trust	−0.038*	−0.011	−0.013	0.035
	(0.02)	(0.02)	(0.02)	(0.02)
Political interest	0.025	−0.12*	0.053	0.12*
	(0.04)	(0.05)	(0.05)	(0.05)
Egalitarian gender beliefs	0.041*	0.033	0.028	0.13***
	(0.02)	(0.02)	(0.03)	(0.03)
Personal economic expectations	−0.11*	−0.11	−0.035	−0.15
	(0.05)	(0.07)	(0.06)	(0.08)
Sociotropic economic expectations	0.12**	−0.016	0.15**	0.14**
	(0.04)	(0.03)	(0.06)	(0.05)
Age	0.0021	−0.0023	0.00031	−0.010**
	(0.00)	(0.00)	(0.00)	(0.00)
Female	−0.030	−0.10	−0.088	−0.072
	(0.08)	(0.08)	(0.10)	(0.12)
Education	−0.019	0.018	0.022	−0.041
	(0.02)	(0.02)	(0.03)	(0.04)
Income	0.026	0.26***	0.021	−0.034
	(0.04)	(0.05)	(0.05)	(0.06)
Constant	1.76***	1.12***	1.19**	0.81*
	(0.27)	(0.32)	(0.37)	(0.39)
Observations	786	778	414	552

Note: Standard errors in parentheses; * $p < .05$, ** $p < 0.01$, *** $p < .001$.
Source: Arab Barometer, Waves II and III.

categories would look more favorably toward democracy although they would likely do so for different reasons. The patterns of support for democracy by the religious outlook categories harmonize with these expectations.

Model 2 in table 6.3 captures the sentiment of attitudes toward democracy by the outlook categories from the vantage point of 2013. Here, although the coefficient for support for democracy by religious communitarians relative to the social communitarians in Egypt is still positive, it is no longer significant at $p < .05$. The experiences of democratic participation for individuals within this outlook, which hopes to implement policy change, may have somewhat reduced the robustness of their enthusiasm that democracy was the best course of action to enact the necessary changes. According to the Arab Barometer, the mean scores of individuals in the category of social communitarian were far lower in 2013 than they were in 2010. For those supporting the conditions of the status quo, the transitional period only strengthened their relative antagonism to the democratic experience and desire to return to the previous order. On the other hand, support for democracy among the other two categories, religious individualists and post-Islamists, showed less fatigue in 2013 and showed stronger coefficients in relative comparison. Within the course of the Egyptian transition, it does not appear that support for democracy waned as much among those who more strongly support religious pluralism; if anything, the transitional period continued to show the value of democratic institutions for individuals among the outlook categories who supported religious pluralism more strongly.

Models 3 and 4, the Tunisian contexts, show some important contrasts to what is observed for Egypt. During the 2010–2011 period of the second wave of the survey, the relationship between social communitarians and the secular authoritarian Tunisian state made the two outlooks most favorable to religion in the public sphere (religious communitarians and post-Islamists) far more supportive of democracy than the social communitarian reference category. In the Tunisian context, the religious individualists, due to their greater support for keeping religion in the private sphere, would be the outlook most aligned in comparing the merits of the secular Tunisian state with the prospect of democratization and the likelihood of religion filling a more prominent role in such a change. Thus, although the coefficient of support for democracy among the religious individualists is positive, it is not $p < .05$ significantly different than the perspective of the social communitarians in Tunisia.

By 2013, major shifts in attitudes toward democracy had occurred across the individuals grouped into each of these outlook categories, as can be observed in model 4. The Tunisian transitional period appears to have led all religious outlook categories to wane in their support of democracy relative to the social communitarians. For religious individualists and post-Islamists, the coefficient switches to negative, although not significant, and the religious communitarian category stays positive but loses significance. This fairly dramatic change is caused by shifts in attitude on both sides of the reference category, with overall attitudes toward democracy higher among the social communitarians in the 2013 survey than those in 2010.

The data and the statistical analysis presented here are not fully conducive to pinpointing the exact mechanisms that engendered these patterns. The developments in postuprising Tunisia could help us explain these results. Coming from a religious communitarian, post-Islamist, and religious individualist perspective, political developments during the transitional period might have engendered uncertainties that caused each of these groups to take stock of the relative merits of democracy. This is in fact a healthy sign for democratization creating a dynamic similar to the notion of critical citizens (Norris 2011), who question the utility and functioning of democracy. The effective (in)ability to implement religious policy at the state level, the costs to religious groups of being involved with politics and governance, and the dangers of revising the previous regime's secular status quo likely buffeted the enthusiasm of these three groups toward democratization. At the same time, the developing power balance between the various outlook perspectives and the pressure toward reconciliation among different groups likely encouraged social communitarians to believe that democratization might be a stable solution that could prevent any of the other groups from holding sway. This was especially true as it was becoming clear that political groups with the status quo position in Tunisia would be able to stay influential and relevant within the new democratic system.[8]

One interesting pattern that is consistent across the Egyptian and Tunisian case is that the transition experience creates a relative waning interest in democracy for religious communitarians. In-depth studies concerning the preferences of religious communitarian individuals as well as studies of communitarian organizations will certainly help put this result in perspective. The benefits of transitioning from an authoritarian state to a democracy for groups that see the merits of majoritarian rule for policy change might have proved to be stronger in theory as democratization approached, and it likely became elusive in practice and experience. Even when Islamist parties received strong electoral support and took governing positions in each country, the ability to enact policy, govern with accountability, and maintain support from citizens turned out to be a far more difficult endeavor than likely anticipated. Such dynamics inherent in democracy appear to have caused some souring in the democratic preferences of religious communitarians in both Egypt and Tunisia. These results and our own reading of them should be taken with a grain of salt due to a lack of additional data and inability to conduct robustness tests. However, it can be reasonably inferred from the estimation results in table 6.3 that the difference between the three religious outlooks and the social communitarians is significantly different between Wave II and Wave III. In the case of Egypt, we do not have a significant result, but all else being equal, the predicted level of support for democracy among religious communitarians relative to social communitarians is slightly larger than in Wave II. In Tunisia, even though the comparable coefficient is smaller, overall support for democracy increases.

Conclusion

Overall, several conclusions follow the analysis presented here. Although the results of the analysis in table 6.3 do not uniformly agree with the overall outcomes from the analysis in chapter 5, the results strongly support several of the most foundational arguments laid out beginning in chapter 1. The present chapter drives home the key assertion that change in context and time matters a great deal in the relationship between religion and attitudes. Between the populations in the representative samples from 2010–2011 and 2013 in Tunisia and Egypt, not only have the distributions of religious outlooks changed, but the consequences in attitude positions of those outlooks changed in significant ways in both cases, particularly in Tunisia. Relative to one's political context, the attitudes toward regime-type preferences are formed by different calculations depending on the likely consequences of the status quo or change in such issues as religious policy or support for pluralism and the amount of religious activity one desires to see in the public sphere. In changing circumstances, outlooks can adjust, but also the implications of those outlooks on attitudes toward policy can adjust, and this is the case because the role of religion and its influence on the individual is largely relational and dynamic, not simply substantive or doctrinal and static.

The fact that these outlooks and their relationship to attitude formation are not static but dynamic also drives home another point about measuring the association between religion and these questions of broad political preferences. The relational nature of religion's influence on attitudes necessitates a description of these relationships between coefficients as snapshots rather than stable associations. In a given context, as also observed among Naqshbandis in chapter 2, there could be many reasons for individuals from religious groups to support democracy; many authoritarian contexts could provide the relational impetus for most devout individuals to support democracy, but even then, they would undoubtedly do so for different reasons and vantage points. Events and experiences as lived out during transitions and changes or openings and restrictions would also encourage recalculations of one's positions.

Certainly, Tunisia and Egypt are dramatic examples of transition and change that undoubtedly contributed to the marked shifts in outlook distributions and their associational attitudes toward politics. As we discussed in the case of Indonesia, religious outlooks may evolve more slowly as the general political and social paradigm change. From Pancasilla to the democratization period, Nahdlatul Ulama, Muhammadiya, and other groups continuously realigned their preferences and views. In any case, however, changes in national politics that could facilitate the recalibration of attitudes in democracies, and even authoritarian states, are more frequent than is often assumed. Therefore, public opinion surveys that establish clear associations between religion and attitudes should be seen as benchmarks to understand how nations and societies are changing over time rather than determinative discoveries. There is likely always contingency in the relationships between these numbers in the data.

Our analysis of temporal change in religious outlooks also has important implications when considered in tandem with religious political organizations. While it would be difficult to argue for a one-on-one match between religious outlooks and organizational preferences, it can be reasonably inferred from the analysis that there will be some synergy between the two levels. Presumably, there will be distinct outlooks within each organization or movement rather than a single outlook uniformly defining the membership of groups, and thus, it is not surprising that many movements, organizations, and political parties are replete with factions, schisms, and splits often instigated by these different outlooks (Wickham 2013). The internal distribution of these outlooks will shape the general ideological or strategic preferences of these organizations, and from time to time, significant events may result in a reshuffling of these outlooks leading to organizational change or new strategies. The analysis in this chapter shows that this insight could be applied to such large-scale social movements as the Muslim Brothers, such political parties as Ennahda, such highly diverse ideological groupings as the Salafis, and groups struggling to become movements but swinging between peaceful participation and violent means, such as Ansar in Tunisia.

Finally, this chapter points out once again that the more careful measurement of those identified as religious in surveys highlights differences and patterns in attitudes that are critical to understanding dynamics in any society. Relationships between religion and attitudes toward democracy are complex, and greater nuance in measurement is necessary to see the patterns that help us understand the contextual dynamics that are at work in these societies. Each chapter has brought to bear the relevance of attending to pluralism among the pious from a different analytical viewpoint. In this chapter, we have seen its significance in understanding relationships between attitudes across a national population over time. The subsequent chapter will also drive this home in applying this pluralistic measurement framework for attitudes toward state economic policy.

Notes

1. This slogan can be translated as "Bread, freedom, and dignity." Of course, many other slogans were used, and individuals in different states and locales put forth different messages. Nevertheless, the overwhelming majority of such slogans were democratic in orientation.

2. It is important to note that while both the Muslim Brothers and Salafi organizations and leaders were hesitant to enter the revolutionary fray in Egypt, most did not attempt to dissuade their members and supporters from individually joining in the protests. Taking such a position may have caused unrest within their organizations.

3. While Wickham (2004, 2013) does not use our terminology, her careful studies of the MB over time have illustrated the conflict among moderates and hardliners regarding the issue of a pluralistic approach, which captures an essential difference between these two outlooks.

4. Quintan Wiktorowicz (2005), for example, defines al-Qaeda as a Salafi community.

5. This difference could also be related to the differences in the survey sample and different question wording/response categories.

6. In our discussion, we assume that outlooks are largely formed by domestic factors. However, the Israel-Palestine conflict as an international problem is also a salient domestic issue in many MENA countries. The discussion in the above paragraph is about the shifting position of the Freedom and Justice Party before the elections, and a pro-Palestinian discourse presumably will appeal to the post-Islamist outlook. Keeping commitments with

Israel would probably make the most sense to social communitarians, and Morsi's speech might be seen as an attempt to appeal to individuals holding this outlook.

7. As such, this means any inferences we attempt to draw at the lowest end of the distribution should be tempered by the fact that the class probabilities we see are driven by very few observations.

8. Our interpretation of the results certainly requires further clarification and additional tests. With data that are more suitable for the analysis of temporal change in outlooks and attitudes than the existing survey data, scholars could refine and further develop the theory introduced in this volume to explain these shifts or test the robustness of these results.

7

ISLAM AND DISTRIBUTIVE PREFERENCES

> There is for every nation a fitna, and for my nation that fitna is wealth.
> The Prophet Muhammad, according to At-Tirmidhi (36:33)

RELIGIOUS DOCTRINE AND DOGMA OFTEN EXPLICITLY OR IMPLICITLY deal with issues related to the distribution of wealth within society. Islam has particularly been noted for its egalitarian streak, especially in the realm of distributive justice (Ciftci 2019; Davis and Robinson 2006; Fish 2011; Hasan 1971; Qutb 2000; Shariati 1979). Children taking Islamic lessons are frequently exposed to stories of the Prophet Muhammad's lack of pomp and preference for giving to others over hording for himself. Sunni Muslims revere the second caliph, 'Umar Ibn al-Khattab, not just for his prowess on the battlefield but for the austere lifestyle he espoused despite his wealth. There are numerous verses in the Koran and in the sunna (words and deeds of the Prophet Mohammed) that place strong emphasis on charity and redistribution. For example, wealthy individuals are expected to pay a certain proportion of their income (generally 2.5 percent) as zakat (a special kind of almsgiving) to certain individuals: "Whatever you spend of good is [to be] for parents and relatives and orphans and the needy and the traveler. And whatever you do of good—indeed, Allah is knowing of it" (Koran 2:215). Al-Bukhari (1996, 2:24:537) reports that the Prophet Muhammad was heard saying: "Allah has made it obligatory for them to pay zakat from their property; it is to be taken from the wealthy among them and given to the poor." The emphasis of the Abrahamic religions on giving to those who are less fortunate might lead to the assumption that individuals who espouse such religious beliefs would express political preferences that favor the redistribution of wealth by the state. Such an assumption, however, has been challenged by the empirical evidence that explores this connection (Pepinsky and Welborne 2011).

Perhaps no relationship in the body of literature on religion and economic preferences has been more roundly supported than the negative correlation between religious observance and support for state-led redistribution (Scheve and Stasavage 2006; Stegmueller et al. 2011). While some scholars have found this relationship to be conditional (Gaskins, Golder, and Siegel 2013a), those who are more pious are generally less likely to support economic redistribution. Although there are many potential explanations for this correlation, the reasons most often cited are that (1) religious groups provide a form of social insurance to their members, obviating the need for state institutions to provide such services (Huber and Stanig 2011); and (2) the psychological benefits associated with religion reduce the costs of unfavorable economic outcomes (Scheve and Stasavage 2006). Nevertheless, while the pious may generally be less likely to support state-led economic redistribution, the potential relationship between religion and distributive preferences extends beyond the intensity of an individual's religious faith. Heterogeneity in outlooks regarding the role that religion should play in molding society means that it is not enough to explore the relationship between the intensity of a Muslim's faith and her or his preferences for redistribution.

The Islamic religious outlooks that have been developed and discussed in previous chapters play a role in shaping social and political preferences and likely also play a significant role in shaping economic policy preferences. One of the underlying reasons that recent studies have focused on the intensity of an individual's faith—that is, measures of religiosity—rather than intrareligious belief systems is the rationalist framework that has guided these studies. Eschewing the Weberian focus on denominational doctrinal differences, these studies have focused on the utility that religious communities provide to their members. As such, religious participation has been considered particularly important in the analysis of how religion affects distributive preferences. Moreover, recent studies have found religiosity to be a more salient factor than religious denomination in influencing support for redistribution (Scheve and Stasavage 2006; Stegmueller et al. 2011). While denominational or sectarian differences may not be significant determinants of distributive preferences, the Islamic religious outlooks developed herein are rooted in the social preferences and experiences of individuals. Thus, it is not doctrinal or denominational differences that drive this inquiry but how religiously oriented preferences over the social order and social relations influence these economic preferences.

The religious outlooks conceptualized within this book have categorized pious Muslims into four different outlooks via a two-dimensional examination of social religious preferences. The two relevant dimensions are preferences for pluralism and support for religion in the public sphere. Within this classification scheme, religious communitarians are those who prefer cultural homogeneity and a religious public sphere. Social communitarians also support cultural homogeneity but do not benefit from an increased presence of religion in the public domain. Religious individualists prefer pluralism over homogeneity and do not support a religious public sphere. Finally, those in the outlook category of post-Islamist, like religious individualists, prefer pluralism but also desire a religious public sphere. Factor and latent class analyses using the survey data support this two-dimensional, four-category classification of religious outlooks.

The theoretical and empirical examination that follows reveals an interesting and nuanced relationship between these religious outlooks and preferences for state-led redistribution. The outlooks that are more prone to authoritarian attitudes, religious communitarians and social communitarians, are, perhaps unsurprisingly, more likely to prefer that there be little change to the current distributive policy. While the relationship between these religious outlooks and a preference for change in policy is relatively straightforward, the relationship between the outlooks and preferences for state-led redistribution appear to be more complicated. In the case of the socially minded and pluralistic post-Islamists, the availability of private religious organizations with robust social service apparatuses appears to play a significant role in shaping the relationship between the adoption of the outlook and preferences for state-led redistribution. In particular, an analysis of Egypt and Tunisia reveals that post-Islamists are generally supportive of state-led redistribution when private channels for redistribution are closed and unsupportive of redistribution when private channels are open. Thus, while there appear to be some broad tendencies regarding distributive preferences for each of the outlooks, the political context appears to play a substantial role in shaping these relationships.

Communitarianism and Preferences for Stability

Given the preference for cultural homogeneity exhibited by both religious and social communitarians, it may be posited by some that communitarians should be economically egalitarian relative to their post-Islamist and religious individualist neighbors. This position, however, ignores the conceptual difference between cultural homogeneity and distributive homogeneity. While the communitarian classes prefer uniformity in the acceptance of social norms, as the analyses in chapters 3 and 5 demonstrated, such uniformity often produces preferences for authoritarian policies. Such authoritarianism is likely not relegated to the political sphere; it manifests itself socially in a preference for hierarchical relationships among citizens. While these relationships may produce stability and predictability in the daily lives of residents, they are inherently inegalitarian (Schwartz 2006). Nevertheless, the defining feature of the communitarians is their preference for stability and regularity over change and diversity.

This preference for stability among the communitarian classes should lead to a stronger preference for the status quo to be maintained. Thus, rather than having strong preferences for or against greater levels of redistribution, both religious communitarians and social communitarians should prefer the current state of affairs over any type of change. To analyze the strength of this preference for change in distributive policy, the analysis herein utilizes the third wave of the Arab Barometer. Preferences for redistribution were measured using a question in the Arab Barometer that asked: "Assuming there is a 0–10 scale to measure the appropriate level of tax burden, where 0 means that the government should impose higher taxes on the rich to generate resources to spend on the poor, and where 10 means that the rich already create job opportunities and economic growth, and that the government shall lessen the taxes they pay and allow them to retain more of their net worth. Where would you put yourself on such a scale?"[1] The order of the responses was then reversed so that a 10 represents the strongest preference for higher taxation and a 0 represents the strongest preference for lower taxation.

Figure 7.1 provides a descriptive representation of the distribution of preferences concerning redistribution for members of the four religious outlook classes. The curves show the Gaussian kernel density functions for the respondents' answers, which allowed for the smooth representation of how preferences were distributed. Both social communitarians and religious communitarians have demonstrably larger proportions of their members occupying the middle values, representing little desire for change in either the direction of higher or lower taxation. The proportion of post-Islamists in the middle value of the scale is also large relative to religious individualists. Nonetheless, religious individualists and post-Islamists are

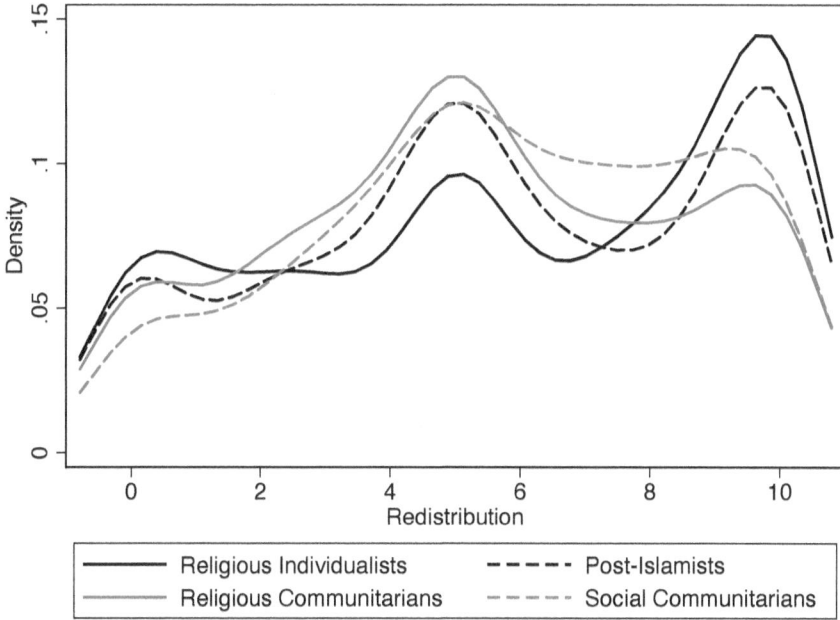

Figure 7.1. Kernel Density Function for Preferences for Redistribution

substantially more likely to be found at the extremes. In fact, the modal response for both religious individualists and post-Islamists was to strongly support higher taxation. Nevertheless, there was little variation in the mean values for each of the religious outlooks, which ranged from 5.37 (religious communitarians) to 5.89 (religious individualists) and represents a slight preference for state-led redistribution for each of the outlooks. Where greater variation between the classes can be observed is in the standard deviations associated with the means of their responses. Tests run on the equality of the standard deviations of the responses for each class revealed statistically significant results ($p < 0.05$) using Levene's robust test statistic for the differences between religious communitarians and both post-Islamists and religious individualists.[2] The same significant relationship was observed when post-Islamists and religious individualists were compared to social communitarians. Religious communitarians and social communitarians, which both had the smallest standard deviations, were not significantly nor substantively different in their deviations from their means.

In order to test the prediction that the communitarian classes are less extreme in their preferences for change, a multivariate OLS regression analysis was conducted using the same explanatory variables that were used in chapter 5, including the country fixed effects. In addition to the explanatory variables used in previous analyses, a variable measuring tribal membership was added due to the role tribes may play in providing social insurance and services to their members (Barnett, Yandle, and Naufal 2013).[3] The primary variables of interest in the analysis are dummy variables that capture the latent religious outlook classes (post-Islamists, religious individualists, and religious communitarians), and social communitarians are reserved as the reference category.

A simple measure capturing a preference for distributive change was then constructed by subtracting 5 from the value of an individual's answer regarding redistribution and then taking the absolute value of that number so that the values range from 0 (lowest desire for change) to 5 (greatest desire for change). This allowed for the testing of the intensity of an individual's preference for change from the status quo. In addition, the relative extremity of an individual's distributive preferences was examined through a measure of how far an individual's preference resides from the median pious individual in the respondent's country by taking the absolute value of the difference between each individual's response from the median for respondents included in the analysis (distance median). Furthermore, given that tests revealed differences in the dispersion of class preferences, the distances of individuals from their religious outlook class median within their countries were also analyzed (distance class median). Finally, the analysis explores criticism of the government's redistributive policies by utilizing the answers to a question asking respondents to evaluate the government's performance in narrowing the gap between the rich and the poor, and these responses range from 0 (very good) to 3 (very bad).[4] This allowed for an analysis of whether these religious outlooks were correlated with the expression of dissent regarding the state's redistributive efforts. The results of these analyses are presented in models 1–4 of table 7.1.

As expected, after controlling for confounders, post-Islamists and religious individualists expressed stronger preferences for changing the distributive policy of the state, and these results were statistically significant at the $p < 0.001$ level. Moreover, religious communitarians were not significantly more or less extreme in their preference for change than social communitarians, and the average difference between these groups was substantively very small. These results are mirrored in the analysis of deviations from the median of all respondents (model 2). While these stronger preferences

Table 7.1. Religious Outlooks and Redistribution

	Model 1 Distributive Change	Model 2 Distance Median	Model 3 Dist. Class Median	Model 4 Criticize Policy	Model 5 Redistribution	Model 6 Redistribution
Post-Islamist	0.182**	0.215***	0.200**	0.0249	-0.0322	0.0429
	(0.061)	(0.060)	(0.061)	(0.025)	(0.092)	(0.105)
Religious individualist	0.386***	0.381***	0.353***	0.197***	0.118	-0.340**
	(0.072)	(0.073)	(0.075)	(0.027)	(0.116)	(0.127)
Religious communitarian	0.00229	-0.0284	-0.0133	-0.0252	-0.397***	-0.284**
	(0.051)	(0.052)	(0.052)	(0.021)	(0.078)	(0.087)
Tribal	-0.280***	-0.330***	-0.310***	-0.0244		-0.396***
	(0.060)	(0.059)	(0.060)	(0.025)		(0.100)
Religiosity	0.0464***	0.0528***	0.0509***	0.00603		-0.00782
	(0.013)	(0.013)	(0.014)	(0.005)		(0.023)
Personal trust	0.0560	0.0768#	0.0168	-0.0947***		-0.0260
	(0.045)	(0.044)	(0.046)	(0.019)		(0.078)
Political trust	-0.0178*	-0.0174*	-0.0199**	-0.0699***		-0.0531***
	(0.007)	(0.007)	(0.008)	(0.003)		(0.013)
Political interest	0.0201	0.0368#	0.0143	0.00944		0.113**
	(0.022)	(0.022)	(0.023)	(0.009)		(0.039)
Egalitarian gender beliefs	0.0278*	-0.00645	-0.0162	-0.00644		0.0265
	(0.011)	(0.011)	(0.012)	(0.004)		(0.019)

Table 7.1. (continued)

	Model 1 Distributive Change	Model 2 Distance Median	Model 3 Dist. Class Median	Model 4 Criticize Policy	Model 5 Redistribution	Model 6 Redistribution
Economic perceptions	-0.111***	-0.0482	-0.0518#	-0.180***		-0.101#
	(0.030)	(0.029)	(0.030)	(0.013)		(0.052)
Prospective economic perceptions	-0.0231	0.0196	0.0446*	-0.0425***		-0.0729*
	(0.019)	(0.019)	(0.020)	(0.008)		(0.034)
Age	-0.00231	-0.00445**	-0.00340*	0.000587		0.00159
	(0.002)	(0.002)	(0.002)	(0.001)		(0.003)
Female	-0.0428	-0.00313	-0.0319	0.00130		-0.149*
	(0.042)	(0.042)	(0.044)	(0.017)		(0.073)
Education	-0.0186	-0.0358**	-0.0276#	0.00558		-0.0153
	(0.014)	(0.014)	(0.014)	(0.005)		(0.024)
Income	-0.0384#	-0.00244	0.0121	-0.0361***		-0.116**
	(0.023)	(0.023)	(0.024)	(0.009)		(0.041)
Country dummies	Yes	Yes	Yes	Yes	No	Yes
Observations	8,032	8,032	8,032	8,141	9,601	8,032
Adjusted R-squared	0.062	0.043	0.037	0.296	0.004	0.072

Notes: Standard errors in parentheses; # $p < 0.1$, * $p < 0.05$, ** $p < 0.01$, *** $p < .001$. Country dummies are presented in the appendix, table A7.4.
Source: Arab Barometer, Wave III.

for changing distributive policy translate into more critical opinions of the government's performance regarding combating inequality among religious individualists, post-Islamists were not significantly more likely to express dissatisfaction with the government's performance (model 4).[5] In addition, supporting the initial analysis of the relative dispersion of the classes, after adding potential confounders, religious individualists and post-Islamists were more likely to reside further away from their class mean than social communitarians ($p < 0.001$), while religious communitarians were not. Thus, not only are religious communitarians and social communitarians more likely to prefer maintaining current redistributive policies; they are more homogenous in their preferences as a class. While these analyses provide evidence in support of the hypothesis that the communitarian classes should have less favorable attitudes toward changing redistributive policy, they do not test the relationship between these classes and support for state-led redistribution.

Religious Outlooks and Support for Redistribution in the Arab World

Given that the modal response for both religious individualists and post-Islamists was to support higher taxes at the maximum level, there may be some expectation that these religious outlooks would be more likely, on average, to support redistribution than social communitarians and religious communitarians. The relationship between religious outlook and support for redistribution, however, is more nuanced than it may initially appear. Model 5 of table 7.1 presents a regression analysis where *redistribution* is the dependent variable of interest, and only the religious outlook class variables are included in the model. While not all of the relationships are significant, religious individualists are, on average, the most likely to support redistribution, and post-Islamists and religious communitarians are less likely to support redistribution than social communitarians. For this analysis, only the religious communitarian class was significantly different from the social communitarian class. It should be noted, however, that if we were to have used religious communitarians as the reference category in model 5, the results for each of the classes would be significant. Nevertheless, when control variables are added to the analysis (model 6), the signs for the coefficients for religious individualists and post-Islamists change. While religious individualists are the group most likely to support redistribution, when controlling for other explanatory variables in the regression analysis, being a religious individualist is associated with a statistically significant decrease in the predicted level of support for redistribution. In addition, religious communitarians also tend to have lower levels of support for redistribution. Thus, when holding all other variables constant, the relationship between preferences for redistribution and religious individualism and communitarianism appears to be substantively similar, and post-Islamists tend to hold similar attitudes to social communitarians.

Why might shifts of the magnitude exhibited in the analysis be observed when other variables are added to the model? Further analysis of the data revealed two fundamental reasons for these shifts. First, the religious outlooks explored are associated with varying degrees of economic optimism. Among the religious outlooks, religious individualists tend to be the most pessimistic about the state of the current economy and the future of the economy. Of course, such a discussion highlights the potential for collinearity to be masking the relationship between these classes and redistribution. More importantly, however, it may indicate that the effects of the religious outlook on their distributive preferences are mediated by their evaluations of the economy. Thus, religious individualists may prefer to reduce state-led redistribution when economic sentiment is held constant, yet religious individualism may also be associated with more negative economic sentiment, and this negative economic sentiment may indirectly increase the support of religious individualists for state-led redistribution. Such an analysis is beyond the scope of this immediate project yet may prove to be fruitful in subsequent analyses. Second, the context in which class members find themselves appears to play a role in shaping how religious outlooks affect preferences for redistribution. Not only are certain environments more likely to produce different compositions of religious outlooks, but these religious outlooks appear to have different relationships with distributive preferences in different states. It should also be noted that, while religiosity was not a significant predictor of distributive preferences in the model, it verges on significance at the $p < 0.1$ level and is statistically significant in other model specifications. Both context and collinearity between religiosity and other variables in the model, as with the results related to religious outlooks, may be masking the underlying relationship between religiosity and distributive preferences.

In addition, on average, those who identify most closely with their tribes tend to be less supportive of redistribution ($p < 0.001$), supporting the contention that the existence of a private social safety net may reduce support for state-led redistribution. Moreover, those who had high levels of political trust ($p < 0.001$), evaluations of the economy ($p < 0.001$), or income ($p < 0.01$) were also, on average, less likely to support redistribution.[6] Thus, the results do indicate that self-interested models of human behavior and preference formation do appear to provide some explanatory power when analyzing preferences for redistribution in the Arab world. Finally, while there is evidence that women are, on average, less likely to support redistribution ($p < 0.05$), those holding more egalitarian attitudes regarding gender may be more supportive of state-led redistribution ($p < 0.1$).

While this analysis provides some preliminary insights into how religious outlooks may generally relate to preferences for redistribution, the relationship between religious outlooks and preferences for state-led redistribution are shaped by the political, social, and economic contexts of the individuals adopting these outlooks. In the analysis above, post-Islamists were not significantly more or less likely to prefer redistribution than social communitarians. The following section will examine how the political landscape may influence whether post-Islamists are more or less supportive of redistribution than members of other outlooks.

Post-Islamists and the State: The Cases of Egypt and Tunisia

While Egypt and Tunisia appeared to have taken similar political trajectories for the three decades that preceded the 2013 Egyptian military coup d'état, there were crucial differences in their recent political histories that significantly affected both the social and political conditions of these states. Among these differences is the extent to which Islamist mobilization in the social sphere was tolerated. Whereas Egypt's relatively strong judiciary and economic challenges led to an environment that allowed Islamists to effectively organize and provide social services, especially among the middle classes (Brooke 2017; Masoud 2014), the Tunisian regimes of Bourguiba and Ben Ali were effectively able to stifle the growth of Islamist social organizations (Gasiorowski 1992). This, in turn, led to differences in the expectations of post-Islamists as to who should be providing social services to those in need. A more robust discussion of the differences between these states was presented in chapter 6, yet a brief synopsis is presented below.

Anwar Saadat found himself in a precarious situation upon ascending to Egypt's presidency in 1970. As the uninspiring heir to the seat held by pan-Arabism's most renowned figure, Gamal Abdel Nasser, he was tasked with the daunting responsibility of setting Egypt on a path that contradicted the regime's political propaganda of the two decades that preceded his reign. While some of these changes fundamentally altered Egypt's foreign and regional policy, the changes to Egypt's economic and institutional landscape that were implemented by Saadat were no less profound. The socialist leanings of the regime gave way to pragmatism as Egypt's economic stagnation produced repeated economic crises and political turmoil (Moore 1986). Rather than turn exclusively to stop-gap measures, Saadat attempted to engage in large-scale institutional reform targeted at encouraging foreign and domestic investment by credibly committing to the rule of law and the protection of property rights (Moustafa 2007). Chief among these reforms was the creation of a judiciary with enough independence to prevent excessive predation by the regime (Moustafa 2007).

The economic liberalization efforts instituted by Saadat and Hosni Mubarak extended beyond providing for greater judicial independence and were complemented by extensive privatization efforts (Moore 1986). The opening of the Egyptian economy did produce significant foreign investment, and by 1997 foreign portfolio investment accounted for approximately 30 percent of Egypt's market capitalization (Pripstein-Posusney 1999). Yet, while a modicum of success was achieved in terms of drawing in foreign capital, Egypt's privatization largely failed to produce the desired results (Belev 2000, 2001). The decentralization of the privatization process across state-owned enterprises in Egypt produced roadblocks to economic liberalization (Belev 2000, 2001). Distributing authority over the privatization process across a wide range of actors with varying interests and perspectives prevented the privatization of the majority of state-owned enterprises that had been intended to transition to private control. Political battles over how privatization should take place, or whether it should take place at all, ensued. Tepid and inconsistent state involvement in the economy also produced an environment where crony capitalism rather than market competition thrived (Chekir and Diwan 2014). Moreover, entities that were privatized did not outperform those that remained completely under the control of the state (Omran 2004, 2007).

While Egypt's economic liberalization policies may have failed to produce the desired results, the creation of an independent judiciary had positive externalities for potential adversaries of the regime. Although the institutions of the state remained largely authoritarian through the reigns of Saadat and Mubarak, the establishment of a more independent judiciary created the infrastructure for protecting the political rights and liberties afforded by Egypt's 1971 constitution (Moustafa 2007). More specifically, for Islamists seeking to mobilize support, it allowed them to commit to the establishment of a robust presence outside of government that could be protected by the courts. Indeed, private avenues of organization were exploited by groups like the Muslim Brothers to develop vast networks of social service provision affording them significant support from various constituencies (S. Berman 2003; Brooke 2017). These networks both complemented the services provided by the government and competed with the government without necessarily aiming to displace the regime (S. Berman 2003). As such, groups like the Muslim Brothers appeared to settle into a comfortable position within Egypt's civil society, and such organizations depended on the government's inability to provide adequate social welfare for entry. While members and supporters of the Muslim Brothers and other religious organizations may have preferred the presence of redistributive mechanisms within their society, they relied on private social organizations for redistribution. Such arrangements offered Islamists the ability to not only compete with the government in the provision of social services but also dictate which communities received assistance.

Similar economic forces to those experienced by Egypt led Tunisia down the path of economic liberalization in the 1980s and 1990s. However, in contrast to Egypt's reforms, Tunisia attempted to open up their economy through a centralized privatization process and without the expansion of judicial independence (Belev 2000, 2001; King 2003). The centralization of the privatization process allowed for the expedited transition of enterprises from state ownership to private control (Belev 2000). While these economic policies succeeded in achieving their immediate goals to a greater extent than in Egypt, the reforms did not produce an independent judiciary capable of adequately restraining the regime's actions.

Tunisia's Islamists ultimately were not allowed to integrate themselves into the state's political institutions and civil society during the reigns of Bourguiba and Ben Ali. Lacking the institutional support and historical organization necessary to fend off the regime's persistent attacks, groups like the Mouvement de la Tendance Islamique (MTI) were unable to effectively and persistently mobilize socially and politically. While Ben Ali's coup was accompanied by an olive branch to the MTI, he was able to dismantle the pluralistic Islamist organization within five years (Ware 1988). Unlike Egypt, in Tunisia, groups like the MTI could not rely on the judiciary to shield them from Ben Ali's attempt to fend off the burgeoning Islamist movement. Tunisia's judiciary lacked the independence of Egypt's judiciary under Saadat and Mubarak and could not be expected to protect the political rights of the MTI. Not only did this effectively stave off the entry of Islamists into Tunisia's legislature, unions, and bureaucracy; it prevented the formation of private Islamic organizations capable of providing social services to their potential constituents. As such, MTI's potential constituency did not have robust private social organizations to turn to for social welfare, and they became effectively reliant on the state to provide social and redistributive services. It should be noted that Ennahda's subsequent electoral success in the aftermath of the Arab Spring indicates that such a constituency was far from negligible in size and potential strength.

How would pious individuals form their distributive preferences given the different contexts observed in Tunisia and Egypt? Among the four religious outlooks, post-Islamists are the group most likely to adapt their social behavior to a country's political landscape. Their support for religion in the public domain should translate into support for Islamic organizations, and their preference for political and social pluralism should produce support for political mobilization more broadly. Thus, post-Islamists should be the outlook that is most engaged socially and politically as a group since they lack deference to the authoritarian state and possess a desire for a religious public presence.

Islamic social and political organizations that have adopted mechanisms for redistribution or social service provision may find themselves competing with the state's institutions in their attempts to provide for the general welfare of their constituencies. Whether the aims of such organizations are political or religious in nature, where their strategy to win supporters or adherents relies on the provision of such services, the state's behavior will influence the effectiveness of this strategy. For example, the Egyptian Muslim Brothers' provision of social services in middle-class neighborhoods signaled their competence to the electorate and improved their electoral performance, yet this strategy relied on the relative inefficiency of social services provided by the state (Brooke 2019). An explicit political objective, however, need not be tied to the provision of social services for their effectiveness to be shaped by their political and economic context. Daniel Chen's (2010) examination of Islamic religious participation and economic conditions in Indonesia highlights the importance of the economic landscape in shaping the effectiveness of redistributive mechanisms by religious groups. In his analysis of Indonesian Pengajians, groups formed for the communal study of the Koran and that act as primary religious organizers for the provision of economic assistance, Chen finds that the availability of credit via financial institutions reduces the effect of economic distress on participation in Pengajians. The provision of financial assistance and social services by public and private institutions may reduce religious participation in groups when these groups provide related forms of assistance.

In the absence of mechanisms for redistribution by religious organizations, economic redistribution provided for by the state should theoretically increase the utility of religious observation for any pious person by decreasing the utility of income generation. Where restrictions on social and political mobilization prevent organized private redistribution, increases to state-led redistribution may produce increased religious observation. This, in turn, should increase the utility associated with the religious observation of post-Islamists, who derive greater benefits from religious observation with others. Where restrictions on social and political mobilization are less extensive, and Islamic organizations are allowed to form networks dedicated to the provision of social services, state-led redistribution may reduce the strength of Islamist organizations and the amount of religious observation associated with them (Brooke 2019; Chen 2010; Clark 2004; Masoud 2014). Furthermore, Huber and Stanig (2011) note that the presence of religious institutions may reduce the reliance of religious adherents on social services provided by the state. Therefore, post-Islamists, while potentially being generally supportive of redistribution, may not view redistribution by the state as being necessary or desirable when private religious institutions provide assistance to individuals.

In Tunisia, where Islamic social mobilization was constrained, redistribution by the state may have been viewed by post-Islamists as being desirable for extrinsic and intrinsic reasons. The lack of available private Islamic social service provision meant that redistribution should be provided by the state. Egyptian post-Islamists could rely on organizations like the Muslim Brothers to efficiently and effectively provide social services to their constituents. This likely acted as a tool for religious and political mobilization that drew the pious to the religious organizations that provided such services and may have contributed to the political success they achieved by demonstrating their competence (Brooke 2017). Moreover, with a political apparatus attached to social service provision, state-led social service provision and redistribution acted as a potential competitor to the services provided by Islamic organizations. As such, while post-Islamists in Tunisia came to support the growth of state-led redistribution, Egyptian post-Islamists saw

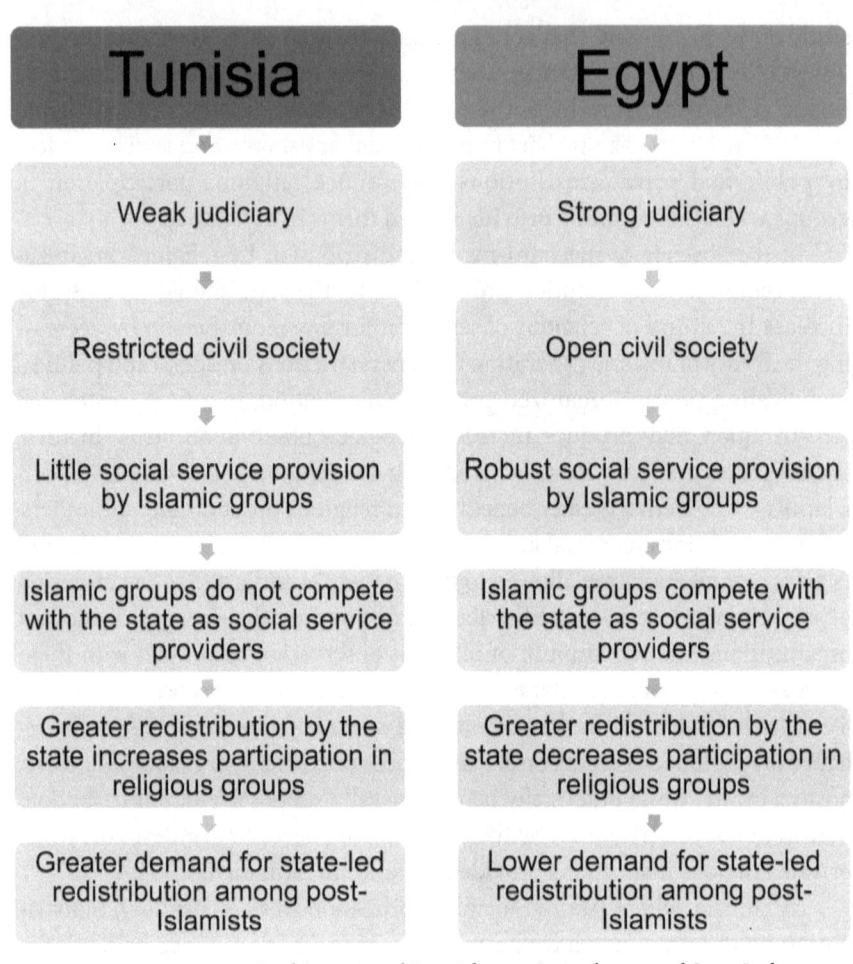

Figure 7.2. Restrictions on Civil Society and Post-Islamist Attitudes toward State-Led Redistribution

Islamic organizations rather than the state as the appropriate mechanism for redistribution. A simplified representation of the broader theoretical linkages that lead to the predictions noted above are represented in figure 7.2.

Using data from Wave III of the Arab Barometer survey that was analyzed in the previous section, an analysis was conducted to determine whether post-Islamists were more or less likely to support state-led redistribution than other pious Muslims in Tunisia and Egypt. The theoretical expectations developed above predict that post-Islamists in Tunisia should, on average, be more supportive of redistribution than other pious Muslims.

In Egypt, it was anticipated that post-Islamists would be less supportive of redistribution than other pious Muslims. Given that this analysis is primarily concerned with the political preferences of post-Islamists, all other pious religious outlooks were reserved as the reference category.

The results of the analysis presented in table 7.2 are generally supportive of the hypotheses developed in this section. Support for redistribution among post-Islamists does appear to be highly sensitive to context. Among pious Egyptians, post-Islamists are significantly less likely to support redistribution at the $p < 0.01$ level (models 1 and 2). When the control variables are added to the model (model 2), Egyptian post-Islamists are predicted to score 0.83 points lower than other pious Egyptians. For pious Tunisians, when control variables are added to the model (model 4), post-Islamists are predicted to express a preference for redistribution approximately 0.99 points higher than other pious Tunisians. The result for the post-Islamist dummy variable was significant at the $p < 0.05$ level for both models run on Tunisian respondents. The difference in redistributive preferences between post-Islamists in Tunisia and Egypt is the one variable that exhibits a contextual difference of this magnitude.

When controlling for post-Islamist outlooks, religiosity in Egypt is associated with a slightly more positive attitude toward redistribution, but this result is not statistically significant at the $p < 0.1$ level. In Tunisia, religiosity, when controlling for post-Islamist outlooks, is associated with lower levels of support for redistribution, and this result was statistically significant at the $p < 0.01$ level. Thus, religiosity was associated with lower levels of support for redistribution in Tunisia but not in Egypt when controlling for the social dimensions of religiosity through the post-Islamist outlook dummy variable. When the most viable method for redistribution is concentrated in the hands of the state, individuals who derive the most utility from the social practice of religion prefer more redistribution, yet religiosity, on average, reduces support for state-led redistribution. These specific results provide some support for both the argument that religion offers psychological benefits that may reduce the desire for redistribution and the argument that social organizations obviate the need for state-led redistribution (Huber and Stanig 2011; Scheve and Stasavage 2006). When social organizations are not present, redistribution is desired to a greater extent by post-Islamists than others, but religiosity decreases support for redistribution. Such a result highlights the importance of the development of religious outlooks that account for the social orientation of religious devotion to understand how religion influences beliefs and preferences. Moreover, it

Table 7.2. Preference for Redistribution in Egypt and Tunisia

	Model 1 Egypt	Model 2	Model 3 Tunisia	Model 4
Post-Islamist	−0.692**	−0.827**	0.795*	0.991*
	(0.240)	(0.291)	(0.340)	(0.385)
Tribal		−0.435		0.487
		(0.523)		(2.046)
Religiosity		0.0991		−0.161#
		(0.071)		(0.086)
Personal trust		0.0478		0.105
		(0.256)		(0.338)
Political trust		0.0388		0.000915
		(0.044)		(0.048)
Political interest		−0.534***		0.215
		(0.136)		(0.138)
Egalitarian gender beliefs		−0.0830		0.00563
		(0.063)		(0.066)
Economic perceptions		0.257		−0.250
		(0.179)		(0.216)
Prospective economic perceptions		−0.296**		−0.00775
		(0.091)		(0.129)
Age		−0.00861		0.0117
		(0.008)		(0.010)
Female		0.0128		−0.413
		(0.208)		(0.306)
Education		−0.00152		0.0755
		(0.065)		(0.095)
Income		−0.156		−0.487**
		(0.133)		(0.151)
Observations	868	748	639	528
Adjusted R-squared	0.008	0.055	0.008	0.030

Notes: Standard errors in parentheses; # $p < 0.1$ * $p < 0.05$, ** $p < 0.01$, *** $p < .001$.
Source: Arab Barometer, Wave III.

calls for further examination of the nuances of individual and social religiosity and for scholars to exercise care in the construction of their Islamic religiosity measures.

Other results associated with the analysis that are of note are those related to political interest and the economy. Among pious Egyptians, political interest was associated with lower levels of support for state-led redistribution

($p < 0.001$), yet among pious Tunisians, there was no statistically significant correlation between political interest and preferences for state-led redistribution. This may also highlight how the specific political institutions of the state, even among authoritarian regimes, may influence preferences for redistribution. In both Egypt and Tunisia, the results of the analyses indicate that economic factors may influence preferences for redistribution. Specifically, in Egypt, higher evaluations of future economic prospects appeared to decrease support for redistribution ($p < 0.01$). Among Tunisians, income was negatively correlated with support for redistribution ($p < 0.001$). Neither age, gender, education, nor either of the trust variables were statistically significant for the analyses of Egypt and Tunisia.

Not only does post-Islamism appear to play a role in shaping attitudes toward redistribution; the magnitude of the relationship is relatively large in both countries. While post-Islamism was significantly correlated with support for state-led redistribution in both Egypt and Tunisia, it was associated with lower levels of support in Egypt and higher levels of support in Tunisia. In Egypt, where strong religious organizations were able to provide social services across the country, post-Islamists saw these organizations, not the state, as the appropriate vehicles for redistribution. Where such private religious organizations could not operate, the provision of social services by the state produced intrinsic and extrinsic benefits for post-Islamists, and such social services could not be provided by those who were ideologically and religiously aligned with them.

Conclusion

This chapter explored the relationship between Islamic religious outlooks and economic distributive preferences. While it is clear that the political and social context should affect which religious outlooks are prevalent within a society, context should also play a role in how religious outlooks influence the preferences and beliefs of those who espouse such outlooks. This should hold true whether the dependent variable for an analysis focuses on economic, political, or social preferences. Despite the contextual nature of the effect of religious outlooks on beliefs and preferences, the analysis in this chapter was able to provide evidence of some general relationships while exploring one of many potential contextual relationships.

Religious outlooks that espouse hierarchical authoritarian preferences should be associated with greater deference for the political status quo. In turn, this should lead to a preference for distributive stability rather than preferences that support or are antagonistic toward redistribution. As such, those who hold religious communitarian or social communitarian outlooks should be less likely to support increases or decreases in levels of redistribution. In addition, while context will shape the degree to which certain outlooks will be associated with support for redistribution, religious communitarians do appear to be, on average, generally less supportive of state-led redistribution. Further analysis of how political repression may influence support for state-led redistribution showed that where Islamic social organizations are able to flourish, those who are most supportive of Islamic civil society, post-Islamists, may be less supportive of state-led redistribution. Where private channels for redistribution are closed, post-Islamists were generally more supportive of redistribution. Thus, Egyptian and Tunisian post-Islamists adopted different attitudes toward state-led redistribution.

The analysis of Egypt and Tunisia provided a brief exploration of how context may influence the relationship between these religious outlooks and political preferences. In Egypt and Tunisia, variance in institutional protections offered to Islamic organizations led to divergent relationships between post-Islamism and distributive preferences, a relationship that could not be illustrated in the basic analysis. Further analysis of how context interacts with these religious outlooks should be explored in the future, and scholars should strongly consider developing multilevel models with cross-level interactions when conducting global analyses of religion and politics. Context, however, should not simply be viewed as an examination of cross-society variation but variation over time. The changing political situations in Egypt and Tunisia should slowly alter the preferences and beliefs of post-Islamists in both countries. Moreover, the analysis of Egypt and Tunisia did not attempt to identify the root cause of support for state-led redistribution among post-Islamists when private social provision is unavailable. Whether the benefits of redistribution that extend to post-Islamists arise out of a greater enjoyment of their religious practice when others participate or their prosocial tendencies drive them to generally be more supportive of redistribution due to their internalization of social justice norms within Islam is a question left unanswered (see Ciftci 2019). It is also unclear whether religion offers some individuals a psychological coping mechanism that allows them to accept poor economic outcomes (Scheve and Stasavage 2006) or whether religious social service provision simply provides an alternative safety net. These topics are worthy of exploration in the future.

While the analyses in this chapter clearly have implications related to political behavior and economic preferences in the MENA region, the results of the analyses conducted can also help shed light on the broader discussion of religion and egalitarianism. Nevertheless, further examination is needed to explore the generalizability of these findings. If similar religious outlooks characterize other faiths, there may be common linkages between religious outlooks across faiths. Moreover, rather than explore whether there exists an unconditional connection between religion and economic preferences, the historical relationships between faith communities and state institutions may provide greater insights into the role that the pious see for the state. In addition, just as the legacies of states will influence the preferences of religious communities, the historical role that religious groups have played will also shape expectations as to the role these groups should play in the lives of the pious. Conversely, while religious outlooks may shape beliefs regarding social service provision and redistribution, the provision of such services may also affect which religious outlooks individuals may adopt. Although a broader exploration of these issues is beyond the scope of this empirical exploration, the analysis presented in this chapter contributes to this important line of inquiry.

Notes

1. Q240 in the Arab Barometer, Wave III.
2. Levene's test statistic is used to evaluate the equality of variances among populations from which different samples are drawn.
3. Q5015 in the Arab Barometer, Wave III.
4. Q2043 in the Arab Barometer, Wave III.
5. Tangential analyses not presented in this chapter found a statistically significant difference between religious individualists and post-Islamists.
6. These results should be viewed in the context of other findings that show that those who benefit from authoritarian institution should be the most likely to possess high levels of political trust in those institutions (Buehler 2016; Jamal 2007).

CONCLUSION

THIS BOOK IS INSPIRED BY TWO IDEAS. FIRST, neither Islam nor its practice is monolithic. Second, religion should inform attitudes in distinct ways since manifestations of Islam and its individual-level practices are plural. As such, this book comes from a position of dissatisfaction with the treatment of Muslim religiosity as a monolithic construct and the assumption of uniformity vis-à-vis its effects on political preferences in the social science scholarship. In his seminal book, *What Is Islam?*, Shahab Ahmed (2015, 5) states that he wanted to "say the word 'Islam' in a manner that expresses the historical and human phenomenon that is Islam in its plenitude and complexity of meaning." Just as Ahmed ambitiously conceptualized Islam as a phenomenon with diverse implications and practices grounded in historical and social contexts, we aimed to treat the influence of religion among the devout as relationally oriented and best expressed through a variety of religious outlooks representing individual preferences toward social relations and religion's place in politics. Our approach, attending to the pluralistic positions among the devout in survey research, expands our knowledge of the study of Islam and politics in ways unattainable through the standard treatment of religiosity as a static and uniform indicator of religious attitudes, outlooks, or behavior.

Throughout the chapters of this book, we have demonstrated that conceptualizing the influence of religion among the devout in a pluralistic manner—accounting for context and the nature of an individual's intrafaith community—provides significant analytical leverage in understanding how religion shapes political attitudes. Consequently, one important argument of this book is that it is important to pay attention to nuances about how individuals perceive, interpret, and live their religion. This study deploys pluralistic outlooks within the religious population of interest as a theoretical instrument to provide a fine-tuned and nuanced explanation of Muslim political attitudes in MENA.

By working from this analytical foundation, this study has challenged the notion that a single conceptualization of religiosity, either as a theoretical construct or a quantifiable index, will successfully capture the influence of religion on attitudes regarding broad socioeconomic and political preferences. We have proposed that religion and religious association lead to a plurality of outlooks. This observation, conveniently ignored by the Orientalist and essentialist students of Islam of the last century, has, nonetheless, been part of the common wisdom throughout Islamic history. For example, the influential Andalusian philosopher Ibn Rushd (Averroes, 1126–1198) famously argued that there could be three valid paths to truth: philosophy, mysticism, and law.[1] Beyond the varieties of doctrinal positions or what religion as a truth claim entails, there has been widespread diversity in the ways people understand and practice Islam. Across an expansive geography ranging from Europe to Southeast Asia, a complex web of interactions with native cultures brought about rich layers of differences in the Muslim world. Over centuries and into contemporary times, Islam and its practices have been anything but monolithic. The perception of Islam as such or describing Muslim faith and worldviews within a singular notion of religiosity is in effect a trend of the modern age and particularly a legacy of Orientalist scholarship.

At first sight, our contention about the plurality of religious outlooks may appear to be a statement of the obvious. However, as we have discussed throughout the book, unlike the well-developed literature in the US, studies conducted in the Muslim world and the MENA region have rarely empirically tackled the issue of the influence of religion with a premise of pluralism in the opinions of the devout within intrafaith communities. While this problem may be due in part to the limitations of the empirical studies themselves, as they usually work with limited data that prevent them from capturing complex variation in belief and practice (Ciftci, Wuthrich, and Shamaileh 2019; Tessler 2015), the problem also reflects the tendency of students of essentialist approaches and modernization theories to build their assumptions regarding the influence of religion from monolithic understandings of the role of faith in society (Gellner 1983; Lewis 2010).

It is our contention that acknowledging the plurality of religious outlooks matters a great deal to the extent that these outlooks have the capacity to shape political attitudes and behavior, especially in the MENA countries, where average religiosity is found by public opinion surveys to be remarkably high. Therefore, studying the influence of Islam on individuals by unfolding various religious outlooks among the devout has analytical value beyond that of a simple conceptual exercise or a scholarly attempt to refute the essentialist approach. This book argues that studying Muslim religious outlooks will help researchers advance our understanding about the interplay of Islam and politics, and more specifically, it will inform the debate on Islam and democracy. The analysis is likely to help observers of Muslim politics to move beyond the existing limited approaches to provide explanations and unfold mechanisms regarding the religion's role in shaping public opinion in MENA and beyond. This approach is conveniently suited to capture the explanatory mechanisms about attitudes and such phenomena as regime type, international actors, economic policies, repression, human rights, and violence.

A lack of attention paid to nuance in the manifestations of religious outlooks and their effects on political attitudes is not limited to the scholarly community. Even political actors whose worldviews are rooted in religious belief tend to neglect these religious outlooks in making policy decisions. The history of the Iranian revolution nicely illustrates this point. It took the Islamic Republic of Iran less than ten years to circumvent the logic that undergirds the very reason for the revolution in the first place. At the very first succession of power of the Velāyat-e faqīh (the guardianship of jurist), the position was filled by the midlevel cleric Ali Khamenei. The entire justification of the existence of a supreme jurist overseeing the republic was that a person of utmost spiritual merit would be most fit to rightly guide the nation, its laws, and governance. At the death of Ayatollah Khomeini, there were numerous ayatollahs and grand ayatollahs who could have taken his place. Allegedly due to the wishes of Khomeini himself, the leaders of the Islamic Republic chose President Khamenei instead. The reason for this was simple: the leaders of the revolution had initially assumed that high religious credentials would lead such religious elites to approach the policy and governance of an Islamic republic in the same way. Ayatollah Khomeini had yet to even consolidate the Islamic Republic before this assumption was proved to be patently false. The regime, even to this day, constantly faces much of its stiffest criticism from many in the country with the highest religious credentials. Furthermore, it is also clear that there is little chance of the next successor being chosen primarily according to the level of their religious credentials.

Another illustrative case worth mentioning comes from Turkish politics. During the Gezi protests and in the latest elections in Turkey, the ruling Justice and Development Party relied on its religious conservative credentials (or, in other words, its "Muslimhood" as White (2004) refers to it) to assume that the core supporters of the party would act or vote in a certain way. On the contrary, there were Islamist groups with different outlooks actively participating in antigovernment protests or voting for non-Islamist parties, including the People's Democracy Party, which represented the Kurds and their political identity. What the AKP leadership and the strategists failed to see was the diversity of opinion among the devout that resulted in behavior that did not conform to the expectations of a presumed monolithic outlook.

One could also consider this faulty simplification and the attempt to search for a single "Muslim outlook" in the West in the context of anti-Muslim sentiment. Research on Islamophobia points to the common misperceptions about Islam or Muslims as the root cause of anti-Muslim sentiment in the West (Allen 2010; Halliday 1999). The assumption underlying such perceptions reduces Islam to a uniform faith or devout Muslims to a single-minded actor or agent (Ciftci 2012). The failing multicultural policies, as implemented by the states in the West to facilitate the integration of Muslim minorities and reduce the social tensions, usually build on the faulty assumption that all Muslims conform to a single outlook and that Muslim religiosity leads to uniform attitudes and behavior. The foundation of the Islamic Republic, the failing strategies of the AKP in Turkey, and the rise of anti-Muslim sentiments have suffered from the same mistaken assumptions about religiosity that have plagued much of the scholarship on Muslim-majority countries, Muslim politics, and religious communities more broadly; that is, many Muslims and non-Muslims alike have assumed that religiosity leads to attitudinal uniformity. This book has intended to provide an antidote to these mistaken assumptions regarding religiosity and its impact on political attitudes.

Religious Outlooks and Political Attitudes

One of the main arguments of this book is that simple measures of religiosity mask the pluralism that exists regarding piety and political preferences among the devout. We have attempted to highlight this plurality in two ways. First, we examined the variation in the political attitudes and social orientations of the Naqshbandi order, a powerful Sufi strand of Sunni Muslim devotion with multiple faith communities in Turkey. This analysis helped us highlight the differences in the political attitudes and approaches of these communities while holding the level of religious devotion constant. Throughout the analyses presented in this study, we found significant resemblance in the plurality of outlooks beyond the case of Naqshbandis in Turkey to include varieties of religious outlooks among distinct groups, including Salafis, new movements of Muslim youth, Indonesian Islamists, and Islamist political parties in the Arab uprisings.

The study of the Naqshbandis is supplemented by expanding the insights from this case into a novel theory of religious outlooks in chapter 2. Using recent advances in social theory (Bayat 2007; Davis and Robinson 2006) and literature concerning religious economies (Iannocone 1998: Stark and Finke 2000), this study attempted to explain the variation among devout individuals regarding the public role of religion and attitudes toward religious pluralism or social conformity. Based on plurality/conformity and religion's public / private dimensions, religious outlooks are conceptualized into four groups. Those who value plurality in social life and desire to confine religion to the private sphere are religious individualists, whereas devout individuals who also value plurality but want a public role for religion are post-Islamists. On the flip side, individuals who desire social conformity with a private role for religion are social communitarian, as opposed to social conformists who view religion as public—namely, religious communitarians. One of the primary contentions of this book is that the plurality of religious outlooks among the pious has implications for political preferences, and this should be the primary source of significant variation in these preferences among individuals who would normally be placed within the single category of religious.

Religious outlooks defined in this book are neither solely informed by doctrine, nor do they arise in a vacuum. Rather, it is hypothesized that context matters a great deal in generating variation in these outlooks. Just as there are visible differences in outlooks among the members of the Naqshbandi communities in Turkey, similar differences will emerge in other settings. For example, the two largest religious communities in Indonesia have quite distinct social preferences. Muhammadiyah is a progressive/reformist movement, whereas Nahdlatul Ulama (NU) is traditional. Both communities, however, adhere to Sunni Islam and encourage pious behavior. While one could naturally expect differences in religious outlooks and political attitudes *between* these communities, what is striking is the different outlooks observed *within* these communities. For example, in recent years, a new generation of scholars affiliated with NU espoused liberal views and promoted human rights and tolerance. This is quite different than the attitude of the average ulama member. Another group within the same community took a different approach and shifted the group's Koranic *halaka* (circle) focus from

Islamic jurisprudence to the issues of *itiqad* (creed), inadvertently bringing about less tolerant social views among some members (Syechbubakr 2018). The case of the Salafis provides another interesting example. Usually known for their political quietism if not indifference to politics, Salafi groups were seen as holding uniform views about religion, social relations, economic life, and politics. When the Arab uprisings provided an opportunity, a rich array of outlooks came to the surface among the Salafis (Al-Anani and Malik 2013). It is likely that Salafi groups always had different outlooks, but they chose to ride the wave of opportunities that came with the social change. One can, thus, reasonably expect to see variation in religious outlooks and the related political attitudes in other contexts.

As has been noted, the literature on Islam and religiosity has found little evidence of a linear and consistent relationship between Islamic piety and political preferences. The fact that religiosity is not always statistically significant in advanced quantitative studies, however, does not indicate that religion is not important in influencing political attitudes. While religion's influence on individual's practice and spirituality occurs through its substance (i.e., the doctrine and ideals), religion's more significant influence on broader political attitudes and perspectives might be through its relationships, the communal association of religious members, and the interaction with the social environment. This study has attempted to illustrate that religious outlooks and the resulting political attitudes are often shaped by one's relational context. Doctrine and religiosity may also matter, operating as essentially necessary conditions for the nature of an individual's religious associations, but to the extent that the doctrine and religiosity matter, it is likely that they matter as a determinant of particular choices and modes of religious association and its attendant consequences.

The relational factors shaping religious outlooks are not static; therefore, neither are the distributions of these outlooks in society. As could be seen in chapter 6 and in the discussion of the Naqshbandis in chapter 2, when the social and political context changes, so do outlooks and attitudes. Religion does shape individuals' attitudes toward issues of major social and political import, but it does so in different ways in different contexts. The examples presented from Turkey, Egypt, and Tunisia provide evidence of these changing dynamics. There are significant differences in attitudes and behavior of the Tunisian Salafi group Ansar al-Sharia and the al-Nour Party in Egypt, another Salafi organization. While doctrine establishes the selection of the community that the individual chooses to associate with, it is primarily the consequence of communal association and one's religious community's status in society that generates the limited range of options for political action. The pattern of political quietism often employed by Salafis is best predicted by these groups' minority or marginal status within their societies. Changes to openings in the political system could lead to shifts from quietism to political participation in the system as in Egypt, where Salafis have enough social traction to believe they can have an influence, or it could lead to a shift from quietism to violence in a system like Tunisia, where Salafis' vision for society is so marginal and excluded from the establishment that radical and revolutionary action seems to be the only possible recourse to enact one's vision of the good society. As scholars seek to understand these dynamics, they will also understand better how countries where religion is a formidable social force may develop politically.

The relational approach employed in this volume also leads to highly nuanced accounts concerning the dynamics among Islam, democracy, and authoritarianism. For example, the degree to which individuals view religion as a social endeavor and are willing to accept social heterogeneity is likely to play a significant role in determining their perceptions of how religion should be incorporated into the political realm. These socially oriented factors are perhaps more salient than other elements of religion, such as how pious an individual is or whether they possess fundamentalist beliefs. Thus, while extreme positions with respect to preferences for social homogeneity may indeed lead to more authoritarian preferences, those who are extremely pious or hold beliefs outside the mainstream are not necessarily more likely to oppose democracy or democratic values. The acts of religious youth in different contexts, such as Iran, Egypt (Bayat 2007), and Turkey (Yenigun 2017), who reconcile pluralism with devotion provide strong evidence in favor of this statement. On the flip side, support for secular authoritarianism among the less religious may be indicative of opposition to democracy due to concerns that liberalization and the consequences of majority rule could possibly lead to increased Islamization of public policy and laws.

This interpretation goes to the heart of the scholarship on Islam and democracy. Students of Islam and democracy would benefit by examining how different religious outlooks, formed relationally, will inform attitudes in distinct ways rather than engaging in endless speculations about the shortcomings of an essentialist approach. Now that the essentialist approach toward Islam and governance has empirically been put to rest, this study suggests a new paradigm in approaching the relationship between religion and attitudes—one that admits the pluralism within Islamic faith and its practices. As noted in this book, there have been initial attempts to account for this plurality and its attitudinal as well as behavioral effects (Tessler 2015). To the extent that this book endorses the validity of this new direction, along with its findings, it has contributed a significant piece to the literature on Islam and politics in the region.

The Way Forward

According to the Koran (16:110), Muhammad and his followers made the pilgrimage to Medina due to the fitna they experienced in Mecca. In this context, fitna referred to the oppression they had endured as outcasts. Yet when they reemerged in Mecca as victors, surely the fitna that was likely of greatest concern to Muhammad's followers was related to potential divisions within the community. This book has made frequent reference to the concept of fitna, and this is because the term's fluidity, its emphasis on relational dynamics, and its centrality in the political sphere within the Muslim world highlights how an individual's religious outlook shapes her or his political preferences. An outlook that sees religious autonomy to be of utmost importance should be associated with political preferences that are diametrically opposed to one rooted in maintaining religious unity, even when shaped by the same doctrine and dogma. Yet these outlooks are not static. Local conditions will influence which outlooks individuals are likely to espouse. Thus, as an inherently social endeavor, the religious outlooks adopted by individuals should both influence and be influenced by their contexts.

While the focus of this exploration was on delineating the religious outlooks present within the Islamic world, such outlooks are likely to be present for members of any faith. Ultimately, our classification system is not rooted in religious doctrinal difference but, rather, the role that individuals see for religion in their communities. Such differences in outlooks regarding the role of religion are applicable to the pious adherents of other religions. Scholars specializing in religion and politics of other regions, including Latin America, Africa, and South Asia, may find it worthwhile to apply our conceptual and theoretical framework to advance our understanding of the different ways religion may play a role in shaping political attitudes and behavior. While this book primarily focused on pious Muslims in Arab-majority societies, many of the intuitions that drove this study apply equally to individuals in other Muslim-majority countries and to the adherents of other faiths. Broad conceptualizations of religious identity may serve as a good starting point for analyzing the intersection of religious and political attitudes, but the large variance in religious attitudes within many faiths makes analyses of intrafaith differences necessary to adequately understand how religious beliefs influence political, economic, and social preferences. In addition to survey evidence from the Arab Barometer, the in-depth study of variations in Naqshbandi religious outlooks and examples from Islamist organizations in Iran and Indonesia strongly confirm this position.

Much of this project dealt with the determinants of support for democratic institutions, but, as chapter 7 demonstrated, these religious outlooks may shape policy preferences as well. Consequently, the framework of our theory can be extended to explore attitudes and actions related to political violence, economics, social interactions, and other political phenomena. We contend that analyses of the relationship between religion and political violence, political party identification, and policy preferences that account for the social preferences adopted by different segments of the devout may prove to be very fruitful. Yet, as with support for particular political institutions, context also affects how religious outlooks may influence the policy preferences that individuals adopt. Scholars interested in examining the effects of religion on economics, violence, and social choice may consider studying the general and contextual effects of religious outlooks on policy preferences.

State and individual behaviors amid the COVID-19 pandemic present new research opportunities about religious outlooks and their contextual determinants. How do religious groups respond to the imperatives of a significant health crisis? Do their relations with the government or their attitudes in social life influence their response? More importantly, what role do religious outlooks play in their behavior? How do pious individuals with different outlooks adjust their preferences, or do they engage in different behavior according to their outlooks? We have seen several examples of religious communities refusing to abide by social distancing and quarantine rules, including the Tablighi Jamaat in India and Pakistan, the Shincheonji Church of Jesus in South Korea, and various Christian churches in the US. Some groups viewed the pandemic as a punishment from God, while others chose to follow the advice of the government and experts. Some faith leaders chose to challenge the state policies restricting religious attendance by law. The reactions of the pious varied tremendously within and between faith communities in this environment. Religious outlooks mattered a great deal in these responses. More importantly, however, these outlooks were shaped by the existing relational influences, state policies about religion and religious groups, and other contextual factors. It should be noted that some of these factors are also evolving in the new reality created by the COVID-19 world. As such, there are unique opportunities to investigate the changing dynamics about religion and political attitudes across the world.

The empirical and theoretical analyses in this book present Muslim populations that are far less homogenous in their religious and political preferences than has generally been presented in the discourse on Islam and politics. Although significant differences regarding preferences for democracy and distribution were illustrated, further exploration of the relationship between Muslim identity and preferences over regime type would likely be fruitful. Democracies and autocracies take on different institutional configurations, and many of these differences may affect the role that religion plays in a society. Moreover, while an analysis of cross-country variations in the aggregate levels of our relevant categories of religious outlooks was beyond the scope of this immediate analysis, a reasonable expectation would be that group membership plays a role in explaining differences in aggregate levels of support for democracy between states. The intensity of such differences, however, should be contingent on the ideological location of the regime and perceptions of the ideal point of society. Thus, while Muslim states made up of more pluralistic groupings may be more likely to produce or sustain democracy, such a result may depend on beliefs regarding the ability of democracy to produce religious public goods relative to its most likely competing regime option.

Notes

1. In a succinct description per the plurality of religious outlooks, the famous Sunni theologian Abū al-Ḥasan al-Ashʿarī (874–936) said, "After their Prophet, the people disagreed about many things; some of them led others astray, while some dissociated themselves from others. Thus, they became distinct groups and disparate parties—except that Islam gathers them together and encompasses them all." This translation is reported in Ahmed (2015).

APPENDIX A

Chapter 3

Table A3.1. LCA Estimation Results with the Full Sample of Respondents

Variables	Response Categories	Religious Individualist	Post-Islamist	Religious Communitarian	Social Communitarian
The government and parliament should enact laws in accordance with Islamic Law.	Strongly disagree	0.34	0.02	0.00	0.05
	Disagree	0.24	0.03	0.06	0.28
	Agree	0.29	0.19	0.64	0.58
	Strongly agree	0.14	0.76	0.30	0.09
Applying shari'a more strictly.	Strongly don't support	0.30	0.02	0.00	0.06
	Don't support	0.28	0.05	0.04	0.30
	Support	0.25	0.17	0.43	0.54
	Strongly support	0.18	0.76	0.53	0.10
Non-Muslims should have less rights.	Strongly disagree	0.68	0.38	0.08	0.15
	Disagree	0.21	0.26	0.50	0.56
	Agree	0.05	0.17	0.35	0.26
	Strongly agree	0.06	0.18	0.08	0.03
Religious practices are private and should be separated from social and political life.	Strongly disagree	0.03	0.31	0.06	0.06
	Disagree	0.02	0.20	0.46	0.18
	Agree	0.09	0.14	0.43	0.57
	Strongly agree	0.86	0.36	0.05	0.18
Laws regulating marriage and divorce shall be based on an accurate explanation of the Islamic shari'a.	I disagree to a certain extent	0.22	0.02	0.01	0.10
	I agree to a certain extent	0.32	0.14	0.19	0.31

Appendix A

Table A3.1. (continued)

Variables	Response Categories	Religious Individualist	Post-Islamist	Religious Communitarian	Social Communitarian
	I absolutely agree	0.46	0.84	0.80	0.59
Country better off with religious people in public office.	Strongly disagree	0.71	0.19	0.01	0.19
	Disagree	0.20	0.18	0.33	0.65
	Agree	0.06	0.26	0.60	0.16
	Strongly agree	0.03	0.37	0.06	0.01
Difference and variation between Islamic scholars with regard to their interpretation of religious matters is a good thing.	I absolutely disagree	0.15	0.09	0.06	0.08
	I disagree to a certain extent	0.17	0.09	0.14	0.22
	I agree to a certain extent	0.26	0.24	0.51	0.54
	I strongly agree	0.42	0.59	0.29	0.17
Religious Minorities such as Christians and Shi'a have the right to practice their religion freely.	I absolutely disagree	0.06	0.14	0.12	0.07
	I disagree to a certain extent	0.04	0.10	0.14	0.18
	I agree to a certain extent	0.17	0.22	0.48	0.50
	I strongly agree	0.73	0.54	0.26	0.25
Which of the following sentences is the closest to your point of view? 1. I prefer a religious political party over a non-religious political party 2. I prefer a non-religious political party over a religious political party 3. I don't agree with either.	Strongly prefer a non-religious party	0.34	0.05	0.02	0.10

Table A3.1. (continued)

Variables	Response Categories	Religious Individualist	Post-Islamist	Religious Communitarian	Social Communitarian
	Prefer a non-religious party	0.29	0.06	0.06	0.33
	I prefer neither	0.23	0.18	0.20	0.23
	I prefer a religious party	0.07	0.17	0.33	0.22
	I strongly prefer a religious party	0.08	0.54	0.38	0.13
Religious institutions should not influence voters.	Strongly disagree	0.02	0.13	0.01	0.05
	Disagree	0.02	0.17	0.23	0.12
	Agree	0.07	0.22	0.68	0.62
	Strongly agree	0.89	0.48	0.09	0.21

Note: The numbers represent class shares according to the LCA estimation.
Source: Arab Barometer, Wave III.

Table A3.2. Factor Analysis Estimation Results from Exploratory Factor Analysis

Variable	Factor1	Factor2	Factor3	Factor4	Uniqueness
lci2	0.4995				0.6690
lci3	0.5551				0.6536
lci4		0.4954			0.8228
lci5			0.5922		0.6356
lci6	0.5127				0.8524
lci8		0.3644			0.6391
lci9				0.4437	0.8172
lci10				0.4452	0.7334
lci11					0.7272
lci12			0.5779		0.7202

Note: The numbers represent factor loadings.
Source: Arab Barometer, Wave III.

Chapter 4

Table A4.1. Class Probabilities from the Baseline Model (Individual Correlates and Country Fixed Effects)

Variable	Response Categories	LCA Code	Religious Individualist	Post-Islamist	Social Communitarian	Religious Communitarian
The government and parliament should enact laws in accordance with Islamic Law.	Strongly disagree	lci2	0.31	0.01	0.06	0.00
	Disagree		0.21	0.03	0.27	0.04
	Agree		0.24	0.23	0.57	0.66
	Strongly agree		0.24	0.73	0.10	0.30
Applying shari'a more strictly.	Strongly don't support	lci3	0.23	0.01	0.06	0.00
	Don't support		0.21	0.04	0.27	0.04
	Support		0.27	0.20	0.55	0.44
	Strongly support		0.29	0.74	0.13	0.53
Non-Muslims should have fewer rights.	Strongly disagree	lci4	0.70	0.34	0.19	0.04
	Disagree		0.19	0.28	0.60	0.46
	Agree		0.05	0.19	0.18	0.40
	Strongly agree		0.07	0.19	0.02	0.10
Religious practices are private and should be separated from social and political life.	Strongly disagree	lci5	0.03	0.33	0.06	0.05
	Disagree		0.03	0.24	0.18	0.51
	Agree		0.08	0.15	0.56	0.41
	Strongly agree		0.86	0.27	0.21	0.03

Table A4.1. (continued)

Variable	Response Categories	LCA Code	Religious Individualist	Post-Islamist	Social Communitarian	Religious Communitarian
Laws regulating marriage and divorce shall be based on an accurate explanation of the Islamic shari'a.	I disagree to a certain extent	lci6	0.15	0.02	0.08	0.00
	I agree to a certain extent		0.30	0.16	0.28	0.16
	I absolutely agree		0.54	0.82	0.64	0.84
Country better off with religious people in public office.	Strongly disagree	lci8	0.73	0.13	0.17	0.03
	Disagree		0.18	0.16	0.60	0.37
	Agree		0.05	0.32	0.22	0.55
	Strongly agree		0.03	0.38	0.01	0.04
Difference and variation between Islamic scholars with regard to their interpretation of religious matters is a good thing.	I absolutely disagree	lci9	0.14	0.07	0.09	0.06
	I disagree to a certain extent		0.12	0.08	0.19	0.17
	I agree to a certain extent		0.25	0.25	0.50	0.57
	I strongly agree		0.50	0.59	0.22	0.20
Religious Minorities such as Christians and Shi'a have the right to practice their religion freely.	I absolutely disagree	lci10	0.04	0.13	0.06	0.17
	I disagree to a certain extent		0.04	0.11	0.15	0.20

Table A4.1. (continued)

Variable	Response Categories	LCA Code	Religious Individualist	Post-Islamist	Social Communitarian	Religious Communitarian
	I agree to a certain extent		0.16	0.26	0.49	0.50
	I strongly agree		0.76	0.50	0.30	0.13
Which of the following sentences is the closest to your point of view? 1. I prefer a religious political party over a non-religious political party 2. I prefer a non-religious political party over a religious political party 3. I don't agree with either.	Strongly prefer a non-religious party	lci11	0.30	0.03	0.09	0.02
	Prefer a non-religious party		0.25	0.05	0.28	0.09
	I prefer neither		0.25	0.16	0.21	0.29
	I prefer a religious party		0.07	0.19	0.22	0.33
	I strongly prefer a religious party		0.13	0.57	0.20	0.27
Religious institutions should not influence voters.	Strongly disagree	lci12	0.03	0.11	0.05	0.01
	Disagree		0.02	0.19	0.11	0.21
	Agree		0.05	0.26	0.60	0.70
	Strongly agree		0.90	0.43	0.25	0.09

Source: Arab Barometer, Wave III.

Appendix A | 213

Chapter 5

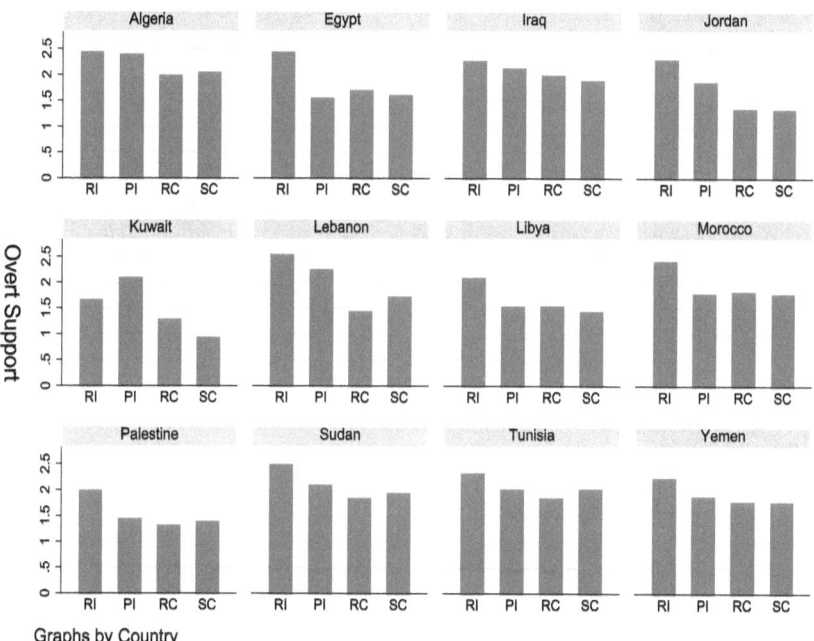

Figure A5.1. Religious Outlooks and Mean Overt Support for Democracy by Country. Source: Arab Barometer.

Table A5.1. Fixed Effects for Table 5.2 (Pious Sample)

	Model 1	Model 2	Model 3	Model 4	Model 5	Model 6
Egypt	−0.318***	−0.216***	−0.204**	0.347**	0.280*	0.298*
	(0.062)	(0.065)	(0.065)	(0.116)	(0.124)	(0.124)
Iraq	0.0323	0.150*	0.133*	−0.144	−0.200	−0.219
	(0.058)	(0.060)	(0.061)	(0.119)	(0.125)	(0.125)
Jordan	−0.554***	−0.462***	−0.440***	0.0700	0.000551	0.0289
	(0.055)	(0.058)	(0.059)	(0.100)	(0.108)	(0.109)
Kuwait	−0.700***	−0.591***	−0.591***	0.244*	0.165	0.168
	(0.060)	(0.062)	(0.062)	(0.114)	(0.121)	(0.121)
Lebanon	−0.234**	−0.137	−0.117	0.0599	−0.0261	−0.00166
	(0.074)	(0.077)	(0.078)	(0.139)	(0.145)	(0.146)
Libya	−0.462***	−0.350***	−0.362***	−0.00649	−0.0772	−0.0875
	(0.067)	(0.071)	(0.071)	(0.118)	(0.126)	(0.127)

Table A5.1. (continued)

	Model 1	Model 2	Model 3	Model 4	Model 5	Model 6
Morocco	−0.0222	0.0942	0.0915	0.592***	0.515***	0.515***
	(0.059)	(0.063)	(0.063)	(0.114)	(0.123)	(0.123)
Palestine	−0.646***	−0.564***	−0.554***	−0.331**	−0.405***	−0.391**
	(0.061)	(0.064)	(0.064)	(0.114)	(0.122)	(0.123)
Sudan	0.0337	0.128*	0.116	−1.216***	−1.285***	−1.297***
	(0.060)	(0.063)	(0.064)	(0.115)	(0.123)	(0.123)
Tunisia	−0.176*	−0.0823	−0.0584	−0.0425	−0.0903	−0.0612
	(0.070)	(0.073)	(0.074)	(0.123)	(0.131)	(0.131)
Yemen	−0.141*	−0.0309	−0.0327	−0.357**	−0.415***	−0.417***
	(0.061)	(0.065)	(0.065)	(0.114)	(0.122)	(0.122)
Constant	1.035***	0.971***	−3.277***	0.316	0.491	−4.502***
	(0.110)	(0.154)	(0.781)	(0.195)	(0.265)	(1.323)

Notes: Standard errors in parentheses; * $p < .05$, ** $p < 0.01$, *** $p < .001$. Algeria is the reference category.
Source: Arab Barometer, Wave III.

Table A5.2. Correlation between Items in the Democracy Measure and the LCA

	(Extrinsic) democ4_13	(Extrinsic) democ4_14	(Extrinsic) democ4_16	(Overt) democ11	(Overt) democ12
lci2	0.0127	−0.00276	0.0280**	0.0126	0.0412***
lci3	0.0244**	0.0376***	0.0302***	0.00924	−0.00742
lci4	0.00255	−0.00997	−0.0105	−0.105***	0.193***
lci5	0.00854	0.0128	0.00804	0.0858***	−0.0404***
lci6	0.0218**	0.0170*	0.0312***	−0.0577***	−0.00388
lci7	0.0186*	−0.00516	0.0297***	−0.0429***	0.00400
lci8	0.00212	0.0268**	−0.00341	−0.0450***	0.0962***
lci9	0.00254	0.0259**	−0.0280**	0.133***	0.00173
lci10	−0.0300***	0.0501***	−0.0165	0.176***	−0.0618***
lci11	−0.0148	0.00262	0.0212*	−0.0863***	0.0811***
lci12	−0.00833	0.0245**	0.00854	0.145***	−0.111***
N	14,205	14,205	14,205	14,205	14,205

Note: * $p < 0.05$, ** $p < 0.01$, *** $p < 0.001$.
Source: Arab Barometer, Wave III.

Table A5.3. Fixed Effects for Table 5.3 (Regression Analysis with Nonpious Muslims)

	(1) Overt Support	(2) Extrinsic Support
Egypt	−0.179**	0.416***
	(0.054)	(0.102)
Iraq	0.0686	−0.205*
	(0.048)	(0.094)
Jordan	−0.498***	0.147
	(0.048)	(0.086)
Kuwait	−0.724***	0.197*
	(0.051)	(0.097)
Lebanon	−0.0673	0.133
	(0.058)	(0.112)
Libya	−0.378***	0.0993
	(0.055)	(0.097)
Morocco	0.0740	0.647***
	(0.051)	(0.099)
Palestine	−0.570***	−0.265**
	(0.049)	(0.094)
Sudan	0.0385	−1.182***
	(0.054)	(0.102)
Tunisia	−0.0809	0.0587
	(0.055)	(0.097)
Yemen	−0.193***	−0.272**
	(0.053)	(0.096)
Constant	1.066***	0.578***
	(0.096)	(0.165)

Notes: Standard errors in parentheses; * $p < .05$, ** $p < 0.01$, *** $p < .001$. Algeria is the reference country.
Source: Arab Barometer, Wave III.

Robustness Checks

The same analysis was run on the full sample of data. The results of this analysis are presented below. These results mirror the analysis presented above and largely corroborate our theoretical expectations. Religious individualists and post-Islamists appear to be more supportive of democracy than social communitarians and religious communitarians.

Table A5.4. OLS Regression and Logit Estimations (Full Sample)

	Model 1	Model 2	Model 3	Model 4	Model 5	Model 6
	Overt Support			Extrinsic Support		
Religious Individualist	0.557***	0.557***	0.568***	0.174*	0.169*	0.179**
	(0.038)	(0.039)	(0.039)	(0.068)	(0.069)	(0.069)
Post-Islamist	0.262***	0.269***	0.278***	0.372***	0.372***	0.380***
	(0.033)	(0.034)	(0.034)	(0.055)	(0.056)	(0.056)
Religious communitarian	−0.0104	−0.00361	−0.000880	0.478***	0.473***	0.475***
	(0.028)	(0.028)	(0.028)	(0.048)	(0.049)	(0.050)
Religiosity		0.00112	0.120***		−0.0101	0.101
		(0.005)	(0.032)		(0.009)	(0.058)
(Religiosity)^2			−0.00527***			−0.00495
			(0.001)			(0.003)
Personal trust	−0.0131	−0.00413	−0.00145	0.0998*	0.0867*	0.0891*
	(0.025)	(0.026)	(0.026)	(0.043)	(0.044)	(0.044)
Political trust	0.0215***	0.0203***	0.0201***	0.000593	0.00235	0.00215
	(0.004)	(0.004)	(0.004)	(0.007)	(0.007)	(0.007)
Political interest	0.00340	0.000775	0.00109	−0.102***	−0.0992***	−0.0990***
	(0.012)	(0.013)	(0.013)	(0.020)	(0.020)	(0.021)
Egalitarian gender beliefs	0.0833***	0.0833***	0.0828***	−0.00508	−0.00884	−0.00936
	(0.006)	(0.006)	(0.006)	(0.010)	(0.011)	(0.011)
Economic perceptions	−0.0621***	−0.0650***	−0.0654***	−0.0804**	−0.0723*	−0.0726*
	(0.017)	(0.018)	(0.018)	(0.028)	(0.029)	(0.029)
Prospective economic perceptions	0.0143	0.0132	0.0128	0.0187	0.0193	0.0190
	(0.011)	(0.011)	(0.011)	(0.018)	(0.018)	(0.018)
Age	0.00244**	0.00244**	0.00265**	0.00335*	0.00393**	0.00413**
	(0.001)	(0.001)	(0.001)	(0.001)	(0.002)	(0.002)
Female	−0.0371	−0.0403	−0.0486*	0.167***	0.162***	0.154***
	(0.023)	(0.023)	(0.023)	(0.039)	(0.040)	(0.040)
Education	0.0342***	0.0349***	0.0348***	−0.0660***	−0.0632***	−0.0634***
	(0.007)	(0.008)	(0.008)	(0.013)	(0.013)	(0.013)
Income	−0.0133	−0.0129	−0.0129	−0.0313	−0.0270	−0.0271
	(0.013)	(0.013)	(0.013)	(0.022)	(0.022)	(0.022)
Country dummies	Yes	Yes	Yes	Yes	Yes	Yes
Observations	11,668	11,308	11,308	12,246	11,850	11,850
Adjusted R-squared	0.101	0.101	0.102			

Notes: Standard errors in parentheses; * $p < .05$, ** $p < 0.01$, *** $p < .001$. Fixed effects presented in table A5.5.
Source: Arab Barometer, Wave III.

The results of these multivariate estimations are robust to alternative specifications. First, the results remain qualitatively similar when using alternative specifications of the dependent variable. Inglehart and Welzel's (2003) operationalization of overt support included two additional items, tapping into the respondents' views regarding military regimes and their opinion about the statement "democracy may have problems, but it is better than other regimes" (Q516.4). Since the former is not available in the third wave of the Arab Barometer, we created an alternative index with three questions (the two questions used in the construction of our dependent variable and Q516.4) and replicated the multivariate analysis with this measure. The results remain unchanged. We also ran multilevel regressions and models with survey weights, used the posterior probability of class membership in place of absolute class categorizations, and tried alternative specifications by adding or dropping certain variables. In each of the specifications noted above, the core results remain robust, highlighting the conceptual utility of dissecting religious outlooks and corroborating the theoretical expectations presented within this chapter.

Fixed effects for table A5.4 are presented below in table A5.5.

Table A5.5. Fixed Effects for Table A5.4 (Full Sample)

	Model 1	Model 2	Model 3	Model 4	Model 5	Model 6
Egypt	−0.209***	−0.138*	−0.133*	0.398***	0.383***	0.390***
	(0.054)	(0.056)	(0.056)	(0.102)	(0.106)	(0.106)
Iraq	0.0786	0.162***	0.155**	−0.178	−0.192*	−0.197*
	(0.048)	(0.049)	(0.049)	(0.094)	(0.098)	(0.098)
Jordan	−0.514***	−0.451***	−0.438***	0.118	0.0955	0.109
	(0.048)	(0.050)	(0.050)	(0.086)	(0.091)	(0.091)
Kuwait	−0.735***	−0.661***	−0.661***	0.193*	0.148	0.149
	(0.051)	(0.052)	(0.052)	(0.097)	(0.100)	(0.100)
Lebanon	−0.163**	−0.0960	−0.0582	0.188	0.149	0.185
	(0.060)	(0.062)	(0.063)	(0.113)	(0.117)	(0.119)
Libya	−0.397***	−0.321***	−0.320***	0.0733	0.0427	0.0451
	(0.055)	(0.057)	(0.057)	(0.097)	(0.102)	(0.102)
Morocco	0.0547	0.142**	0.142**	0.628***	0.603***	0.604***
	(0.051)	(0.053)	(0.053)	(0.098)	(0.104)	(0.104)
Palestine	−0.559***	−0.502***	−0.497***	−0.283**	−0.311**	−0.305**
	(0.049)	(0.051)	(0.051)	(0.094)	(0.099)	(0.099)

Table A5.5. (continued)

	Model 1	Model 2	Model 3	Model 4	Model 5	Model 6
Sudan	0.00847	0.0709	0.0769	−1.217***	−1.240***	−1.233***
	(0.053)	(0.056)	(0.056)	(0.102)	(0.107)	(0.107)
Tunisia	−0.132*	−0.0674	−0.0615	0.0956	0.0775	0.0843
	(0.055)	(0.057)	(0.057)	(0.098)	(0.102)	(0.102)
Yemen	−0.216***	−0.137*	−0.132*	−0.269**	−0.299**	−0.293**
	(0.053)	(0.055)	(0.055)	(0.096)	(0.100)	(0.100)
Constant	0.938***	0.875***	0.239	0.268	0.377*	−0.220
	(0.094)	(0.109)	(0.202)	(0.163)	(0.188)	(0.359)

Notes: Standard errors in parentheses; * $p < .05$, ** $p < 0.01$, *** $p < .001$. Algeria is the reference category.
Source: Arab Barometer, Wave III.

Chapter 6

Table A6.1. Class Probabilities from LCA Estimation, Wave II

		Egypt				Tunisia			
		RI	PI	RC	SC	RI	PI	RC	SC
Members of other religions	Yes	0.99	0.89	0.94	0.96	0.91	0.92	0.81	0.77
Enact laws in accordance with sharia	Strongly disagree	0.00	0.08	0.01	0.00	0.05	0.10	0.00	0.01
	Disagree	0.33	0.19	0.02	0.10	0.45	0.20	0.20	0.29
	Agree	0.43	0.15	0.32	0.55	0.49	0.37	0.34	0.64
	Strongly agree	0.24	0.57	0.65	0.35	0.01	0.33	0.45	0.06
Religious leaders should not interfere in voters' decisions	Strongly disagree	0.02	0.07	0.06	0.01	0.03	0.08	0.06	0.00
	Disagree	0.01	0.02	0.14	0.16	0.12	0.00	0.61	0.13
	Agree	0.11	0.00	0.47	0.80	0.23	0.05	0.14	0.82
	Strongly agree	0.86	0.91	0.33	0.03	0.62	0.86	0.20	0.05
Religious leaders should have influence over government decisions	Strongly disagree	0.29	0.48	0.03	0.05	0.12	0.76	0.00	0.01
	Disagree	0.57	0.34	0.37	0.51	0.85	0.09	0.28	0.70
	Agree	0.09	0.00	0.41	0.43	0.03	0.11	0.52	0.28
	Strongly agree	0.05	0.18	0.19	0.01	0.00	0.04	0.20	0.01

Table A6.1. (continued)

		Egypt				Tunisia			
		RI	PI	RC	SC	RI	PI	RC	SC
Religious practices are private and should be separate from public life	Strongly disagree	0.00	0.07	0.10	0.00	0.00	0.03	0.22	0.00
	Disagree	0.01	0.08	0.43	0.17	0.05	0.00	0.45	0.26
	Agree	0.58	0.02	0.11	0.74	0.28	0.12	0.12	0.66
	Strongly agree	0.42	0.83	0.35	0.08	0.67	0.86	0.20	0.08
Religious minorities should be free to practice their religion	I absolutely disagree	0.00	0.02	0.00	0.00	0.03	0.02	0.07	0.00
	I disagree to a certain extent	0.01	0.02	0.00	0.05	0.01	0.01	0.12	0.04
	I agree to a certain extent	0.34	0.08	0.14	0.42	0.24	0.05	0.25	0.77
	Strongly agree	0.66	0.88	0.86	0.52	0.71	0.92	0.57	0.19

Notes: Probabilities based on LCA estimation results from Arab Barometer, Wave II. RI, religious individualist; PI, post-Islamist; RC, religious communitarian; SC, social communitarian.
Source: Arab Barometer, Wave II.

Table A6.2. Class Probabilities from LCA Estimation, Wave III

		Egypt				Tunisia			
		RI	PI	RC	SC	RI	PI	RC	SC
Non-Muslims should have less rights	Strongly disagree	0.84	0.42	0.03	0.58	0.51	0.57	0.26	0.00
	Disagree	0.11	0.54	0.80	0.21	0.32	0.07	0.29	0.70
	Agree	0.01	0.04	0.16	0.16	0.10	0.10	0.36	0.26
	Strongly agree	0.04	0.01	0.00	0.04	0.06	0.26	0.10	0.04
Enact laws in accordance with sharia	Strongly disagree	0.07	0.05	0.00	0.34	0.31	0.09	0.00	0.05
	Disagree	0.14	0.19	0.13	0.24	0.20	0.11	0.00	0.56
	Agree	0.31	0.53	0.72	0.10	0.46	0.02	0.81	0.31
	Strongly agree	0.48	0.23	0.15	0.32	0.03	0.78	0.19	0.07
Religious leaders should not interfere in voters' decisions	Strongly disagree	0.03	0.00	0.00	0.28	0.19	0.13	0.06	0.00
	Disagree	0.03	0.00	0.13	0.38	0.00	0.08	0.11	0.19
	Agree	0.00	0.21	0.84	0.28	0.08	0.02	0.52	0.67
	Strongly agree	0.95	0.79	0.04	0.06	0.73	0.77	0.31	0.14
Religious leaders should have influence over government decisions	Strongly disagree	0.52	0.48	0.01	0.42	0.73	0.51	0.11	0.11
	Disagree	0.21	0.44	0.75	0.33	0.20	0.06	0.44	0.68
	Agree	0.00	0.08	0.25	0.20	0.00	0.14	0.42	0.21

Table A6.2. (continued)

		Egypt				Tunisia			
		RI	PI	RC	SC	RI	PI	RC	SC
Religious practices are private and should be separate from public life	Strongly agree	0.27	0.00	0.00	0.05	0.06	0.30	0.03	0.00
	Strongly disagree	0.02	0.01	0.03	0.48	0.01	0.25	0.26	0.00
	Disagree	0.05	0.08	0.28	0.21	0.00	0.10	0.28	0.25
	Agree	0.00	0.60	0.68	0.24	0.21	0.07	0.44	0.57
	Strongly agree	0.93	0.31	0.01	0.07	0.78	0.59	0.02	0.17
Religious minorities should be free to practice their religion	I absolutely disagree	0.00	0.00	0.01	0.12	0.01	0.23	0.03	0.04
	I disagree to a certain extent	0.00	0.01	0.02	0.39	0.08	0.07	0.16	0.13
	I agree to a certain extent	0.05	0.46	0.63	0.13	0.25	0.20	0.42	0.59
	Strongly agree	0.95	0.53	0.34	0.36	0.66	0.50	0.39	0.24

Notes: Probabilities based on LCA estimation results from Arab Barometer, Wave III. RI, religious individualist; PI, post-Islamist; RC, religious communitarian; SC, social communitarian.
Source: Arab Barometer, Wave III.

Chapter 7

Table A7.1. Analysis of Standard Deviation of Redistribution by Class

Class	Standard Deviation		
Religious individualists	3.45		
Post-Islamists	3.28		
Religious communitarians	3.08		
Social communitarians	2.96		
Levene's Test Statistic			
	Religious Individualists	*Post-Islamists*	*Religious Communitarians*
Religious individualists			
Post-Islamists	14.00*		
Religious communitarians	66.32*	24.56*	
Social communitarians	86.75*	38.61*	2.94*

Note: * $p < 0.05$.
Source: Arab Barometer, Wave III.

Table A7.2. Analysis of Full Sample

	Model 1	Model 2	Model 3	Model 4	Model 5	Model 6
	Distributive Change	Distance Median	Dist. Class Median	Criticize Policy	Redistribution	Redistribution
Post-Islamist	0.227***	0.251***	0.225***	0.0444*	−0.0333	−0.0535
	(0.050)	(0.049)	(0.050)	(0.021)	(0.077)	(0.087)
Religious individualist	0.552***	0.464***	0.427***	0.189***	0.334***	−0.210#
	(0.062)	(0.063)	(0.066)	(0.023)	(0.101)	(0.112)
Religious communitarian	−0.00268	−0.0491	−0.0386	−0.0320#	−0.305***	−0.252***
	(0.042)	(0.043)	(0.043)	(0.018)	(0.065)	(0.073)
Tribal	−0.215***	−0.251***	−0.262***	−0.0110		−0.217*
	(0.053)	(0.052)	(0.052)	(0.022)		(0.088)
Religiosity index	0.0125#	0.0179*	0.0213*	−0.00157		0.0231#
	(0.008)	(0.008)	(0.009)	(0.003)		(0.014)
Personal trust	0.0535	0.0460	0.0112	−0.0963***		0.0206
	(0.039)	(0.038)	(0.039)	(0.016)		(0.067)
Political trust	−0.0181**	−0.0171**	−0.0156*	−0.0693***		−0.0437***
	(0.006)	(0.006)	(0.006)	(0.003)		(0.011)
Political interest	0.0161	0.0369*	0.0185	0.000868		0.103**
	(0.018)	(0.019)	(0.020)	(0.007)		(0.033)
Egalitarian gender beliefs	0.0266**	−0.00870	−0.0161#	−0.000387		0.0411*
	(0.009)	(0.009)	(0.010)	(0.004)		(0.017)
Economic perceptions	−0.113***	−0.0548*	−0.0519*	−0.175***		−0.143**
	(0.026)	(0.025)	(0.026)	(0.011)		(0.044)
Prospective economic perceptions	−0.0219	0.0103	0.0214	−0.0429***		−0.0568#
	(0.016)	(0.016)	(0.017)	(0.007)		(0.029)
Age	−0.00103	−0.00273*	−0.00263#	0.000276		0.00117
	(0.001)	(0.001)	(0.001)	(0.001)		(0.002)
Female	−0.0408	0.00501	0.000904	−0.00148		−0.0858
	(0.035)	(0.035)	(0.037)	(0.014)		(0.061)

Table A7.2. (continued)

	Model 1	Model 2	Model 3	Model 4	Model 5	Model 6
	Distributive Change	Distance Median	Dist. Class Median	Criticize Policy	Redistribution	Redistribution
Education	−0.0234*	−0.0353**	−0.0227#	0.00260		−0.0358#
	(0.012)	(0.012)	(0.012)	(0.005)		(0.020)
Income	−0.0506**	−0.0251	−0.00362	−0.0340***		−0.0911**
	(0.020)	(0.020)	(0.020)	(0.008)		(0.034)
Egypt	0.0950	0.105	0.0775	0.0318		0.472**
	(0.091)	(0.091)	(0.095)	(0.036)		(0.154)
Iraq	0.388***	0.378***	0.404***	−0.0794*		−0.0861
	(0.081)	(0.081)	(0.081)	(0.035)		(0.140)
Jordan	0.160*	0.143#	0.153*	−0.0104		1.062***
	(0.076)	(0.074)	(0.074)	(0.034)		(0.124)
Kuwait	0.759***	0.599***	0.563***	−0.307***		0.160
	(0.087)	(0.090)	(0.090)	(0.038)		(0.144)
Lebanon	0.826***	0.0828	−0.188	0.175***		2.124***
	(0.103)	(0.106)	(0.117)	(0.038)		(0.172)
Libya	0.720***	0.725***	0.725***	−0.141***		−0.244
	(0.093)	(0.093)	(0.093)	(0.038)		(0.158)
Morocco	1.136***	0.282**	0.260**	−0.0106		2.355***
	(0.091)	(0.091)	(0.100)	(0.034)		(0.146)
Palestine	0.699***	0.749***	0.760***	−0.0767*		0.402**
	(0.086)	(0.087)	(0.087)	(0.038)		(0.149)
Sudan	0.957***	0.990***	0.973***	0.000138		0.268
	(0.093)	(0.093)	(0.093)	(0.038)		(0.166)
Tunisia	0.315***	0.416***	0.457***	−0.197***		0.205
	(0.087)	(0.087)	(0.087)	(0.038)		(0.152)
Yemen	0.373***	0.282***	0.264**	−0.0375		0.883***
	(0.084)	(0.083)	(0.085)	(0.036)		(0.143)
Constant	2.381***	2.340***	2.241***	3.439***	5.665***	5.538***
	(0.165)	(0.165)	(0.174)	(0.066)	(0.049)	(0.293)
Observations	11,158	11,158	11,158	11,307	13,259	11,158
Adjusted R-squared	0.061	0.040	0.037	0.292	0.004	0.078

Note: Standard errors in parentheses; # $p < 0.1$, * $p < .05$, ** $p < 0.01$, *** $p < .001$.
Source: Arab Barometer, Wave III.

Table A7.3. Analysis of Full Sample (Egypt and Tunisia)

	Model 1	Model 2	Model 3	Model 4
	Egypt		Tunisia	
Post-Islamist	−0.631**	−0.801**	0.761**	0.665*
	(0.223)	(0.268)	(0.255)	(0.285)
Tribal		−1.054*		−1.046
		(0.444)		(1.431)
Religiosity		0.0945		−0.00507
		(0.057)		(0.043)
Personal trust		0.148		0.0310
		(0.241)		(0.260)
Political trust		0.0503		0.0405
		(0.041)		(0.036)
Political interest		−0.466***		0.101
		(0.130)		(0.105)
Egalitarian gender beliefs		0.0104		0.0262
		(0.061)		(0.053)
Economic perceptions		0.0422		−0.239
		(0.170)		(0.161)
Prospective economic perceptions		−0.245**		0.0181
		(0.086)		(0.099)
Age		−0.00952		0.00562
		(0.008)		(0.008)
Female		0.0976		−0.392#
		(0.201)		(0.217)
Education		−0.0658		−0.0232
		(0.063)		(0.070)
Income		−0.0696		−0.294**
		(0.124)		(0.112)
Constant	5.971***	6.597***	5.248***	5.354***
	(0.103)	(1.085)	(0.102)	(0.819)
Observations	1,021	877	1,138	941
Adjusted R-squared	0.006	0.047	0.008	0.014

Note: Standard errors in parentheses; # $p < 0.1$, * $p < .05$, ** $p < 0.01$, *** $p < .001$.
Source: Arab Barometer, Wave III.

Table A7.4. Fixed Effects for Table 7.1

	Model 1	Model 2	Model 3	Model 4	Model 5
Egypt	0.105	0.157	0.110	0.0184	0.452**
	(0.105)	(0.105)	(0.107)	(0.042)	(0.172)
Iraq	0.594***	0.599***	0.611***	−0.0988*	−0.0316
	(0.102)	(0.102)	(0.105)	(0.044)	(0.177)
Jordan	0.278**	0.292***	0.309***	0.0236	1.058***
	(0.089)	(0.087)	(0.089)	(0.040)	(0.142)
Kuwait	1.015***	0.830***	0.817***	−0.257***	0.253
	(0.104)	(0.108)	(0.108)	(0.046)	(0.170)
Lebanon	1.064***	0.337*	0.172	0.210***	2.147***
	(0.126)	(0.132)	(0.149)	(0.046)	(0.210)
Libya	0.880***	0.892***	0.838***	−0.126**	−0.00306
	(0.114)	(0.114)	(0.115)	(0.046)	(0.193)
Morocco	1.241***	0.503***	0.481***	0.0280	2.220***
	(0.106)	(0.109)	(0.119)	(0.041)	(0.170)
Palestine	0.686***	0.757***	0.757***	−0.0314	0.538**
	(0.105)	(0.106)	(0.106)	(0.047)	(0.176)
Sudan	1.076***	1.133***	1.111***	0.0116	0.259
	(0.105)	(0.106)	(0.106)	(0.043)	(0.184)
Tunisia	0.515***	0.615***	0.600***	−0.215***	0.380*
	(0.109)	(0.110)	(0.112)	(0.048)	(0.190)
Yemen	0.487***	0.379***	0.362***	0.00790	0.995***
	(0.101)	(0.099)	(0.102)	(0.043)	(0.168)
Constant	1.808***	1.689***	1.701***	3.340***	6.099***
	(0.232)	(0.232)	(0.245)	(0.094)	(0.402)

Notes: Standard errors in parentheses; * $p < .05$, ** $p < 0.01$, *** $p < .001$. Algeria is the reference category.
Source: Arab Barometer, Wave III.

APPENDIX B

Chapter 5

$$U_i = -(x_i - x_i^*)^2 - c(x_i - x_D)^2 - a_i\left(\frac{\Sigma_{-i}(x_{-i} - \bar{x})^2}{n-1}\right) + b_i x_i^* \sqrt{\sum_{-i} x_{-i}}$$

Proposition 1: When all other variables are held constant, an individual's support for liberal democracy is decreasing in her preference for social cohesion.

Proof of Proposition 1.

Individuals have one choice variable, x_i, and the function is strictly concave given that $c \geq 0$ ($\frac{d^2U}{dx_i^2} = -2 - 2c$). In equilibrium, individuals will choose

$$\frac{dU}{dx_i} = -2x_i + 2x_i^* - 2cx_i + 2cx_D = 0$$

$$x_i = \frac{x_i^* + cx_D}{1+c}$$

The absolute distance between any two individuals in equilibrium will be

$$|x_1 - x_2| = \frac{|x_1^* - x_2^*|}{1+c}$$

The distance between any two individuals is weakly decreasing in c. This trivially implies that $Var(x_{-i})$ is weakly decreasing in c. Thus, the utility of c is weakly increasing in a. It is important to note that the distance between these two individuals does not hinge on the position of the regime. As c increases, the distance between these individuals decreases in c independent of where D's preferred policy is located.

Proposition 2: When all other variables are held constant, increasing an individual's preference for religion in the public sphere increases her likelihood of preferring a regime type based on its effect on the contributions of others.

Proof of Proposition 2

Where $x_i < x_{\sim d}$, an increase in c will lead to an increase in x_i in equilibrium, and where $x_i > x_{\sim d}$, an increase in c will decrease x_i in equilibrium. If $\bar{x}_d < \bar{x}_{\sim d}$, x_{-i} will, on average, increase in $c_{\sim d}$. If $\bar{x}_d > \bar{x}_{\sim d}$, x_{-i} will, on average, decrease in $c_{\sim d}$. These conditions require an $x_d < x_{\sim d}$ and $x_d > x_{\sim d}$ respectively. Since the utility of x_{-i} is increasing in b, as b increases the value of x_{-i} increases. As b increases, the proportion of the utility derived from x_{-i} also increases when all other variables and parameters are held constant. Thus, as b increases, the utility associated with choosing the D which maximizes x_{-i} is also increasing, and the utility associated with choosing the D which minimizes x_{-i} is decreasing. Thus, it follows trivially that i's relative preference for the regime type that increases x_{-i} is increasing in b.

Corollary 1

a. Social communitarians should be relatively less supportive of democracy.
b. Religious communitarians should be relatively less supportive of democracy.
c. Post-Islamist should be relatively more supportive of democracy.
d. Religious individualists should be relatively more supportive of democracy.

Assume that propositions 1 and 2 are true. All individuals draw some utility and, therefore, have some basis for supporting d since all individuals prefer placing themselves at their own ideal point, x_i^*. Moreover, an individual from each of the groups has the potential to gain more or less than members of each of the other groups from d relative to $\sim d$, depending on the parameters of the model. Without loss of generality, let us assume four individuals share the same ideological position, x^*, but belong to the four different subsets of individuals discussed in this article: a social communitarian (1), a religious communitarian (2), a habituated post-Islamist (3), and a religious individualist (4): $x_1^* = x_2^* = x_3^* = x_4^*$. Let us also assume that there are only two levels of a and b, high and low, where social communitarians are characterized by high levels of a and low levels of b, religious communitarians have high levels of both a and b, habituated post-Islamists have low levels of a and high levels of b, and religious individualists have low levels of a and b. Given that an individual's preference for d is decreasing in a and that players 1 and

2 have high levels of a, their preference for democracy is lower than that of players 3 and 4 when ignoring the component of the utility function associated with b. Assuming proposition 2 holds true, whether higher levels of b are associated with a greater or weaker preference for d depends on whether x_{-i} is increasing in b. Thus, if we treat the positions ~d as random, we would not expect an increase in b to be associated with greater or lesser utility associated with d relative to ~d. Therefore, given that $a_1 = a_2 > a_3 = a_4$, on average, we would expect the utility associated with d to be higher for players 3 and 4 than players 1 and 2.

If we do not treat ~d as a random variable, players 3 and 4 can only prefer d to a greater extent than players 1 and 2 under very narrow conditions. Where d decreases x_{-i}, given that $a_1 = a_2 > a_3 = a_4$, players 1 and 2 will always derive greater utility from ~d relative to player 4, player 2 will always derive greater utility from ~d relative to player 3, and player 1 will derive greater utility from ~d_i relative to player 3 only when the relative gains from x_{-i} are sufficiently large or the losses associated with $\frac{\Sigma_{-i}(x_{-i} - \bar{x})^2}{n-1}$ are sufficiently small (or the differences between a_1 and a_3 are sufficiently small or b_1 and b_3 are sufficiently large). Where d increases x_{-i}, both player 1 and player 2 derive greater utility from ~d than player 3, player 1 will always derive greater utility from ~d than player 4, and player 2 will derive greater utility from ~d unless the relative gains from x_{-i} are sufficiently large or the losses associated with $\frac{\Sigma_{-i}(x_{-i} - \bar{x})^2}{n-1}$ are sufficiently small (or the differences between a_2 and a_4 are sufficiently small or b_2 and b_4 are sufficiently large). Therefore, players 3 and 4 derive greater utility from d relative to ~d than players 1 and 2 under most conditions. An individual's preference for democracy is decreasing in that individual's preference for homogeneity, a, under all conditions. This leads us to predict that, on average, religious individualists and habituated post-Islamists prefer liberal democracy to a greater extent than social and religious communitarians.

Corollary 2

a. Social communitarians should be less likely to support a regime type for extrinsic reasons.
b. Religious communitarians should be more likely to support a regime type for extrinsic reasons.

c. Post-Islamists should be more likely to support a regime type for extrinsic reasons.
d. Religious individualists should be less likely to support a regime type for extrinsic reasons.

Assume that proposition 2 is true. Given that $b_i x_i^* \sqrt{\Sigma_{-i} x_{-i}}$ is the only component of the utility function that provides for extrinsic benefits associated with d, and that b is by definition greater for religious communitarians and habituated post-Islamists than religious individualists and social communitarians, it follows trivially that for any x_{-i}, the difference between the extrinsic utility that religious communitarians and habituated post-Islamists derive from the regimes is larger for them than the difference in the utility derived by social communitarians and religious individualists.

A Brief Note on the Robustness of the Model

The model is robust to a number of functional form specifications. The specifications presented above identify a simple and reasonable specification of individuals' utility functions. So long as the cost of deviating from the regime's preferred point increases at an increasing rate, some individuals prefer religious homogeneity, and some individuals prefer that religion be present in the public domain, these results should hold. Even if we were to assume some level of dependence between preferences for religion's presence in the public domain and preferences for religious homogeneity, the fundamental qualitative predictions of the model would still hold: authoritarianism is more fundamentally tied to preferences for uniformity in action than a desire for the public domain to be characterized by a specific set of religious practices. In such a scenario, where perhaps a is treated as an increasing function in b, it would trivially follow that b's effect on preferences for democracy will either depend on the context or the degree to which a preference for religion in the public sphere increases the preference cohesion.

BIBLIOGRAPHY

Abbas, Akeel. 2014. "Deconstructing Despotic Legacies in the Arab Spring." In *Routledge Handbook of the Arab Spring*, edited by Larbi Sadiki, 446–457. Abingdon, UK: Routledge.

Ahmed, Shahab. 2017. *What Is Islam? The Importance of Being Islamic*. Princeton, NJ: Princeton University Press.

Akaike, Htrotugu. 1973. "Maximum Likelihood Identification of Gaussian Autoregressive Moving Average Models." *Biometrika* 60 (2): 255–265.

Akturk, Sener. 2015. "Religion and Nationalism: Contradictions of Islamic Origins and Secular Nation-Building in Turkey, Algeria, and Pakistan." *Social Science Quarterly* 96 (3): 778–806.

Akyeşilmen, Nezir, and Arif Behiç Özcan. 2014. "Islamic Movements and Their Role in Politics in Turkey." *Selcuk University Social Sciences Institute Journal* 31:29–38.

Al-Anani, Khalil, and Maszlee Malik. 2013. "Pious Way to Politics: The Rise of Political Salafism in Post-Mubarak Egypt." *Digest of Middle East Studies* 22 (1): 57–73.

Al-Bukhari, Imam. 1996. *Sahih al-Bukhari (The English Translation of Sahih Al Bukhari with the Arabic Text)*. Translated by Muhammad Muhsin Khan. Riyadh: Dar-us-Salam.

Allen, Christopher. 2010. *Islamophobia*. Farnham, UK: Ashgate.

Al-Rasheed, Madawi. 2006. *Contesting the Saudi State: Islamic Voices from a New Generation*. New York: Cambridge University Press.

Al-Tirmidhi, Imam. 2008. *Sunan Al Tirmidhi: The True Collection*. Translated by Haytham Kreidley. Beirut, Lebanon: Dar Al Kotob Al-Ilmiyah.

Anderson, Lisa. 2011. "Demystifying the Arab Spring: Parsing the Differences between Tunisia, Egypt, and Libya." *Foreign Affairs* 90 (3): 2–7.

Angrist, Michele Penner. 2013. "Understanding the Success of Mass Civic Protest in Tunisia." *Middle East Journal* 67 (4): 547–564.

An-Náim, Abdullahi Ahmed. 2008. *Islam and the Secular State*. Cambridge, MA: Harvard University Press.

Ansari, Ali M. 2010. *Crisis of Authority: Iran's 2009 Presidential Election*. London: Chatham House.

Arrow, Kenneth J. 1971. *Essays in the Theory of Risk-Bearing*. Chicago: Markham.

Averroes. 2001. *The Book of the Decisive Treatise Determining the Connection between the Law and Wisdom: and, The Epistle Dedicatory*. Provo, UT: Brigham Young University Press.

Aviv, Efrat. 2018. "The İsmailağa Community and Its Relationship with the AK Party." *Democracy and Security* 14 (3): 276–299.

Ayoob, Mohammed. 2009. *The Many Faces of Political Islam: Religion and Politics in the Muslim World*. Ann Arbor: University of Michigan Press.

Barnett, Andy, Bruce Yandle, and George Naufal. 2013. "Regulation, Trust, and Cronyism in Middle Eastern Societies: The Simple Economics of 'Wasta.'" *Journal of Socio-Economics* 44:41–46.

Bayat, Asef. 2007. *Making Islam Democratic: Social Movements and the Post-Islamist Turn.* Stanford, CA: Stanford University Press.
———. 2013a. "The Arab Spring and Its Surprises." *Development and Change* 44 (3): 587–601.
———. 2013b. *Life as Politics: How Ordinary People Change the Middle East.* Stanford, CA: Stanford University Press.
———. 2017. *Revolution without Revolutionaries: Making Sense of the Arab Spring.* Stanford, CA: Stanford University Press.
Belev, Boyan. 2000. *Forcing Freedom: Political Control of Privatization and Economic Opening in Egypt and Tunisia.* Lanham, MD: University Press of America.
———. 2001. "Privatization in Egypt and Tunisia: Liberal Outcomes and/or Liberal Policies?" *Mediterranean Politics* 6 (2): 68–103.
Belge, Ceren, and Ekrem Karakoç. 2015. "Minorities in the Middle East: Ethnicity, Religion, and Support for Authoritarianism." *Political Research Quarterly* 68 (2): 280–292.
Benson, Peter L, and Dorothy Lowe Williams. 1982. *Religion on Capitol Hill: Myths and Realities.* San Francisco: Harper and Row.
Berkes, Niyazi. 1964. *The Development of Secularism in Turkey.* Montreal: McGill-Queen's University Press.
Berman, Eli. 2000. "Sect, Subsidy, and Sacrifice: An Economist's View of Ultra-Orthodox Jews." *Quarterly Journal of Economics* 115 (3): 905–953.
Berman, Sheri. 2003. "Islamism, Revolution, and Civil Society." *Perspectives on Politics* 1 (2): 257–272.
Bishara, Azmi. 2001. *Sectarianism without Sects.* New York: Oxford University Press.
Blaydes, Lisa, and Drew A. Linzer. 2008. "The Political Economy of Women's Support for Fundamentalist Islam." *World Politics* 60 (4): 576–609.
Bolck, Annabel, Marcel Croon, and Jacques Hagenaars. 2004. "Estimating Latent Structure Models with Categorical Variables: One-Step versus Three-Step Estimators." *Political Analysis* 12 (1): 3–27.
Boubekeur, Amel. 2016. "Islamists, Secularists and Old Regime Elites in Tunisia: Bargained Competition." *Mediterranean Politics* 21 (1): 107–127.
Bratton, Michael, and Robert Mattes. 2001. "Support for Democracy in Africa: Intrinsic or Instrumental?" *British Journal of Political Science* 31 (3): 447–474.
Brooke, Steven. 2017. "From Medicine to Mobilization: Social Service Provision and the Islamist Reputational Advantage." *Perspectives on Politics* 15 (1): 42–61.
———. 2019. *Winning Hearts and Votes: Social Services and the Islamist Political Advantage.* Ithaca, NY: Cornell University Press.
Brownlee, Jason, Tarek Masoud, and Andrew Reynolds. 2015. *The Arab Spring: Pathways of Repression and Reform.* Oxford, UK: Oxford University Press.
Buckley, David. 2016. "Demanding the Divine? Explaining Cross-National Support for Clerical Control of Politics." *Comparative Political Studies* 49 (3): 357–390.
Buehler, Matt. 2016. "Do You Have 'Connections' at the Courthouse? An Original Survey on Informal Influence and Judicial Rulings in Morocco." *Political Research Quarterly* 69 (4): 760–772.
———. 2018. *Why Alliances Fail: Islamist and Leftist Coalitions in North Africa.* Syracuse, NY: Syracuse University Press.
Bush, Sarah Sunn, and Amaney A. Jamal. 2015. "Anti-Americanism, Authoritarian Politics, and Attitudes about Women's Representation: Evidence from a Survey Experiment in Jordan." *International Studies Quarterly* 59 (1): 34–45.

Çağaptay, Soner. 2002. "Reconfiguring the Turkish Nation in the 1930s." *Nationalism and Ethnic Politics* 8 (2): 67–82.
Çakır, Ruşen. 1990. *Ayet ve Slogan: Türkiye'de İslami Oluşumlar*. Istanbul: Metis Yayınları.
Campbell, David E. 2004. "Acts of Faith: Churches and Political Engagement." *Political Behavior* 26 (2): 155–180.
———. 2013. "Social Networks and Political Participation." *Annual Review of Political Science* 16:33–48.
Cavatorta, Francesco. 2015. "Salafism, Liberalism, and Democratic Learning in Tunisia." *Journal of North African Studies* 20 (5): 770–783.
Chekir, Hamouda, and Ishac Diwan. 2014. "Crony Capitalism in Egypt." *Journal of Globalization and Development* 5 (2): 177–211.
Chen, Daniel L. 2010. "Club Goods and Group Identity: Evidence from Islamic Resurgence during the Indonesian Financial Crisis." *Journal of Political Economy* 118 (2): 300–354.
Chin, James. 1997. "Politics of Federal Intervention in Malaysia, with Reference to Sarawak, Sabah and Kelantan." *Journal of Commonwealth & Comparative Politics* 35 (2): 96–120.
Ciftci, Sabri. 2010. "Modernization, Islam, or Social Capital: What Explains Attitudes toward Democracy in the Muslim World?" *Comparative Political Studies* 43 (11): 1442–1470.
———. 2012. "Islamophobia and Threat Perceptions: Explaining Anti-Muslim Sentiment in the West." *Journal of Muslim Minority Affairs* 32 (3): 293–309.
———. 2013. "Secular-Islamist Cleavage, Values, and Support for Democracy and Shari'a in the Arab World." *Political Research Quarterly* 66 (4): 781–793.
———. 2019. "Islam, Social Justice, and Democracy." *Politics and Religion* 12 (4): 549–576.
Ciftci, Sabri, and Ethan M. Bernick. 2015. "Utilitarian and Modern: Clientelism, Citizen Empowerment, and Civic Engagement in the Arab World." *Democratization* 22 (7): 1161–1182.
Ciftci, Sabri, F. Michael Wuthrich, and Ammar Shamaileh. 2019. "Islam, Religious Outlooks, and Support for Democracy." *Political Research Quarterly* 72 (2): 435–449.
Claret-Campana, Maria, and Athina Lampridi-Kemou. 2017. "Islamist Forces in Contemporary Egypt: The End of Conventional Dualities." In *Political Islam in a Time of Revolt*, edited by Ferran Izquierdo Brichs, John Etherington, and Laura Feliu, 127–152. London: Palgrave Macmillan.
Clark, Janine A. 2004. *Islam, Charity, and Activism: Middle-Class Networks and Social Welfare in Egypt, Jordan, and Yemen*. Bloomington: Indiana University Press.
Cleveland, William L., and Martin Bunton. 2009. *A History of the Middle East*. Boulder, CO: Westview.
Collins, Kathleen, and Erica Owen. 2012. "Islamic Religiosity and Regime Preferences: Explaining Support for Democracy and Political Islam in Central Asia and the Caucasus." *Political Research Quarterly* 65 (3): 499–515.
Coppedge, Michael, John Gerring, Staffan I. Lindberg, Svend-Erik Skaaning, Jan Teorell, David Altman, Michael Bernhard, M. Steven Fish, Adam Glynn, Allen Hicken, Carl Henrik Knutsen, Kelly McMann, Pamela Paxton, Daniel Pemstein, Jeffrey Staton, Brigitte Zimmerman, Rachel Sigman, Frida Andersson, Valeriya Mechkova, and Farhad Miri. 2016. *V-Dem Codebook v6*. Varieties of Democracy (VDem) Project. Accessed June 28, 2021. https://www.v-dem.net/media/filer_public/5e/cb/5ecb5afd-ee67-4d35-b864-6a90f4b2b85c/codebook_6.pdf.
———. 2017. V-Dem Dataset v7. Varieties of Democracy (website). Accessed June 28, 2021. https://www.v-dem.net/en/data/archive/previous-data/data-version-7/.

Corstange, Daniel. 2014. "Foreign-Sponsorship Effects in Developing-World Surveys: Evidence from a Field Experiment in Lebanon." *Public Opinion Quarterly* 78 (2): 474–484.
Davis, Nancy J., and Robert V. Robinson. 1996. "Are the Rumors of War Exaggerated? Religious Orthodoxy and Moral Progressivism in America." *American Journal of Sociology* 102 (3): 756–787.
———. 2006. "The Egalitarian Face of Islamic Orthodoxy: Support for Islamic Law and Economic Justice in Seven Muslim-Majority Nations." *American Sociological Review* 71 (2): 167–190.
Dayton, C. Mitchell, and George B. Macready. 1988. "Concomitant-Variable Latent-Class Models." *Journal of the American Statistical Association* 83 (401): 173–178.
Dekmejian, R. Hrair. 1994. "The Rise of Political Islamism in Saudi Arabia." *Middle East Journal* 48 (4): 627–643.
Djupe, Paul A., and Ryan L. Claassen. 2018. *The Evangelical Crackup? The Future of the Evangelical-Republican Coalition.* Philadelphia: Temple University Press.
Djupe, Paul A., and Christopher P. Gilbert. 2008. *The Political Influence of Churches.* New York: Cambridge University Press.
Dreyer, Jaco S. 2011. "Public Theology and the Translation Imperative: A Ricoeurian Perspective." *HTS Teologiese Studies / Theology* 67 (3): 98–106.
Driessen, Michael D. 2014. "Regime Type, Religion-State Arrangements, and Religious Markets in the Muslim World." *Sociology of Religion* 75 (3): 367–394.
———. 2018. "Sources of Muslim Democracy: The Supply and Demand of Religious Policies in the Muslim World." *Democratization* 25 (1): 115–135.
El-Ghobashy, Mona. 2005. "The Metamorphosis of the Egyptian Muslim Brothers." *International Journal of Middle East Studies* 37 (3): 373–395.
———. 2011. "The Praxis of the Egyptian Revolution." *Middle East Report* 258:2–13.
Feldman, Noah. 2020. *The Arab Winter: A Tragedy.* Princeton, NJ: Princeton University Press.
Feldman, Stanley. 2003. "Enforcing Social Conformity: A Theory of Authoritarianism." *Political Psychology* 24 (1): 41–74.
Feldman, Stanley, and Karen Stenner. 1997. "Perceived Threat and Authoritarianism." *Political Psychology* 18 (4): 741–770.
Feuer, Sarah J. 2018. *Regulating Islam: Religion and the State in Contemporary Morocco and Tunisia.* Cambridge, UK: Cambridge University Press.
Filali-Ansary, Abdou. 2012. "The Languages of the Arab Revolutions." *Journal of Democracy* 23 (2): 5–18.
Fish, M. Steven. 2011. *Are Muslims Distinctive? A Look at the Evidence.* New York: Oxford University Press.
Fox, Jonathan. 2008. *A World Survey of Religion and the State.* Cambridge, UK: Cambridge University Press.
———. 2012. "Religion and State Codebook: Round 2 (Version 5)." May 24, 2012. https://www.thearda.com/ras/downloads/Religion%20and%20State%20Codebook.pdf.
Gasiorowski, Mark J. 1992. "The Islamist Challenge: The Failure of Reform in Tunisia." *Journal of Democracy* 3 (4): 85–97.
Gaskins, Ben, Matt Golder, and David A. Siegel. 2013a. "Religious Participation and Economic Conservatism." *American Journal of Political Science* 57 (4): 823–840.

———. 2013b. "Religious Participation, Social Conservatism, and Human Development." *Journal of Politics* 75 (4): 1125–1141.
Gause, F. Gregory, III. 2011. "Why Middle East Studies Missed the Arab Spring: The Myth of Authoritarian Stability." *Foreign Affairs* 90 (4): 81–90.
Gellner, Ernest. 1983. *Muslim Society*. Cambridge, UK: Cambridge University Press.
George, Alexander L., and Andrew Bennett. 2005. *Case Studies and Theory Development in the Social Sciences*. Cambridge, MA: MIT Press.
Gerring, John. 2006. *Case Study Research: Principles and Practices*. Cambridge, UK: Cambridge University Press.
Gilbert, Christopher P. 1993. *The Impact of Churches on Political Behavior: An Empirical Study*. Westport, CT: Greenwood.
Glas, Saskia, and Amy Alexander. 2020. "Explaining Support for Muslim Feminism in the Arab Middle East and North Africa." *Gender and Society* 34 (3): 437–466.
Grewal, Sharan, Amaney A. Jamal, Tarek Masoud, and Elizabeth R. Nugent. 2019. "Poverty and Divine Rewards: The Electoral Advantage of Islamist Political Parties." *American Journal of Political Science* 63 (4): 859–874.
Grzymała-Busse, Anna. 2015. *Nations under God: How Churches Use Moral Authority to Influence Policy*. Princeton, NJ: Princeton University Press.
Haas, Mark L., and David W. Lesch. 2013. "Introduction." In *The Arab Spring: Change and Resistance in the Middle East*, edited by Mark L. Haas and David W. Lesch, 1–12. Boulder, CO: Avalon.
Habermas, Jürgen. 2006. "Religion in the Public Sphere." *European Journal of Philosophy* 14 (1): 1–25.
Hagenaars, Jacques A., and Allan L. McCutcheon. 2002. *Applied Latent Class Analysis*. Cambridge, MA: Cambridge University Press.
Halliday, Fred. 1999 "Islamophobia Reconsidered." *Ethnic and Racial Studies* 22 (5): 892–902.
Hart, Kimberly. 2013. *And Then We Work for God: Rural Sunni Islam in Western Turkey*. Stanford, CA: Stanford University Press.
Hasan, Ahmad. 1971. "Social Justice in Islam." *Islamic Studies* 10 (3): 209–219.
He, Baogang, Laura Allison-Reumann, and Michael Breen. 2018. "The Politics of Secular Federalism and the Federal Governance of Religious Diversity in Asia." *Federal Law Review* 46 (4): 575–594.
Hefner, Robert W. 2011. *Civil Islam: Muslims and Democratization in Indonesia*. Vol. 40. Princeton, NJ: Princeton University Press.
Hinnebusch, Raymond. 2001. *Syria: Revolution from Above*. London: Routledge.
———. 2015. "The Politics of Identity in Middle East International Relations." In *International Relations of the Middle East*, edited by L. Fawcett, 148–169. Oxford, UK: Oxford University Press.
———. 2020. "Identity and State Formation in Multi-sectarian Societies: Between Nationalism and Sectarianism in Syria." *Nations and Nationalism* 26 (1): 138–154.
Hoffman, Michael, and Amaney Jamal. 2014. "Religion in the Arab Spring: Between Two Competing Narratives." *Journal of Politics* 76 (3): 593–606.
Hofmann, Steven. 2004. "Islam and Democracy: Micro-level Indications of Compatibility." *Comparative Political Studies* 37 (6): 652–676.
Hoot, Humam. "Bashar Al-Assad Haywan Dib Al-Fitna." YouTube video, June 11, 2018. https://www.youtube.com/watch?v=PaXCsjKaodk.

Huber, John D., and Piero Stanig. 2011. "Church-State Separation and Redistribution." *Journal of Public Economics* 95 (7–8): 828–836.

Huckle, Kiku, and Andrea Silva. 2020. "People of Color, People of Faith: The Effect of Social Capital and Religion on the Political Participation of Marginalized Communities." *Religions* 11 (5): 249.

Hülür, H. 1999. "Technology and Naqshbandi Sufism: An Empirical Analysis of İsmailağa and İskenderpaşa Branches." *Selçuk Üniversitesi Fen Edebiyat Fakültesi Edebiyat Dergisi* 13:289–340.

Huntington, Samuel. 1993. "The Clash of Civilizations?" *Foreign Affairs* 72 (3): 22–49.

Iannaccone, Laurence R. 1992. "Sacrifice and Stigma: Reducing Free-Riding in Cults, Communes, and Other Collectives." *Journal of Political Economy* 100 (2): 271–291.

———. 1998. "Introduction to the Economics of Religion." *Journal of Economic Literature* 36 (3): 1465–1495.

Inglehart, Ronald, and Pippa Norris. 2003. *Rising Tide: Gender Equality and Cultural Change around the World*. Cambridge, UK: Cambridge University Press.

———. 2004. *Sacred and Secular: Religion and Politics Worldwide*. New York: Cambridge University Press.

Inglehart, Ronald, and Christian Welzel. 2003. "Political Culture and Democracy: Analyzing Cross-Level Linkages." *Comparative Politics* 36 (1): 61–79.

Introvigne, Massimo. 2006. "Turkish Religious Market(s): A View Based on the Religious Economy Theory." In *The Emergence of a New Turkey: Democracy and the AK Parti*, edited by M. Hakan Yavuz, 23–48. Salt Lake City: University of Utah Press.

Isani, Mujtaba Ali. 2018. *Muslim Public Opinion toward the International Order: Support for International and Regional Actors*. New York: Springer.

Jamal, Amaney. 2006. "Reassessing Support for Islam and Democracy in the Arab World? Evidence from Egypt and Jordan." *World Affairs* 169 (2): 51–63.

———. 2007. "When Is Social Trust a Desirable Outcome? Examining Levels of Trust in the Arab World." *Comparative Political Studies* 40 (11): 1328–1349.

Jamal, Amaney, and Mark Tessler. 2008. "The Democracy Barometers (Part II): Attitudes in the Arab World." *Journal of Democracy* 19 (1): 97–111.

Jelen, Ted G. 1993. "The Political Consequences of Religious Group Attitudes." *Journal of Politics* 55 (1): 178–190.

Johnson, Benton. 1963. "On Church and Sect." *American Sociological Review* 4:539–549.

Kaplan, Sam. 2006. *The Pedagogical State: Education and the Politics of National Culture in Post-1980 Turkey*. Stanford, CA: Stanford University Press.

Karakoç, Ekrem, and Birol Başkan. 2012. "Religion in Politics: How Does Inequality Affect Public Secularization?" *Comparative Political Studies* 45 (12): 1510–1541.

Karakoç, Ekrem, Talha Köse, and Mesut Özcan. 2017. "Emigration and the Diffusion of Political Salafism: Religious Remittances and Support for Salafi Parties in Egypt during the Arab Spring." *Party Politics* 23 (6): 731–745.

Karpat, K. 1959. *Turkey's Politics: The Transition to a Multi-party System*. Princeton, NJ: Princeton University Press.

Kass, Robert E., and Larry Wasserman. 1995. "A Reference Bayesian Test for Nested Hypotheses and Its Relationship to the Schwarz Criterion." *Journal of the American Statistical Association* 90 (431): 928–934.

Kazemipur, Abdolmohammad, and Ali Rezaei. 2003. "Religious Life under Theocracy: The Case of Iran." *Journal for the Scientific Study of Religion* 42 (3): 347–361.

Kedourie, Elie. 1994. *Democracy and Arab Political Culture*. London: Frank Cass.
Kellstedt, Lyman A., John C. Green, James L. Guth, and Corwin E. Smidt. 1996. "Grasping the Essentials: The Social Embodiment of Religion and Political Behavior." In *Religion and the Culture Wars: Dispatches from the Front*, edited by John C. Green, James L. Guth, Corwin E. Smidt, and Lyman A. Kellstedt, 174–192. Lanham, MD: Rowman and Littlefield.
Kepel, Gilles. 1985. *The Prophet and the Pharoah: Muslim Extremism in Egypt*. London: Al Saqi Books.
Khatib, Lina, and Ellen Lust. 2014. *Taking to the Streets: The Transformation of Arab Activism*. Baltimore: Johns Hopkins University Press.
Kılıç, Ali Rıza. 2017. "Din Devlet Ilişkisi Açısından Menzil Cemaati Örneği." Master's thesis, Adıyaman University.
Kim, Heejung, and Hazel Rose Markus. 1999. "Deviance or Uniqueness, Harmony or Conformity? A Cultural Analysis." *Journal of Personality and Social Psychology* 77 (4): 785–800.
King, Stephen J. 2003. *Liberalization against Democracy: The Local Politics of Economic Reform in Tunisia*. Bloomington: Indiana University Press.
Klingemann, Hans-Dieter. 1999. "Mapping Political Support in the 1990s: A Global Analysis." In *Critical Citizens: Global Support for Democratic Governance*, edited by Pippa Norris, 31–56. New York: Oxford University Press.
Konuralp, Okan. 2006. "Türkiye'nin Tarikat ve Cemaat Haritası." *Hürriyet*, September 17, 2006.
Kuru, A. 2009. *Secularism and State Policies toward Religion: The United States, France, and Turkey*. New York: Cambridge University Press.
Lazarsfeld, Paul F. 1950. "The Logical and Mathematical Foundation of Latent Structure Analysis." In *Studies in Social Psychology in World War II*, vol. 4, *Measurement and Prediction*, edited by Samuel A. Stouffer, Louis Guttman, Edward A. Suchman, Paul F. Lazarsfeld, Shirley A. Star, and John A. Clausen, 362–412. Princeton, NJ: Princeton University Press.
Leege, David C., and Michael R. Welch. 1989. "Religious Roots of Political Orientations: Variations among American Catholic Parishioners." *Journal of Politics* 51 (1): 137–162.
Lewis, Bernard. 2010. *Faith and Power: Religion and Politics in the Middle East*. Oxford, UK: Oxford University Press.
Limentani, Giselle B., Moira C. Ringo, Feng Ye, Mandy L. Bergquist, and Ellen O. McSorley. 2005. "Beyond the T-Test: Statistical Equivalence Testing." *Analytical Chemistry* 77 (11): 221A–226A.
Linzer, Drew A., and Jeffrey B. Lewis. 2011. "PoLCA: An R Package for Polytomous Variable Latent Class Analysis." *Journal of Statistical Software* 42 (10): 1–29.
Lord, Ceren. 2017. "Between Islam and the Nation: Nation-Building, the Ulama and Alevi Identity in Turkey." *Nations and Nationalism* 23 (1): 48–67.
———. 2018. *Religious Politics in Turkey: From the Birth of the Republic to the AKP*. Cambridge, UK: Cambridge University Press.
Lust, Ellen. 2011. "Missing the Third Wave: Islam, Institutions, and Democracy in the Middle East." *Studies in Comparative International Development* 46 (2): 163–190.
Mallat, Chibli. 2015. *Philosophy of Nonviolence: Revolution, Constitutionalism, and Justice beyond the Middle East*. New York: Oxford University Press.

Masoud, Tarek. 2014. *Counting Islam: Religion, Class, and Elections in Egypt.* Cambridge, UK: Cambridge University Press.

Masoud, Tarek, Amaney Jamal, and Elizabeth Nugent. 2016. "Using the Qur'ān to Empower Arab Women? Theory and Experimental Evidence from Egypt." *Comparative Political Studies* 49 (12): 1555–1598.

McCarthy, Rory. 2018. *Inside Tunisia's Al-Nahda: Between Politics and Preaching.* Cambridge, UK: Cambridge University Press.

McClendon, Gwyneth, and Rachel Beatty Riedl. 2019. *From Pews to Politics: Religious Sermons and Political Participation in Africa.* Cambridge, UK: Cambridge University Press.

Meeker, M. 2002. *A Nation of Empire: The Ottoman Legacy of Turkish Modernity.* Los Angeles: University of California Press.

Merone, Fabio. 2017. "Between Social Contention and Takfirism: The Evolution of the Salafi-Jihadi Movement in Tunisia." *Mediterranean Politics* 22 (1): 71–90.

Mitchell, Richard Paul. 1993. *The Society of the Muslim Brothers.* New York: Oxford University Press.

Moaddel, Mansoor. 2010. "Religious Regimes and Prospects for Liberal Politics: Futures of Iran, Iraq and Saudi Arabia." *Futures* 42 (6): 532–544.

Moore, Clement Henry. 1986. "Money and Power: The Dilemma of the Egyptian Infitah." *Middle East Journal* 40 (4): 634–650.

Morikawa, Toshihiko, and Michihiro Yoshida. 1995. "A Useful Testing Strategy in Phase III Trials: Combined Test of Superiority and Test of Equivalence." *Journal of Biopharmaceutical Statistics* 5 (3): 297–306.

Moustafa, Tamir. 2007. *The Struggle for Constitutional Power: Law, Politics, and Economic Development in Egypt.* Cambridge, MA: Cambridge University Press.

Muslim, Imam Abul-Husain. 2007. *Sahih Muslim.* Translated by Nasiruddin Al-Khattab. Riyadh: Dar-us-Salam.

Nordland, Rod. 2012. "Egypt's Islamists Tread Lightly, but Skeptics Squirm." *International Herald Tribune*, July 30, 2012.

Norris, Pippa. 2011. *Democratic Deficit: Critical Citizens Revisited.* New York: Cambridge University Press.

Okruhlik, Gwenn. 2002. "Networks of Dissent: Islamism and Reform in Saudi Arabia." *Current History* 101 (651): 22–28.

Omran, Mohammed. 2004. "The Performance of State-Owned Enterprises and Newly Privatized Firms: Does Privatization Really Matter?" *World Development* 32 (6): 1019–1041.

———. 2007. "Privatization, State Ownership, and Bank Performance in Egypt." *World Development* 35 (4): 714–733.

Owen, Ann L., and Julio R. Videras. 2007. "Culture and Public Goods: The Case of Religion and the Voluntary Provision of Environmental Quality." *Journal of Environmental Economics and Management* 54 (2): 162–180.

Ozgur, Iren. 2012. *Islamic Schools in Modern Turkey: Faith, Politics, and Education.* New York: Cambridge University Press.

Parsa, Misagh. 2016. *Democracy in Iran.* Cambridge, MA: Harvard University Press.

Pepinsky, Thomas B., R. William Liddle, and Saiful Mujani. 2012. "Testing Islam's Political Advantage: Evidence from Indonesia." *American Journal of Political Science* 56 (3): 584–600.

Pepinsky, Thomas B., and Bozena Welborne. 2011. "Piety and Redistributive Preferences in the Muslim World." *Political Research Quarterly* 64 (3): 491–505.
Pirický, Gabriel. 2012. "The İsmailağa Community: Shifting Religious Patterns in Contemporary Turkey." *Archiv Orientalni: Quarterly Journal of African and Asian Studies* 80 (3): 533–561.
Pripstein-Posusney, Marsha. 1999. "Egyptian Privatization: New Challenges for the Left." *Middle East Report* 210:38–40.
Putnam, Robert D., and David E. Campbell. 2010. *American Grace: How Religion Divides and Unites Us*. New York: Simon and Schuster.
Qutb, Sayyid. 2000. *Social Justice in Islam*. Translated by John D. Hardie. New York: American Council of Learned Societies.
Rabin, Matihew. 2013. "Risk Aversion and Expected-Utility Theory: A Calibration Theorem." In *Handbook of the Fundamentals of Financial Decision Making: Part I*, edited by Leonard C. MacLean and William T. Ziemba, 241–252. Singapore: World Scientific.
Rainey, Carlisle. 2014. "Arguing for a Negligible Effect." *American Journal of Political Science* 58 (4): 1083–1091.
Rizzo, Helen, Abdel-Hamid Abdel-Latif, and Katherine Meyer. 2007. "The Relationship between Gender Equality and Democracy: A Comparison of Arab versus Non-Arab Muslim Societies." *Sociology* 41 (6): 1151–1170.
Robbins, Michael. 2015. "After the Arab Spring: People Still Want Democracy." *Journal of Democracy* 26 (4): 80–89.
Said, Edward W. 1978. *Orientalism*. New York: Pantheon.
Saouli, Adham. 2019. "Sectarianism and Political Order in Iraq and Lebanon." *Studies in Ethnicity and Nationalism* 19 (1): 67–87.
Sartori, Giovanni. 1970. "Concept Misformation in Comparative Politics." *American Political Science Review* 64 (4): 1033–1053.
Scheve, Kenneth, and David Stasavage. 2006. "Religion and Preferences for Social Insurance." *Quarterly Journal of Political Science* 1 (3): 255–286.
Schwarz, Gideon. 1978. "Estimating the Dimension of a Model." *Annals of Statistics* 6 (2): 461–464.
Schwartz, Shalom. 2006. "A Theory of Cultural Value Orientations: Explication and Applications." *Comparative Sociology* 5 (2–3): 137–182.
Shamaileh, Ammar. 2017. *Trust and Terror: Social Capital and the Use of Terrorism as a Tool of Resistance*. New York: Routledge.
———. 2019. "Never Out of Now: Preference Falsification, Social Capital and the Arab Spring." *International Interactions* 45 (6): 949–975.
Shariati, Ali. 1979. *On the Sociology of Islam*. Translated by Hamid Algar. Berkeley, CA: Mizan.
Somer, Murat. 2017. "Conquering versus Democratizing the State: Political Islamists and Fourth Wave Democratization in Turkey and Tunisia." *Democratization* 24 (6): 1025–1043.
Spierings, Niels. 2014. "The Influence of Islamic Orientations on Democratic Support and Tolerance in Five Arab Countries." *Politics and Religion* 7 (4): 706–733.
Stark, Rodney, and Roger Finke. 2000. *Acts of Faith: Explaining the Human Side of Religion*. Berkeley, CA: University of California Press.
Stegmueller, Daniel, Peer Scheepers, Sigrid Roßteutscher, and Eelke De Jong. 2012. "Support for Redistribution in Western Europe: Assessing the Role of Religion." *European Sociological Review* 28 (4): 482–497.

Stepan, Alfred, and Juan J. Linz. 2013. "Democratization Theory and the 'Arab Spring.'" *Journal of Democracy* 24 (2): 15–30.
Stepan, Alfred, and Graeme B. Robertson. 2004. "Debate: Arab, Not Muslim, Exceptionalism." *Journal of Democracy* 15 (4): 140–146.
Sunar, Ilkay, and Binnaz Toprak. 1983. "Islam in Politics: The Case of Turkey." *Government and Opposition* 18 (4): 421–441.
Syechbubakr, Ahmed Syarif. 2018. "Nahdlatul Ulama and Muhammadiyah Struggle with Internal Divisions in the Post-Soeharto Era." University of Melbourne, Indonesia at Melbourne. May 28, 2018. http://indonesiaatmelbourne.unimelb.edu.au/nahdlatul-ulama-and-muhammadiyah-struggle-with-internal-divisions-in-the-post-soeharto-era/.
Tessler, Mark. 2002. "Islam and Democracy in the Middle East: The Impact of Religious Orientations on Attitudes toward Democracy in Four Arab Countries." *Comparative Politics* 34 (3): 337–354.
———. 2015. *Islam and Politics in the Middle East: Explaining the Views of Ordinary Citizens*. Bloomington: Indiana University Press.
Tessler, Mark, Amaney Jamal, and Michael Robbins. 2012. "New Findings on Arabs and Democracy." *Journal of Democracy* 23 (4): 89–103.
Tezcür, Güneş Murat, and Taghi Azadarmaki. 2008. "Religiosity and Islamic Rule in Iran." *Journal for the Scientific Study of Religion* 47 (2): 211–224.
Tilly, Charles. 2005. *Trust and Rule*. New York: Cambridge University Press.
Tuğal, Cihan. 2009. *Passive Revolution: Absorbing the Islamic Challenge to Capitalism*. Stanford, CA: Stanford University Press.
Turam, Berna. 2007. *Between Islam and the State: The Politics of Engagement*. Stanford, CA: Stanford University Press.
Volpi, Frederic, and Janine Clark. 2019. "Activism in the Middle East and North Africa in Times of Upheaval: Social Networks' Actions and Interactions." *Social Movement Studies* 18 (1): 1–16.
Ware, Lewis B. 1988. "Ben Ali's Constitutional Coup in Tunisia." *Middle East Journal* 42 (4): 587–601.
White, Jenny B. 2002. *Islamist Mobilization in Turkey: A Study in Vernacular Politics*. Seattle: University of Washington Press.
———. 2004. "The End of Islamism? Turkey's Muslimhood Model." In *Remaking Muslim Politics: Pluralism, Contestation, Democratization*, edited by Robert W. Hefner, 87–111. Princeton, NJ: Princeton University Press.
Wickham, Carrie Rosefsky. 2002. *Mobilizing Islam: Religion, Activism, and Political Change in Egypt*. New York: Columbia University Press.
———. 2004. "The Path to Moderation: Strategy and Learning in the Formation of Egypt's Wasat Party." *Comparative Politics* 36 (2): 205–228.
———. 2013. *The Muslim Brotherhood: Evolution of an Islamist Movement*. Princeton, NJ: Princeton University.
Wiktorowicz, Quintan. 2005. *Radical Islam Rising: Muslim Extremism in the West*. Lanham, MD: Rowman and Littlefield.
Wuthrich, F. Michael. 2015. *National Elections in Turkey: People, Politics, and the Party System*. Syracuse, NY: Syracuse University Press.
Wuthrich, F. Michael, and Sabri Ciftci. 2020. "Islamist Parties, Intraparty Organizational Dynamics, and Moderation as Strategic Behavior." *Mediterranean Politics*, July 9, 2020. https://doi.org/10.1080/13629395.2020.1790165.

Yavuz, M. Hakan. 2003. *Islamic Political Identity in Turkey.* New York: Oxford University Press.
Yenigun, Halil Ibrahim. 2017. "The New Antinomies of the Islamic Movement in Post-Gezi Turkey: Islamism vs. Muslimism." *Turkish Studies* 18 (2): 229–250.
Yildirim, A. Kadir. 2016. *Muslim Democratic Parties in the Middle East: Economy and Politics of Islamist Moderation.* Bloomington: Indiana University Press.
Yong Liow, and Joseph Chin. 2004. "Exigency or Expediency? Contextualising Political Islam and the PAS Challenge in Malaysian Politics." *Third World Quarterly* 25 (2): 359–372.
Yükleyen, Ahmet. 2008. "Sufism and Islamic Groups in Contemporary Turkey." In *The Cambridge History of Turkey*, edited by Resat Kasaba, 381–387. Cambridge, UK: Cambridge University Press.
———. 2010. "Production of Mystical Islam in Europe: Religious Authorization in the Süleymanlı Sufi Community." *Contemporary Islam* 4 (3): 269–288.
Zubaida, Sami. 2012. "The 'Arab Spring' in the Historical Perspectives of Middle East Politics." *Economy and Society* 41 (4): 568–579.
Zürcher, Erik Jan. 2004. *Turkey: A Modern History.* London: I. B. Tauris.

INDEX

Page number followed by *t* indicate a table. Page numbers followed by *f* indicate a figure.

Ahmed, Shahab, 196
Al-Azhar school, 152
Algeria, 105
Alheweny, Abu Ishaq, 2
al-Islamiyya, 152
Al-Mourabitoun group, 2
Al-Wasat, 152
al-Zitouna University, 153
Ansar al-Sharia, 154, 172, 201
Arab Barometer surveys: area of coverage and, 61–62; data analysis and, 69, 70*t*; data and variables to test regime preference theory in, 134–137; data surrounding Arab Spring uprisings and, 158–159; democracy and, 69–71, 122; dynamic political context and, 59–60; methodology for assessing transition data, 159–160, 160*t*; political freedoms and, 71; post-Islamist support for state-led redistribution of wealth and, 190–191, 192*t*; regime type reference and, 69–71, 122, 134–137; religiosity questions and, 71–73, 73*f*; religious perspective questions, 69, 73; as source of data for multidimensional approach, 5; Wave II vs. Wave III, 85–86. *See also* religious outlooks
Arab uprisings: in Egypt and Tunisia, 150–152; Muslim Brothers and, 103, 149–150, 152, 154, 156–157, 172–173; support for democracy in Egypt and, 167–169, 168*f*; support for democracy in Tunisia and, 167–168, 168*f*
Ashmawi, Hisham, 2
Assad, Bashar Al-, 120, 146n4
Ataturk, Kemal, 34, 36
authoritarianism: Arab Barometer data and, 69–71, 122, 134–137; Arab uprisings and, 150; benefit of multidimensional approach to religious attitudes and, 5; costs of religious expression and, 124–126, 126*f*; nonlinear effect of religiosity of attitudes toward, 11, 127, 131, 201; personal utility function of religious expression and, 127; preference for social cohesion/religious uniformity and, 123, 128, 202; preferences regarding constraints on others and, 127; regime preference model predictions and support for, 133–134, 134*t*; religious public good and, 128–129; theory of religious outlooks and support for, 123–131, 201–202, 213*f*, 213*t*, 214*t*, 215*t*

Bayat, Asef, 63–65, 151
Ben Ali regime, 150, 185, 187–188
Bölükbaşı, Osman, 55
Bourguiba, Habib, 153, 185, 187
Büyükkörükçü, Tahir, 47

Christian minority religious communities, 21, 93
civil liberties index, 99
"conceptual stretching," 3
Coşan, Esad, 49
COVID-19 pandemic, 204
Cübbeli Ahmet Hoca (Ahmet Mahmut Ünlü), 1–2, 4, 45

Danish cartoon controversy, 2
Davis, Nancy J., 63–64, 67
Demirel, Süleyman, 54
democracy: Arab Barometer data and, 69–71, 122, 134–137; benefit of multidimensional approach to religious attitudes and, 5; costs of religious expression and, 124–126, 126*f*; nonlinear effect of religiosity of attitudes toward, 11, 127, 131, 201; personal utility function of religious expression and, 127; preference for social cohesion/religious uniformity and, 123, 128, 202; regime

245

democracy (Cont.)
  preference model predictions and support for, 133–134, 134*t*; relational influence of religious community and, 11–12, 197–198; religiosity and support for, 123; religious public good and, 128–129; support for in Egypt during time of uprisings, 167–169, 168*f*; support for in Tunisia during time of uprisings, 167–169, 168*f*; support for religion in public sphere and, 123; theory of religious outlooks and support for, 123–131, 172, 201–202, 213*f*, 213–215*t*

economic optimism, 184, 192*t*, 193, 224*t*, 226*t*
economic policy preferences: communitarianist preference for stability and, 178–180, 183; cross-country variation and, 225*t*, 227*t*; economic optimism and, 184, 192*t*, 193, 224*t*, 226*t*; educational attainment and, 181–182*t*, 192*t*, 224*t*; further research topics regarding religion and, 195; gender and, 181–182*f*, 192*t*, 224*t*, 226*t*; income and, 192*t*, 224*t*, 226*t*; Islam and, 175–176; personal trust and, 192*t*, 224*t*, 226*t*; political context and, 184, 193, 226*t*; political interest, 192–193, 192*t*, 224*t*, 226*t*; political trust and, 185, 192*t*, 224*t*, 226*t*; religiosity and, 176, 181–182*t*, 192*t*, 224*t*; religious outlooks and, 177–180, 181–182*t*, 183–185, 193–194, 223*t*, 224*t*, 226*t*; tribal identification and, 181–182*t*, 184–185, 192*t*, 224*t*

Egypt: Al-Azhar school and, 152; al-Nour Party and, 201; Arab Barometer data surrounding uprisings and, 158–159; Arab uprisings and, 149–152, 154–158; change in class share of religious outlook groups around uprisings, 161*f*, 162–165, 171; diversity of religious communities in, 151; Freedom and Justice Party (FJP), 156; institutionalization of religion and, 152; Muslim Brothers, 103, 149; post-Islamists and economic policy preferences, 185–187, 189–193, 191*f*, 192*t*, 194; religiosity and change of class share of outlooks in, 164–165, 164*f*; religious landscape before uprisings, 152–154; religious outlook classes and, 103, 105; Salafi groups and, 58, 93, 150, 152–153, 156, 201–202; state-religion relations and, 151–152; support for democracy around time of uprisings, 167–168, 168*t*, 170–171

Eliaçık, İhsan, 1–2, 4
Ennahda (Tunisia), 103, 149, 150, 154–156, 165, 165*f*, 173
Erbakan, Necmettin, 36–37, 48–49, 54–56
Erdoğan, Recep Tayyip, 37–38, 45–46, 56–57, 66
Erol, Mehmet Reşit, 41, 45–46
Ez-Zitouna school, 152

Finke, Roger, 16–18, 20, 22–24, 31, 51, 64, 68
fitna, 119–121, 145n3, 146n4, 203
Freedom and Justice Party (FJP), 156–157

Gezi Park protests, 2
government regulation of religion (GRR), 100
Gülen, Fethullah, 32, 56

Hassan, Mohamed, 2
Hezbollah, 120

Ibn Rushd, 197
İmam Hatip Okullari, 34
Indonesia, 93, 188–189, 200–201
interpersonal trust (as variable), 137, 138–139*t*, 192*t*, 224*t*, 226*t*
Iran, 23, 59, 64, 98, 198
Iraq, 105
Islah Party (Yemen), 103, 156
Islam: economic redistribution and, 175–176; Muslim feminism and, 147n18; Orientalist tradition of Western scholarship and, 14–15; pluralism and, 14–15, 196, 203; support for democracy and, 143, 145; term *fitna* and, 119, 119–121, 145n3, 146n4, 203; Western misconception of, 199. *See also* religion
Islamic Action Front (Jordan), 103
Islamism, 5, 63–65, 67

Jordan, 103, 105
Justice and Development Party (AKP, Turkey), 2, 37, 45–47, 50, 54, 56
Justice and Development Party (Morocco), 103

Kaçar, Kemal, 55
Kadiri order (Turkey), 32, 35–36, 38
Khaled, Amr, 2
Khamenei, Ali, 198
Kotku, Mehmet Zahit, 36, 41, 48–49

Lebanon, 103–104, 132
liberalization, 11–12, 24–25
Libya, 105

Madjid, Nurcholish, 93
Malaysia, 98–99, 156
Menemen rebellion (1930), 52–53, 60n4
Middle East and North Africa (MENA), 5, 13–20
Ministry of Religious Affairs (Turkey, MRA), 34, 37–38, 49, 52–54
moral cosmology theory, 62–65
Morocco, 105
Morsi, Mohamed, 2, 156–157
Mouvement de la Tendance Islamique (MTI), 187–188
Mubarak, Hosni, 186
Muhammadiyah, 93, 200
Muslim Brothers, 103, 149, 150, 152, 154, 156–157, 172–173, 187
Muslim feminism, 147n18

Nahdlatul Ulama, 93, 200
Naqshbandi order: about, 30–31, 39; AKP's rise to power and, 51, 51f; classification of subgroups and, 31; democratization and, 54–55; Erenköy, 40, 40f, 43, 43f, 47–48, 51–52, 51f, 64–65; Gülen movement and, 32, 38, 46, 54; importance of sheikh and, 39; inward-outward focus and, 42–43, 43f, 51f; İskenderpaşa, 32, 40–41, 40f, 43–44, 43f, 48–51, 51f, 54–56, 63; İsmailağa, 32, 40, 40f, 43, 43f, 45, 48, 51, 51f, 66, 90n1; Justice and Development Party (AKP) and, 56; level of tension with social environment and, 39–42, 40f, 50, 51f, 57, 92; Menzil, 40f, 41–42, 43, 43f, 45–48, 51, 51f, 66–67; methodological advantages of study of, 31–33; MRA and, 34–35; National Salvation Party (MSP) and, 36; pluralism and, 199–200; political behavior of communities as conditions change, 52–58; political approach of Kurdish orders and, 48; political involvement of communities and, 45–52, 51f, 57–58; recruitment and, 43–44, 48; scholarship on, 33; social activism and, 39; Sufi beliefs and, 30–31; Süleymancı, 40f, 41, 43–44, 43f, 49–50, 51f, 53–54, 56, 63, 66; temporal change in religious outlooks and, 149; Turkish political context and, 33–38, 58–59
Nasser, Gamal Abdel, 186
nationalism, 5
National Salvation Party (MSP), 36, 47, 54
Nurcu orders (Turkey), 36, 38
Nursi, Said (Bediüzzaman), 32

Oktar, Adnan, 1, 4
Orientalism, 14
Özal, Turgut, 37, 47

Pakistan, 98
Pancasilla, 93
Parti Islam Se-Malaysia (PAS), 156
Pengajians, 188–189
personal trust (as variable), 137, 138–139t, 181–182t
Pilavoğlu, Kemal, 36
political equality, 99
political interest (as variable), 131, 137, 138–139t, 181–182t
political trust (as variable), 137, 138–139t, 185
post-Islamist religious outlook: about, 64–65, 95–96, 177; change in class share in Egypt/Tunisia around Arab uprisings, 161f, 162–163; changes in religiosity and class share for, 164, 164f; cross-national variation and, 104–105, 104f; data analysis of Wave III Arab Barometer data and, 64–65, 67–69, 68f; economic policy preferences and, 177–180, 181–182t, 183–193, 190t, 192t, 194; economic policy preferences within political context, 185–194, 190t, 192t, 225t; educational attainment and, 106, 113f; estimation results and category of, 77–78, 78f, 79–81t, 81; feeling of security and, 113–114, 114f; individual and contextual covariates,

post-Islamist religious outlook (*Cont.*)
107–108*t*; Islamism and, 64–65, 67;
preference for religion in the public
sphere and, 130–131; preference for social
cohesion/religious uniformity and, 130;
regime preference model predictions and,
133–134, 134*t*; religiosity data and, 83–85,
83*f*; robustness analysis of model and,
86, 87–88*t*, 89*f*; social trust and, 109–110;
state-religion relations (SRR), 110–112,
111*f*; support for democracy and, 130, 137,
138–139*t*, 140–143, 143, 144*t*, 145; trends
from contextual analysis and, 114–117

radicalization, 24
Ramazanoğlu, Mahmud Sami, 40
redistribution of wealth. *See* economic
policy preferences
regime preference: Arab Barometer data
and, 69–71, 122, 134–137; nonlinear effect of
religiosity on attitudes toward, 11, 127, 131,
201; personal utility function of religious
expression and, 127; preference for
religious homogeneity and support for, 123;
preference for social cohesion/religious
uniformity and, 128, 202; preferences
regarding constraints on others and, 127;
religiosity and, 123, 201; religious public
good and, 128–129; support for religion in
public sphere and, 123; theory of religious
outlooks and support for, 123–131, 201–202,
213*f*, 213*t*, 214*t*, 215*t*
regime preference model: additional tests
of, 143; application of and political
context, 131–132; Arab Barometer data
and, 134–137; description of, 123–131;
interpersonal trust and, 137; political
interest and, 137; political trust and,
137; proof of propositions of, 229–232;
religious diversity and, 131; results of Arab
Barometer data analysis, 137, 138–139*t*,
140–143, 141*f*, 142*t*; robustness of model
and, 232; sectarian divisions and, 132;
theoretical predictions of, 133–134, 134*t*,
146n14, 147n15, 202
religion: Arab uprisings and, 150–151;
benefit of multidimensional approach
to, 3–5; geographical variance in
religion's influence on political beliefs,
10–11; observance of and economic
redistribution, 176; participation in and
political involvement religious elites, 21;
pluralist outlooks and, 196–197, 199–200;
reductionist approaches to, 4; relational
influence on political/social beliefs and,
11–12, 30; relation to common religious
proscriptions, 11; religiosity and theory
of regime preference, 133–134, 134*t*; state
regulation and participation in, 22–26,
26*f*. *See also* religious communities;
religious outlooks
Religion and the State (RAS) data set,
99–100
religiosity: Arab Spring and, 154–155, 155*t*;
economic redistribution and, 176, 192*t*;
support for democracy and, 138–139*t*,
141–142, 142*f*, 143
religious communitarianism outlook:
about, 63, 65–66, 95–96, 177; change in
class share in Egypt/Tunisia around
Arab uprisings, 161*f*, 162–163; changes in
religiosity and class share for, 164–165,
164*f*; cross-national variation and,
104–105, 104*f*; data and latent class
analysis and, 68, 68*f*; economic policy
preferences and, 177–180, 179*f*, 181–182*t*,
183–185, 194; educational attainment and,
106, 113*f*; feeling of security, 113–114, 114*f*;
individual and contextual covariates,
107–108*t*; individual determinants and,
103; preference for religion in the public
sphere and, 130–131; preference for social
cohesion/religious uniformity and, 130;
preference for stability and, 178–180;
regime preference model predictions and,
133–134, 134*t*; religiosity and, 83–85, 83*f*;
results of analysis and, 77–78, 78*f*, 79–81*t*,
81; robustness analysis of model and,
86, 87–88*t*, 89*f*; social trust and, 109–110;
state-religion relations (SRR), 110–112, 111*f*;
support for democracy and, 130, 137, 138–139*t*,
140–143, 143, 144*t*, 145; support for
democracy around time of uprisings and,
170–171; transitions toward democracy

and, 158; trends from contextual analysis and, 114–117
religious communities: church-sect distinction and, 17–18; distribution of according to theory of religious markets, 16–20, 19*f*, 27–28; as indicators of religious outlook, 15; in Iran, 59, 98; relationship with larger society and, 11–12, 204–205; Salafi groups in Egypt and, 58, 93–94; in Saudi Arabia, 23, 94, 98; sociopolitical context and, 21, 94–95; state regulation and, 20, 22–26, 26*f*; tensions with society/state and, 24–25; theory of religious markets and, 15–20, 205; United States example, 58, 92–93; within the Naqshbandi order, 31–32. *See also* Naqshbandi order; religious outlooks
religious expression: and cost of repression, 124–125, 126*f*
religious individualist outlook: about, 65, 67–68, 95–96, 177; cross-national variation and, 104, 104*f*; data and latent class analysis and, 68*f*; economic policy preferences and, 177–180, 179*f*, 181–182*t*, 183–185, 194; educational attainment and, 105, 113*f*; feeling of security, 113–114, 114*f*; government favoritism of religion (GFR), 100; individual and contextual covariates, 107*t*; preference for religion in the public sphere and, 130–131; preference for social cohesion/religious uniformity and, 130; regime preference model predictions and, 133–134, 134*f*; religiosity and, 83*f*, 84–85; results of analysis, 77, 78*f*, 79–81*t*, 81; robustness analysis of model and, 85–86, 87–88*t*, 89*f*; social trust and, 97, 109; sociopolitical factors and, 103; state-religion relations (SRR), 110–112, 111*f*; support for democracy and, 130, 137, 138–139*t*, 140–143, 143, 144*t*, 145; transitions toward democracy and, 158; trends from contextual analysis and, 114–117
religious markets: as analogy for religious pluralism, 16; autonomy and, 18, 19*f*, 20; distribution of, 16–19; religious club goods and, 18–20, 19*f*; social favorability and, 18–20, 19*f*; state regulation and, 28

religious outlooks: Arab Barometer data surrounding uprisings and, 158–159, 203–204; change in level of tension with state/society and, 162; change of class share in Egypt/Tunisia around Arab uprisings, 160–162, 161*f*; changing contexts and, 30, 92–94; civil liberties index, 99, 105; class probabilities from baseline model, 210–212*t*; class probabilities from LCA estimation, 219–222*t*; contextual factors, 97–101, 97*f*; COVID-19 pandemic and, 204–205; cross-national variation, 103–104, 104*f*, 112–113, 205, 217–218*t*; data and latent class analysis, 69–73, 70*t*, 73*f*, 89; economic optimism and, 184; economic policy preferences and, 177; educational attainment and, 105; feeling of security, 113–114, 114*f*; GDP and, 99, 101, 105; government regulation of religion (GRR) and, 100; GSEM (generalized structural equation modeling) and, 71, 91n4; individual factors, 67, 96–98, 97*f*, 209*t*; individual/sociopolitical factors, 94–97, 101, 102*t*, 103–106, 104*f*, 107–108*t*, 109–114, 111*f*, 113*f*, 114*f*, 200; latent class analysis and, 69, 71–76, 74*t*, 76*t*, 77*t*, 82, 207–209*t*; latent class regression and, 96–97, 97*f*, 103; measures of democracy and, 100–101; measures of religiosity and, 67; "modernist" cosmology and, 64–65; moral cosmology theory and, 62–65, 200; overlap and, 81–82; plurality-conformity dimension, 67, 68*f*, 69, 200; policy preferences and, 204; political equality and, 99; public-private attitudinal dimension, 67, 68*f*, 69, 200; regime preference theory and Arab Barometer data, 134–137, 200; Religion and the State (RAS) data set and, 99; religiosity and, 71–73, 73*f*, 77*t*, 82–85, 83*f*, 85*f*, 91n5, 91n7, 163–164, 197; results of analysis, 73–78, 74*t*, 76*t*, 77*t*, 78*f*, 79*t*, 80*t*, 81–82, 81*t*; robustness analysis with Wave II data and, 85–86, 87–88*f*, 89, 216*t*, 217; scholarship and, 197; sex and, 96, 109; social order and, 121–122; social trust and, 97, 109, 109–110; state regulation of religion and, 25–28,

religious outlooks (*Cont.*)
26f, 99; state-religion relations (SRR), 99–100, 110–112, 111f, 203; and support for democracy, 138–139t; temporal change and, 148–149; term *fitna* and, 120–121; trends in contextual analysis and, 114–117, 115f. *See also* post-Islamist religious outlook; religious communitarianism outlook; religious individualist outlook, social communitarianism religious outlook

Risale-i Nur (Epistles of Light) (Nursi), 32

Robinson, Robert V., 63–64, 67

Saadat, Anwar, 185–186
Said, Edward, 14
Salafi groups: changes of Egyptian in response to Arab uprisings, 157, 201; in Egypt, 58, 93, 150, 152–154, 156; jihadi Salafists in Tunisia and, 159; political pluralism and, 158; Salafi televangelists, 2; in Tunisia, 154, 156
Saudi Arabia, 23, 94, 98, 152–153
schools of jurisprudence (*madhāhib*), 14
sex (as variable), 96, 109, 137, 181–182t, 192t
Shafiq, Ahmed, 156
Sheikh Said revolt (1925), 52–53, 60n4
social communitarianism religious outlook: about, 66, 68f, 95–96, 177; change in class share in Egypt/Tunisia around Arab uprisings, 161f, 163–164; changes in religiosity and class share, 164f, 165; cross-national variation and, 104–105, 104f; economic policy preferences and, 177–180, 179f, 181–182t, 183–185, 194; educational attainment, 113f; feeling of security, 113–114, 114f; income and, 109; individual and contextual covariates, 105, 107t; preference for religion in the public sphere and, 130–131; preference for social cohesion/religious uniformity and, 130; preference for stability and, 178–180; regime preference model predictions and, 133–134, 134t; religiosity and, 83f, 84–85; results of analysis, 77–78, 78f, 79–81t, 81; robustness analysis and, 85–86, 87–88t, 89f; social trust and, 109–110;

state-religion relations (SRR), 110–112, 111f; support for democracy and, 130, 137, 138–139t, 140–143, 143, 144t, 145; trends from contextual analysis and, 114–117
social trust, 97, 109, 109–110
Stark, Rodney, 16–18, 20, 22–24, 31, 51, 64, 68
state regulation: cost associated with religious practice, 124–125, 126f; religious outlooks and, 25–27, 26f; on religious communities, 20, 22–25, 26f; state-religion relations (SRR), 110–112, 111f
Sufism, 34–35, 39
Syria, 120

Tessler, Mark, 15
tribal identification, 180, 185, 192t
Trump, Donald, 58
Tunahan, Süleyman Hilmi, 41, 53, 55
Tunisia: Arab Barometer data surrounding uprisings and, 158–159; Arab uprisings and, 149–152, 154–158; before Arab uprisings, 153–154; change in class share of religious outlook groups, 103–105, 160–163, 161f, 171; diversity of religious communities in, 151; Ez-Zitouna school and, 152; institutionalization of religion and, 152; Mouvement de la Tendance Islamique (MTI), 187–188; post-Islamists and economic policy preferences, 185, 187–189, 191–194, 191f, 192t; religiosity and change of class share of outlook groups in, 165, 165f; religious landscape before uprisings, 152–154; Salafi groups in, 156, 202; state-religion relations, 151–152; support for democracy around time of uprisings, 167–171, 168t
Turkey: attitude toward religion of, 33–35; democratization and, 54–55; Democrat Party (DP) of, 35–36; Gezi protests, 198–199; Gülen movement and, 32, 38, 46, 54, 56, 60n1; Justice and Development Party (AKP), 2, 37, 45–47, 50, 54, 56, 60n1, 156, 198–199; Kadiri order of brotherhoods, 32, 35–36, 38, 48; Kurds and, 199; Menemen rebellion (1930) and, 52–53, 60n4; military intervention of 1971 and, 53; Motherland

Party and, 47; MRA of, 34, 37–38, 49, 52–54; Naqshbandi order in, 30–31, 35, 38; National Order Party (Milli Nizam Partisi) of, 36; National Salvation Party (MSP, Milli Selamet Partisi) of, 36, 47, 54; National View movement and, 37; Nation Party and, 55; 1980 military coup and, 36–37; Nurcus and, 36, 38, 49, 56; People's Democracy Party, 199; political dynamics of, 32–38; relationship with religious communities and, 37–38; secularization of, 34; Sheikh Said revolt (1925) and, 52–53, 60n4; Sufi dervish lodges and, 34–35; Sunni attitudes in, 38; Ticani sect of, 36; Turkish Republic and, 34–35; ulema under Ataturk and, 34; Welfare Party of, 37, 55–56

United States, 13–14, 58, 92–93
Ünlü, Ahmet Mahmut (Cübbeli Ahmet Hoca), 1–2, 4, 45
Ustaosmanoğlu, Mahmut, 45

Varieties of Democracy project, 99–100
V-Dem Codebook, 100

Waldensians, 25
Western Europe, 14
women, organizational roles for, 41
World Values Surveys, 9n3
World War I, 34
World War II, 35

Yahya, Harun (Adnan Oktar), 1, 4
Yemen, 103, 156

SABRI CIFTCI is Professor of Political Science and the Michael W. Suleiman Chair at Kansas State University. He is author of *Islam, Justice, and Democracy*.

F. MICHAEL WUTHRICH is Associate Professor of Political Science and Associate Director of the Center for Global and International Studies at the University of Kansas. He is author of *National Elections in Turkey: People, Politics, and the Party System*.

AMMAR SHAMAILEH is Assistant Professor of Politics and International Relations at the Doha Institute for Graduate Studies. He is author of *Trust and Terror: Social Capital and the Use of Terrorism as a Tool of Resistance*.

www.ingramcontent.com/pod-product-compliance
Lightning Source LLC
Chambersburg PA
CBHW031804220426
43662CB00007B/528